Childhood, Citizenship, and the Anthropocene

Children and Young People in the Anthropocene

Series Editors: Peter Kelly, Peter Kraftl, Diego Carbajo Padilla, Veronica Pacini-Ketchabaw and Kate Tilleczek

This series seeks to examine, exemplify and problematise the ways in which childhood and youth are entangled with the Anthropocene. The series is multidisciplinary – bringing together, drawing on and exploring various intersections and entanglements between, sociologies of childhood, youth, education, work, well-being; children's and young people's geographies; feminist and post-feminist theories and methodologies; new materialist and posthuman theories and methodologies. It engages with an array of critical theoretical, methodological and empirical challenges and opportunities that emerge when thinking about children, young people and the Anthropocene.

Titles in the Series
Childhood, Citizenship, and the Anthropocene: Posthuman Publics and Civics
Anna Hickey-Moody, Linda Knight and Eloise Florence

Childhood, Citizenship, and the Anthropocene

Posthuman Publics and Civics

Anna Hickey-Moody, Linda Knight and
Eloise Florence

ROWMAN & LITTLEFIELD
London • New York

Credits and acknowledgements for material borrowed from other sources, and reproduced with permission, appear on the appropriate page within the text.

Published by Rowman & Littlefield
An imprint of The Rowman & Littlefield Publishing Group, Inc.
4501 Forbes Boulevard, Suite 200, Lanham, Maryland 20706
www.rowman.com

British Library Cataloguing in Publication Information Available

Library of Congress Cataloguing-in-Publication Data

Names: Hickey-Moody, Anna, 1977– author. | Knight, Linda, author. | Florence, Eloise, author.
Title: Childhood, citizenship, and the anthropocene : posthuman publics and civics / Anna Hickey-Moody, Linda Knight, Eloise Florence.
Description: Lanham : Rowman & Littlefield Publishing Group, [2022] | Series: Children and young people in the anthropocene | Includes bibliographical references and index. | Summary: "This book mobilizes the theoretical resources offered by theories of little publics and posthuman civics to consider what it means to be a child in the Anthropocene" —Provided by publisher.
Identifiers: LCCN 2021033736 (print) | LCCN 2021033737 (ebook) | ISBN 9781538153604 (cloth) | ISBN 9781538164075 (paperback) | ISBN 9781538153611 (epub)
Subjects: LCSH: Childhood—Social aspects. | Geology, Stratigraphic—Anthropocene. | Human beings.
Classification: LCC HQ767.9 .H53 2022 (print) | LCC HQ767.9 (ebook) | DDC 305.23—dc23
LC record available at https://lccn.loc.gov/2021033736
LC ebook record available at https://lccn.loc.gov/2021033737

Anna and Eloise would like to dedicate this book to the children of the Anthropocene. Linda would like to dedicate this book to Hannah, who makes beautiful art.

Contents

Acknowledgements

We would like to thank Fiona Hillary for sparking our own consolidation of work on this subject. In 2019 Anna Hickey-Moody brought Professor Rosi Braidotti to Media and Communication RMIT, and Fiona worked to co-host this visit by sourcing funding from the School of Art. Fiona curated a series of workshops on Posthuman Publics as part of the Masters of Art in Public Space at RMIT. These workshops were framed as 'laboratories' and explored the theme of posthuman publics. Anna and Rosi ran a workshop day, and the lecture Anna delivered to this cohort inspired chapter 2 in this book. The full programme for the Posthuman Publics laboratory series can be viewed here: https://art.rmit.edu.au/news/posthuman-publics

We would like to thank all the research staff employed in the Interfaith Childhoods project, especially Dr Kate Lonie, Robina Akhter Uller, Dr Joanna Dennis, Thu Le, Dr Christine Horn, Shabana Baig, Dr Angelica Harris-Faull, Marissa Willcox, Dr Mia Harrison, Lucian Marine, Zoe Walshe, Anne-Marie Atkinson, Beverly Irving, Tia Roko, and Katerina Eleftheriadou. Thanks to the Department of Gender and Cultural Studies at the University of Sydney; the Department of Sociology at Goldsmiths, London; and the Education and Social Research Institute at Manchester Metropolitan University for hosting the project outside Melbourne. Thanks to the Department of Media and Communication at RMIT University and the Digital Ethnography Research Centre. Huge thanks to the now 500+ individuals who have participated in the project. Thanks also to Felicity Colman, Joanna Hodge, Maggie McLure, Harry Torrance, Kate Pahl, Rebecca Coleman, Les Back, David Rousell, Nancy Lesko, Dave Griffiths, Dan Harris, Kat Jungnickel, and Natalya Lusty. The project is funded by Australian Research Council Future Fellowship FT16010023 'Early start arts to counter radicalization' and an RMIT Vice Chancellor's Senior Research Fellowship. All names of participants are pseudonyms that Anna has chosen to reflect their ethnic identity. The Interfaith Childhoods research has been assessed and approved by ethics committees at the University of Sydney, Manchester Metropolitan University, Goldsmiths London and RMIT University Melbourne. The research is approved under active project titles: Interfaith arts workshops, community and belonging, ethics application code 21071 and Interfaith futures public art campaign: Imagining diverse communities, ethics application code 21386. Huge thanks to the families and the twenty organizations that have supported this research. The importance of context in ethnographic analysis has meant that previous attempts to fictionalise the identities of the educational institutions have been unsuccessful and appeared naïve. The participants' (children, teachers and parents) identities have remained anonymised at all times and all identifiable images of children have been removed from data used in public. In the chapter on posthuman publics (chapter 2), Anna Hickey-Moody draws on a re-working of material that was originally published, in an earlier form, in the 2016 paper: 'Youth agency and adult influence: A critical revision of little publics', *Review of Education, Pedagogy, and Cultural Studies*, 38:1, 58-72, DOI: 10.1080/10714413.2016.1119643

We would also like to thank the researchers who worked on the Scaling the City project: Carol Brown, Claire Battersby and Mabingo Alfdaniels for their expertise in dance and creative movement, and for being enthusiastic about collaborating across disciplines and locations. Thanks also go to the children who participated: the Urban Activators, the Downtown Mappas and the children of the school in Aotearoa, New Zealand, who were fantastically enthusiastic, creative and hard-working in their ideas and project pieces.

Chapter 1

Mapping Key Debates in Childhood Studies and Posthumanism

Global warming is increasing at an unprecedented rate. The United Nations Intergovernmental Panel on Climate Change (IPCC) has made it clear that we, as a global community, have less than twelve years to prevent irreversible global warming of 1.5 degrees (IPCC 2018). As such, responding to the realities of climate change and reconciling the impacts of climate change on young lives is the major issue facing education experts, parents, children and youth today. Teaching children and young people today requires critical engagement with the climate crisis, precisely because global warming and resulting climate change is the largest and most compelling issue in the contemporary world and will dictate the future lives of children and young people today. Within universities, particularly in the humanities and social sciences, a primary tool for re-thinking approaches to climate change has been to think about the more-than-human or 'posthuman' (Braidotti 2013) world. This term 'posthuman' refers to both the impact that humans have on the world around them (looking beyond the human) and the impact that the non-human world has on humans, and vice-versa. Whether you come to this book looking for new pedagogical approaches, or a seasoned scholar of posthumanism, we hope the practices and debates we canvass here will furnish you with new approaches and ways of thinking.

At the heart of our work is an activist response to climate change: we are working to stop global warming, and we research with an ethics of engagement with children and the non-human world that is grounded in respect and reciprocity. As we have suggested, concepts that are core to posthuman debates are increasing in popularity in the humanities and social sciences, and arguably this is because they have emerged as a response to the environmental destruction and resulting climate change that frames all other political and economic debate in contemporary global society. A key idea in posthuman scholarship is the 'Anthropocene' which is an unofficial unit of geologic time that is measured by the scars since mankind began to damage ecosystems and planetary health. In simple terms, the Anthropocene is the damage caused to the earth's surface by humans. While ideas of posthumanism and the Anthropocene perform inherently critical readings of the contemporary global, social-environmental condition in which we find ourselves, these ideas are also, at times, scorned by scholars working within the environmental humanities. In this first chapter of this book, we argue that dialogue between environmental humanities and posthumanism is needed if we are to undertake research that adequately engages with the lived complexities of social and political life for children and young people in the era of climate change. More than this, as this book demonstrates, there is more to be gained from bringing together the terms of debate embedded in theories of publics and civics, the posthuman and the Anthropocene than there is from perpetuating the idea that these theoretical resources are not able to be brought into dialogue. We explore the generative tension of locating middle ground between conceptual debates and research practices.

CHILDREN IN PUBLICS AND CITIZENSHIP

Theoretical discussions of civics and publics have historically excluded children from their discussion of who and what makes a public and who can be called a citizen. As we explore in chapter 2, children are excluded from traditional notions of publics because they are seen to lack the agency – and therefore 'full' humanity – of adults. Hickey-Moody conceptualised 'little publics' (2013) as a form of counter-publics (Warner 2002; Munoz 1999; Halberstam 2005; Berlant and Warner 1998), a public constituted by those excluded from the typically masculinist, Western, able-bodied and rational humanist publics that were theorised by pragmatist John Dewey (Dewey and Rogers 2012[1927]). Theorising civic participation as a realm occupied only by the politically enfranchised, or what Dewey might call the individual equipped with the 'intelligence' to take part in political affairs, has excluded children from being considered as full, engaged and participant citizens.

In Rethinking Children's Citizenship Tom Cockburn (2013) theorises children as being confined to categories of 'other' that have been historically excluded from citizenship: women, children, slaves, people of colour, people with disabilities. Indeed, Cockburn (2013) argues that liberal citizenship has been defined by the exclusion of Others. Children have been excluded because they are 'incomplete', 'fragile' and 'under-developed', the same characteristics attributed to women and people of colour in order to exclude them from citizenship. Cockburn echoes Murris (2016) and her appraisal of the adult as the 'transcendental signifier' (89) of humanist configurations of childhood: 'The understanding of childhood depends upon definitions of adulthood . . . that is, where childhood ends adulthood begins, and vice versa' (Cockburn 2013, 1). These positions can be seen as reinforcing, or at the very least, being aligned with, the posthumanist critique that children are thought of as the 'almost-adult'; in terms of citizenship and the ability to participate in and form publics, this figures childhood as a state of preparation for the rights and responsibility of public and political life. With this in mind, Cockburn seeks to challenge these 'constructions of children that have served to exclude them from being considered worthy or capable of having responsibilities or laying claim to rights' (6).

Cockburn explicitly links citizenship with agency, arguing that children's agency entitles them to the rights and responsibilities of citizenship and the ability to freely participate in publics. Even newborn babies, Cockburn argues, 'demonstrate the agency that is necessary for citizenship associated with rights, duties and responsibilities' (9). This conceptualisation of citizenship as associated with agency has utility. Many posthuman scholars draw on ideas from the new materialisms, for example, Sencindiver (2017) explains new materialism by characterising it as:

> a[A]n interdisciplinary, theoretical, and politically committed field of inquiry, emerging roughly at the millennium as part of what may be termed the post-constructionist, ontological, or material turn . . . new materialism has emerged mainly from the front lines of feminism, philosophy, science studies, and cultural theory, yet it cuts across and is cross-fertilized by both the human and natural sciences. The revival of materialist ontologies has been animated by a productive friction with the linguistic turn and social constructionist frameworks in the critical interrogation of their limitations engendered by the prominence given to language, culture, and representation, which has come at the expense of exploring material and somatic realities beyond their ideological articulations and discursive inscriptions. (np)

To put this another way, new materialism is located within the humanities and social sciences but has established, increasing, links to the environmental and 'hard' sciences. It is an approach concerned with empirical events, matter and its actions, and extrapolates or builds on the agency of the material world.

When considered through the new materialist lens that assigns agency to the more-than-human (Bennett 2010, 2020), a posthumanist expansion of agency is important Cockburn (2013) engages with children's agency and their subsequent entitlement to citizenship as far as considering the 'enormous contribution to their [parents'] health, welfare and education' and how considering children's citizenship 'forms part of current opportunities for investment, future productivity and the future redemption of debts' (10). If children's agency is expanded beyond the ability to contribute to the lives of parents, for example through the agentic realism of posthuman concepts of childhood, we can afford children the same rights and capacities as adult citizens but also specify the extent to which children's agency has different foci and goals from adult citizenship and agency.

At the heart of Cockburn's (2013) critique is a problematisation of liberal citizenship, which is built upon the masculinist precondition of individual freedoms, a form of 'citizenship that is premised upon and assumes an autonomous individual freely operating in the world without constraint' (14). Liberal citizenship began viewing children, women, and slaves 'as an "other" that is defined entirely as linked, dependent, reliant and constantly under the influences of other people and thus incapable of making contributions to society' (14). Such a citizenship assumes these others cannot contribute because they are interlinked (see, for example, the argument of anti-women's suffrage campaigners that women would simply vote in accordance with the preference of their husbands or fathers). Scholars such as Hultgren (2017) argue that liberal constructs of citizenship are built upon foundations of inclusion and exclusion: 'The very condition of possibility for citizenship is the reduction of some Other (or some set of Others) to non-human or quasi-human status' (188). While posthumanism blurs these boundaries and thus provides inroads for the inclusion of children in these constructs (see chapter 3), Hultgren also cautions against turning attention away from how these distinctions between human and non-human continue to structure citizenship, particularly through marginalisation and persecution of people and the abuse of environmental resources arising from their lack of legal rights. As we establish across this book, posthumanism broadens the political community attached to citizenship to include more-than-humans, directly implicating the institutional forums through which posthuman ethics of citizenship can be carried out and which have continued to exclude children. Hultgren points to Latour's 'parliament of things' and Deleuze's 'idiot' in the more abstract sense, and Hables Gray's 'Cyborg Bill of Rights' in practice as ways of 'opening up spaces where the non-human could be listened to in different, more attentive ways' (191). If children have been excluded from the pantheon of the fully adult human citizen, then they might at least be included in the groups that need to be listened to more attentively.

POSTHUMAN APPROACHES TO CHILDWORLDS

We build on the work of others (Malone 2018; Blaise 2016; Murris 2016; Renold 2018; 2019; Cutter-Mackenzie-Knowles et al. 2019) who have worked to open up posthumanism and new materialism to include children. We take seriously the publics and civics formed by children and engage children as legitimate political actors and citizens. As we outline in chapter 3, empirical methods underpinned by posthumanism provide insight into children's lifeworlds and views because they are attuned to non-verbal and non-discursive forms of communication. It is this embracing of non-verbal communication that is privileged in both the projects at the heart of this book, and which provides one of the avenues through which posthumanist philosophy can enliven empirical methodologies. Non-representational research animates methodologies that think differently about what 'counts' as research data, allowing us to open up fields of social scientific inquiry to those whose public and civic participation occurs through indirect discourse: children. By grounding our methodologies in posthuman thought we are able to open up examinations of the public sphere and civics and citizenship to include children.

POSTHUMAN RESEARCH

As posthuman philosophy and new materialist methodologies moved into the social sciences, some scholars critiqued posthumanism as a research perspective. In 2008, Iris van de Tuin and Sarah Ahmed published an exchange discussing new materialism and its feminist roots. The discussion centres on the question of the strains of apparent anti-biology in the genealogy of critical feminism, and what this means for the then burgeoning field of new materialism and its focus on matter. Ahmed (2008) argues that the new materialisms have been shaped by what she calls the 'inflationary logic' of the assumption that feminist theory has so far refused to engage with biology and matter. In Ahmed's reading, which is quite different from our own reading, new materialism begins from the assumption that 'feminism and postructuralism have reduced "everything" to language and culture . . . and have forgotten the "real" of the real world, or the materiality of what is given' (26). Ahmed takes issue with her reading of a 'feminism has reduced matter to culture' (33) pointing to genealogies of feminist engagement with biology and matter. Ahmed argues that the legacy of feminism is not, or should not be, characterised by 'a knee-jerk' biophobia in response to which new materialism has supposedly evolved (Ahmed cites Elizabeth Grosz (2004) as an example of this argument). Rather, she posits that feminism has long been concerned with biology, and not only with the biological determinism that is used as a social and cultural means of oppression and marginalisation. The use of biological arguments to confirm the patriarchal status quo was a significant concern of second-wave feminist philosophers, and this concern is echoed in critical race theory's studies of 'the uses of "culture" to defend racial hierarchies' (28). But beyond this, Ahmed argues that feminism has long been concerned with 'matter', and that new materialism's supposedly central concern with the omission of matter from feminist critique is, at best, a part-truth. She points to the contemporary work of feminist science studies as a field in which feminist philosophy engages directly with matter. We agree that feminism has always been concerned with the politics of matter, and indeed our reading of new materialisms is that it looks to extend feminist understandings of the politics of matter. In response, van de Tuin points out that despite praising feminist science studies, Ahmed does not work with them, and confines them to an unneccarily narrow field, 'a neo-discipline' (414).

Van de Tuin (2008) offers her own positioning of new materialism as one that 'does not merely affirm the biological or the cultural body, but rather confirms that bodies are constituted in (affective) encounters' (415). New materialism, van de Tuin argues:

> [G]oes beyond both 'pure' materiality and 'just' representation, affirming the matter–representation divide (Claire Colebrook) and allowing the constitution of a transdisciplinary perspective (drawing upon feminist science studies, feminist postcolonial studies, Deleuzian feminism) that is both a new feminist materialism and a critical and creative engagement with second-wave feminist epistemologies. (415)

We extend this position to suggest that the new materialism's 'new' is not in anyway an attempt to distance contemporary scholarship from histories of feminism, but rather a means or creating space from Marxist materialism, which is Ahmed and van de Tuin's exchange traditionally a patriarchal and male-focused scholarly landscape that does not engage with feminism. 'New' refers to the contemporary, empirical, lived and emergent and 'new' also signifies 'feminist, not Marxist'. However, this exchange between Ahmed and van de Tuin highlights the beginning of extended criticism that new materialism has faced in both its epistemological and ontological grounding and its application in realms of feminist theory and critique.

The feminist genealogy of new materialism has meant that many criticisms have been framed around new materialisms' ability to deal with the '"real" of the real world' (Ahmed 2008, 25). In particular, the capacity of new materialisms to examine political issues, specifically race, became a particular concern, in relation to political and power relations within research methodologies themselves. However, our assessment of this argument, and Eva Petersen's paper we discuss below, is that they are based either on active misreadings of the school of thought or a fundamental mis-understanding of what the new materialisms are. Jessica Gerrard and colleagues (2017) argued that new materialisms can't examine political issues in education research because they often focus on micro-politics. We would suggest that all identity politics shape micro-politics and such processes are inherently political. In a reading of new materialisms as a field that constructs 'the field' through a single experimental paper written by Mindy Blaise, Eva Petersen (2018) argues that new materialisms focus on non-human matter that is supremely agentic and that this focus renders materials discrete and separate; something to be intra-acted with, rather than the product of intra-action:

> *In the insistence of the agential realism of matter, the operation of the cut, or the 'determination', is elided and as a result the binary nature/culture remains intact.* (13)

We don't agree with this reading, as all cuts are already nature and culture entanglements, the divide between nature and culture is not possible within a new materialist practice. Petersen (2018) also argues the new materialist positioning of educational research data as supremely agentic entails an inherent depoliticisation of the 'still, sensing researcher body' (13). By removing or sidelining their position in relation to the data, Peterson argues, new materialist researchers effectively attempt to de-politicise their relation to the data, and therefore 'negate their engagement, much like the "objective" "neutral" scientists under the God Trick did' (14). However, we would suggest that the absolute opposite is the case. A new materialist perspective calls for a foundational enmeshment of the researcher body with the co-production of the 'data' and that rather than separating these entities, a new materialist perspective would see them as part of the same assemblage and, indeed, as co-constitutive. Adopting a similar line of critique exercised with greater nuance, Gerrard and colleagues similarly argue that post-qualitative methods risk becoming cut off from 'the worlds and and people being researched' (384), and that such methods do not 'attend to political and historical relations of social power, both in the worlds it constitutes and in the processes of its knowledge production' (384). We have written elsewhere in response to these claims that new materialist methods are depoliticised (Hickey-Moody and Willcox 2019), which are made by Gerrard et al. (2017). To restate our argument, a new materialist perspective is designed to illustrate the relationships between historical and social relationships of power and the material politics and technics of contemporary knowledge production.

Gerrard and colleagues (2017) enquire as to the political and ethical implications of new materialist methods in relation to marginalisation and oppression, suggesting that in their efforts to shift focus to the relationships between the researcher and their research, new materialist methods obscure the political positioning of the power relations at play in research methodologies. It is interesting to note the huge difference between Petersen and Gerrard and colleagues' readings of the positionality of the researcher in new material-ism; Petersen suggesting new materialism erases the researcher completely and Gerrard and colleagues arguing new materialism is all about researching the researcher. We contend both perspectives misunderstand intra-action. Intra-action is the ontological principle in which life, including research assemblages, is dynamically co-created by people and non-human matter in a performance of historical power relations and future possibilities. Gerrard and colleagues particularly point out the academic capital of research with marginalised communities, pointing out how taking on this research is often used as a way for academics to demonstrate 'research authenticity . . . within a hierarchical field of knowledge structured by colonial power' (389). They are concerned with 'how much of the post-qualitative inquiry still includes human "subjects" within the research, but seems to obfuscate important political and ethical considerations surrounding the claims made about these [marginalised] people', (390) and they suggest these research methodologies might obscure the 'the often hidden, banal, or unspoken social relations of power' (391) between the researchers and participants. This is a significant issue for social research that is often the focus of research ethics, and our position would be that new materialisms are not any more subject to unspoken relations of social power than any other social science or empirical research approach. Indeed, bringing a reflexive approach to empirical research is likely to create space to discuss power relations. In our experience, often participants are more inter-ested in community-facing research outputs and learning experiences than research outputs designed for academic readerships and much of our work around engagement speaks to the need to contribute back to community and offer useful forms of research translation. We have argued elsewhere:

> *[N]ew materialist and post qualitative research can be explicitly political and can respond to issues of race, class, gender and sexuality. Further, our aim in positioning feminist new materialism as being inherently political addresses the postcolonial critique that Gerrard and colleagues (2017) raise, suggesting that post qualitative inquiry risks operating less as new mechanisms for generative and subversive post-humanist research and more as being a process of closure and erasure. Opposing this critique, the transformative nature of feminist new materialist methodologies in which art and research converge can be seen in the work of Alaimo and Hekman (2008), Kester (2004), Barrett and Bolt (2014) and Thompson's (2015) writing on art and activism. Thompson (2015) focuses his research on art as a political intervention and shows how art today can (and does) inspire innovation and transformation through activists and empowered communities. We are also interested in the politics embedded in art making and sharing.* (Hickey-Moody and Willcox 2019, 6)

To put this another way, collaborative making with participants that allows participants to shape the ways they make and guide processes of production is not an empirical research method grounded in 'unspoken power dynamics', it is a process of making together in which the researcher is attentive, responsive, interested, supportive, engaged and caring. It is hard work. Structures often need to be in place when working with children to guide children's energy and attention, but there is a significant difference between providing a structure and materials while encouraging and supporting children and exploiting 'unspoken power dynamics'. Children say no and disengage if they are not interested. Gerrard et al. did not explain why new materialisms more than, for example, a survey, an interview or observation undertaken from a poststructuralist or structuralist approach are more reliant on exploitative power relationships than the other popular social science methods we cite. Our sense is the new materialisms are an approach that some scholars love to hate, partly because they don't understand new materialist approaches and partly because they misunderstand these approaches.

Suffice to say that other authors have expressed similar concerns about new materialist methodologies in relation to marginalised communities, power relations and knowledge hierarchies. Of more interest to us is the argument advanced by critical race theorists that movements away from the centrality of the human figure may work to exclude communities who have been historically been sidelined from debates about 'the human'. Astrida Neimanis (2016) rightfully points out that posthumanist thought must remain couched in 'social justice–oriented feminisms that continue to struggle, in quite human terms and in very human contexts, for the ability of human bodies to be allowed to be' (18). Neimanis points to Haraways's (2004) concern at the 'death of the subject' of poststructuralism, pointing out the irony that this turn away from the masterful 'human' subject is occurring 'just at the moment when raced/sexed/colonized speakers begin "for the first time", (. . .) to represent themselves' (Haraway 2004, 57). Black scholars have similarly warned against moving away from the centrality of 'the human' 'after being excluded from humanity for so long' (Neimanis 2016, 18). Lewis Gordon (1998) writes of the death of man in postmodernism that: 'dominant groups can "give up" humarism for the simple fact that their humanity is presumed, while other communities have struggled too long for the humanist prize' (39). We agree with these positions and situate our own research as an extension of the social justice orientation of early feminism. We argue for centring of black, postcolonial and decolonial approaches, some of which are explored in this book through Indigenous perspectives on land, and the politics of affect, yet this is not the primary field to which this book contributes. We are looking to make a substantive contribution to the field of youth studies of the Anthropocene. This field is, of course, characterised by colonizing and decolonizing practices and knowledges which we discuss at various points across this book.

Critical race theorists have also pointed out how the posthuman turn in the humanities and social sciences poses the very real risk of colonial-style exploitation of Indigenous knowledge systems. Some, such as Simone Bignall (2020), have argued that the posthuman turn simply repackages Indigenous relationality and ways of being into Euro-centric philosophies, pointing out how these existing knowledges have been operating for thousands of years. Bignall suggests that the 'humanism' against which posthumanism pushes is not universal, but is aligned with particular cultures: 'Humanism is associated culturally with the philosophy, geography and temporality of modern Western European expansionism emerging in tandem with the 17th century movement of liberal Enlightenment' (2). Bignall demonstrates that Indigenous philosophies have been posthuman for centuries, and that the non-Indigenous posthumanists must actively resist mining these traditions as contemporary posthumanism:

> *Decolonisation calls for a different response from non-Indigenous Australians: to trawl our migrant cultural frameworks for concepts and practices that align favourably with the ways of being, thinking, perceiving and acting within the world observed by First Nations peoples, the Aboriginal sovereigns of the Country that now supports us all.* (Bignall 2020, 3)

Others have expressed concern over, or actively critiqued, new materialism because of its decentering of 'the human' at a time when many marginalised groups are finally obtaining the 'humanist prize' (Gordon 1998, 39), or being included in the term 'human' after having being excluded for so long. Many of these concerns are deeply pragmatic and centred around material processes of exclusion and marginalisation. Vehmas and Watson (2016) argue that posthumanist scholarship has a pursuit to nullify the separation between humans and animals and that this poses a risk to the moral agency of people with disabilities: 'Putting humans and animals in the same box opens up the door for speculations about moral worth where disabled people are likely to be on the losing side' (12). When we query what it means to be 'human', there remains a danger of further marginalisation of disadvantaged communities who have for a long time been excluded from what 'counts' as human. However, our reading is not that posthumanism says animals and humans are the same, but rather that everything is interconnected. Hierarchies exist, but they are connected to other systems still. Moreso, and as we explain in greater detail below, much disability studies scholarship has thrived in relation to the field of posthumanism, and while Vehmas and Watson are quite critical of posthumanism, posthuman disability studies is a field in its own right.

Other critiques, like that advanced by Slavoj Žižek, are concerned less with pragmatic risks and are more interested in perceived conceptual or philosophical failings. Zizek (in Till 2015) argues that new materialism conceptually fails in its attempt to de-centre the human when it stresses the liveliness and agency of non-human matter. Zizek argues that this approach renders non-human matter as 'someone "like us", someone we can "understand"' (in Till 2015, np). However we would contend that this is not at the basis of particle physics theories, as described by Karen Barad in their work on entanglement. The point is not that the computer and the researcher are 'equal' or 'the same', rather, the point is that the way in which the researcher 'works' is mediated through and in relation to the computer – the two are entangled with each other and also with much longer chains of production. For Zizek, the result of new materialism is an actual re-centring of the human, which he argues is the result of viewing the agency of matter as a social phenomenon, 'the result of our "animistic" attitude towards it rather than qualities which exist within it' (Till 2015, np). As sociologist Chris Till points out, Zizek's critique demonstrates the persistence of human interest and human-centred framings, which even seemingly accidentally appear in new materialist thinking and posthumanist philosophy; 'but I can't immediately see how this can be avoided' (Till 2015. np). However, as we have suggested, the point of posthumanism is not to avoid the human, but rather to contest bodily distinction and consider porosity, cyborgian bodies and the human-in-relation to the more-than-human.

Whilst questions around the role of the human subject in posthumanism and critiques of this approach persist, many empirical social scientists have come to see the utility of a posthuman approach as a way of understanding the causal relationships between human and non-human. In 2010, Wolfe argued that posthumanist philosophy is not about seeing or moving beyond the human; posthumanist thought is not, she argues, about moving to the point '"after" our embodiment had been transcended' (xv). Posthumanism 'opposes the fantasies of disembodiment and autonomy inherited from humanism' (xv). As we work with the concept of posthumanism in this book, we see that posthumanism is not about the absence of the human, rather, it is a deeply embodied and material way of understanding 'how' one is a human, and the relationship between humans and non-humans. Many social science scholars have identified the utility of such an approach and applied it to empirical research of class, gender, the nation state, race, colonialism, sexuality and disability.

For example, posthumanism has been taken up enthusiastically across the field of disability studies. Viewing disability through the lens of the posthuman condition, Goodley and colleagues (2014) introduce disability as 'a moment of relational ethics' (342) arguing that many disabled humans 'are already enacting forms of activism, art and relationality that push us all to think imaginatively and critically about a new epoch that we might term the posthuman'. St. Pierre (2015) looks to posthumanism as a way of critiquing communication and social studies, specifically the ways these fields privilege 'rational' speech as the primary form of discourse. 'While humanism venerates speech as the most privileged manifestation of rational human identity', St. Pierre argues, 'it defers the immanent tension in speech between universal and particular by excluding non-normative voices from the realm of rational discourse' (330). Posthumanism directly challenges this exclusion of non-normative voices, privileging instead 'informationally flexible and malleable bodies' (330), indirect discourse and ways of communicating that are not mainstream.

Like Wolfe, we situate posthumanism as a theoretical and empirical perspective born of a specific historical moment. The necessary reshaping of humankind's philosophical and material relationship with the planet has required the engagement of posthumanism in philosophy and social science, as much as in the ecological and biological sciences. Wolfe (2010) argues:

Posthumanism names a historical moment in which the decentering of the human by its imbrication in technical, medical, informatics, and economic networks is increasingly impossible to ignore, a historical development that points toward the necessity of new theoretical paradigms (but also thrusts them on us), a new mode of thought that comes after the cultural repression and fantasies, the philosophical protocols and evasion, of humanism as a historically specific phenomenon. (xv–xvi)

In the face of this remapping of the relationship between humans and the planet, many posthumanities scholars (Muecke and Roe 2020; Braidotti and Bignall 2019; Hickey-Moody et al. 2021) have employed new materialisms as a means of developing new conceptual and methodological framings of research and philosophy. We follow Braidotti (2013), Halberstam (2020) and van de Tuin (2008) in arguing that any tension between language and matter is in fact generative, a conceptual form of Braidotti's (2019) embodied and material 'middle grounds' (52) (we expand on this in chapter 5).

Our research methods and approaches have been designed to respond to conceptual debates and research practices that have emerged as a critique of the Anthropocene. In particular, posthuman and new materialist research perspectives interrogate how we, as researchers, understand 'our relationship with what it is we investigate, and therefore how we perceive our knowledge to be produced' (Hinton and Teusch 2015, 3). Reframing the conceptual standpoint from which research begins reframes the research practices. This mostly involves the rejection of an assumed empirical separation between the researcher and the research 'subject'. The reworking of subjectivity that is entailed in feminist materialist and posthuman research concepts entails the reworking of research practice. Hinton and Teusch (2015) explain:

> *[O]bjects and subjects of inquiry are entangled, emergent, and contingent . . . these 'actors' in knowledge processes cannot be conceived of in solely atomistic or anthropocentric terms. With new feminist materialism's post- humanist attentions, the human no longer assumes priority as the knowing eye/I organizing inquiry.* (3)

We explore in detail in chapter 3 how our methods of making art, movement and creative approaches to research are modalities that centre youth voices while simultaneously decentring the human. We frame our methods conceptually as a philosophy of and in action, ways of enacting and exploring the more-than-human world and how we can think about both children's and non-humans' roles in publics and civics. Our approaches are philosophical-methodological, forms of enactment as modes of performing ideas, sitting in the space between (or the 'middle ground') of method and concept. The relationship between ideas and practice is alive; a generative tension through which new ways of knowing can emerge.

Jasmine Ulmer (2017) writes that 'the posthuman turn has radically – and rapidly – shifted what is possible in research methodology' (832), and this is evident in some work in the social sciences. In response to Savage and Burrows's (2007) suggestion that quantitative sociological methods were becoming obsolete in the face of the deluge of social 'data' being generated online and structuring the post-digital world, many sociologists turned to empirical methods that are open to 'new ontologies of the social' (de Freitas 2017, 27), in response to the historical posthuman moment:

> *Conventional research methods in the social sciences – interviews, surveys and observation – continue to center human intentionality and reinstate human exceptionalism, despite the fact that scholars are increasingly situating their work within the Anthropocene.* (de Freitas 2017, 28)

De Freitas argues that traditional research methods embody humanist and rational ideas of origins, entail acts of exclusion and establish and often re-establish regimes of work and labour, and that together these often reinstate social hierarchies and orders. De Freitas argues that by opening up new ontologies, like those developed in response to the Anthropocene, has the potential to allow new methods to emerge that 'plug into a more-than-human worldly becoming' (29–30). Posthuman research is therefore part of a broader approach to ontology – to discussions of what it means to be – and to epistemology and empiricism, or what it means to know (St. Pierre 2016).

Taylor (2017) argues 'posthumanism invites us (humans) to undo the current ways of doing – and then imagine, invent and do the doing differently' (6, original emphasis). Posthuman empirical methods have, as we would expect, taken many forms. Ringrose and Renold (2019) speak on behalf of a collective of queer and feminist research-activist scholars (Hickey Moody 2015, 2017; Harris and Taylor 2016; Springgay and Zaliwska 2016; Renold 2018; 2019; Gray et al. 2018) to offer 'phEmaterialist' research methods. PhEmaterialism combines feminist posthumanism and the new materialisms and applies them to questions of empiricism in educational research. PhEmaterialist approaches to research fundamentally re-frame what counts as research 'data'. This re-questioning has occurred primarily through an 'arts-based, participatory research field of inquiry and intervention into the live political ecology of education' (Ringrose and Renold 2019, np). Educational research has been a fertile ground for the development of posthuman empiricism, allowing for 'new ways of grasping educational experience [other] than those afforded by humanism' (Taylor 2016, 5; see also Malone et al. 2020).

In part, we explore the ways that posthuman thinking can open up empirical research methodologies with children and around pedagogy. We draw particularly on scholars such as Malone et al. (2020), who not only argue that childworlds are always-already posthuman, but also offer posthuman philosophy as a mode of inquiry, theorising the research practice implications of research childhood and children in the Anthropocene through a posthuman lens. We have put this theorisation to effect on multiple occasions (Hickey-Moody et al. 2020; Hickey-Moody et al. 2021), and this book continues to demonstrate the ways in which such methods open up new connections and frame ways of knowing the complex inner lifeworlds of children.

OUR APPROACH

Chapters 2 and 3 of this book establish the conceptual terrain to which we contribute, and we broadly canvass debates about publics and civics which have developed since the 1920s, often without substantial consideration of children and youth. In chapter 3 we explore civic practices beyond the human. These analytic, 'literature review' chapters are united by our interest in the utility of bringing a posthuman approach to social science concepts. After introducing traditional notions of the public sphere, in chapter 2 we explore how we might conceptualise a posthuman public. We argue that the public sphere has always been more-than-human, building on works that similarly critique the restrictively humanist-focus of traditional public spheres to explore the possibilities of a public sphere that is grounded in constitutive relationships between things: human and non-human. In particular, we draw on works by Deleuze and Guttari, especially their concept of assemblage, and Nancy Fraser's reading of Habermas's public sphere as always-already posthuman, to propose the non-human as key to publics and their political functions.

Our concept of a posthuman public understands the non-human as key to any situation. We show that the public sphere has always been more-than-human, however, it has not been widely theorised as posthuman. Broadly speaking, the idea of 'the public sphere' began as an instrument of inherently humanist, masculinist and classist thought, developed to explain the function of the agora, the ancient Greek marketplace in which bourgeoisie male landholders debated the legal conditions upon which they traded (Habermas 1991[1962], 3). Carrying on the masculinist bourgeoisie tradition, the American pragmatist John Dewey (Dewey and Rogers 2012[1927]) famously developed the concept of the public sphere as a space in which citizens assemble to respond to negative effects of market or governmental activities. The concept became known as a way of illustrating the functions of political life. It took quite some time until the exclusion of communities from the public sphere began to be discussed in relation to the potential inclusion of Indigenous communities, women, children, queers, animals and plants. In extending these discussions of inclusion and opening them up to 'the bewilderment that accompanies the desire to end that world without knowing what comes next' (Halberstam 2020, 32), our discussions are entangled with the work of theorists such as Barrett (2012), Berlant (1997) and Fraser (1990), each of whom shows us what expanded notions of the public sphere may look like.

In chapter 3 we similarly challenge the humanist focus of citizenship and the rights of the 'adult', 'autonomous' individual, to propose a posthuman reading of urban civics. 'Garbage' animals which include pigeons, rats, bats and insects participate in urban life to such an extent that their activities and presence result in the establishment of civic by-laws and acts: buildings are instructed to attach particular fixtures to deter the ability for pigeons to roost; the branches of trees favoured by fruit bats must be pruned to not overhang pathways and allow bat droppings and saliva to fall on humans. Elements and matter too, such as water, wind and seismic movements, are often controlled by urban architecture and planning. These occasionally break their boundaries and cause enormous infrastructural damage, forcing the diversion of traffic, the evacuation of neighbourhoods and the reconstruction of buildings. Inhuman and non-human animal citizens constitute a civic presence and have a history that predates the contemporary cityscape; they are a reminder that cities have colonised spaces that were already social and civic spaces for collectives comprising elements, matters, critters and Indigenous peoples. A posthuman reading of civics therefore not only creates new conceptual ideas of civics, it returns to the historical civic relationalities to think about Braidotti's (2019) call for justice in relation to childhoods and citizenships during what she identifies as the Fourth Industrial Revolution and Sixth Extinction. We mobilise the writings of scholars such as Bennett (2010), Tsing and Yanagisako (1983), Chen (2012), Rankine (2014), Watson (2019) and Haraway (2016) to consider how their respective critical theorisations of citizenship expand notions of civics and who, how or what is a citizen during these extraordinary global changes.

In chapter 4 we turn to methodologies and methods for critical engagements with the concepts of publics and civics that have been developed through the works of Micheal Warner, Lauren Berlant and Wendy Brown, and the postcolonial scholar Simone Bignall. This chapter demonstrates how these points of theoretical critique directly inform the methods for empirical research with children that guided the two research projects and data sets on which this book is based. Hickey-Moody's Interfaith Childhoods project was a multi-sited ethnography that employed arts-based methods with children to express their everyday stories and experiences of belonging. Often shared through images, words, memory, allegory and collaborative exchanges, the 'data' of this project emerged through a method that held space to recognize subjugated, non-mainstream knowledges; a decolonializing approach to a feminist, new materialist methodology concerned with the agency of experience, of places, matter and things. Similarly, Linda Knight's Scaling the City project was a multi-sited research-creation project in Australia and New Zealand that investigated how children use creative practices to move through city spaces and build their civic connection as an urban citizen. Scaling the City is methodologically aligned with research-creation approaches through its generation of experimental and emergent movement works and gestural mapping responses to urban space captured through visual, photographic and video 'data'. Movement and gestural responses allowed for different forms of presence and intervention on the space, with many different traces and imprints left remaining. The two approaches and data sets acknowledge the centrality and importance of vernacular culture and respond to the agency of matter and of political landscapes when children craft their publics and civics. The methodologies recognise that meaning and communication are often non-verbal and are constituted in the vital present in ways that are shaped by complex political, social and cultural histories. We detail the methodologies and the theoretical and conceptual groundings of each method in new materialist and posthuman theories.

Chapter 5 is the first of four subsequent chapters that draw directly on our empirical research. We work with data from the Interfaith Childhoods project to explore children's imaginings of posthuman publics of the future. The chapter examines children's collaborative multi-media visual mappings of ideal urban futures as modes of civic participation. The posthuman urban scapes the children imagined are defined by values of care and collectivity in which humans are entangled in a relationship of care and community with animals, water roads, flying mosques and dragons. Through these imaginings of cities of the future, the children not only imagine publics and civics characterised by a sense of entanglement with the more-than-human, they also call publics to attention. The children's artworks were displayed in art exhibitions and auctioned at an art fair; processes of engagement which called expanding publics to contemplate the children's valuation of city life in the Anthropocene. Set against increasingly stratified educational contexts, the often super diverse urban schools, religious institutions and community centres in which the Interfaith Childhoods research took place are largely removed from higher education institutions, galleries and 'the art world'. Drawing on Harwood and colleagues' (2016) concept of ecologies of learning, this chapter also examines the different kinds of work undertaken by the children's collaborative multi-media visual mappings of ideal urban futures in different contexts: the classroom, the community centre, the art show, the gallery. The pictures speak on behalf of an assemblage of children, and also bring children's worlds into physical and cultural spaces with which they are not yet familiar. The collaborative artworks create new ecologies of learning in which children learn from each other and from the non-human world, and which feature an ethics of care entangled with deep kinship with the more-than-human. As a point around which publics are called to attention, the future cities become direct calls to action for a more deeply ingrained entanglement with the more-that-human for cities that are facing the Anthropocene.

In chapter 6 we work with Knight's Scaling the City project to speculate on emergent concepts of urban civics that are not limited to humanist readings of citizenship and political agency. The children in the project had interactions with non-human and inhuman urban others through their creative and performative curations. They worked with materials, animals and matters, some of which have a long historical presence and connection with the urban space. The curations became a starting point to pay respects to pre-urban civics as the intellectual basis for a posthuman politics that is respectful of non-human and inhuman participation and civic agency. We argue that children need expressive modes that are brought about through the arts to experiment and speculate with the complexities of posthuman ideas, to imagine and actively work towards urban possibilities. Expressive curations reposition the child as central and bring different conceptions of citizenship into focus as they negotiated these urban zones. We explore the ways that urban children develop civic connection and identity through creative movement and visual mapping in civic spaces, and how gesturally mapping wild spaces examines the ways in/non-human citizens contribute to urban civics.

In chapter 7 we explore how posthuman publics as a concept can be used to map both the start and end of the concept of childhood. We argue that the Anthropocene brings with it the impossibility of a childhood originally imagined by scholars such as Jean-Jacques Rousseau. Childhood as a concept, and in some respects, as a developmental trajectory, no longer exists, save for in some extremely privileged, largely White and bourgeoisie contexts. We present a 'proof of concept' that childhood has been killed by the Anthropocene and that child publics have always-already been posthuman through data from the Interfaith Childhoods project. This includes close consideration of refuges built and narrated by children in the Interfaith Childhoods project, thinking through their invisible and visible aspects of home, identity and workshops in which children created outdoor artwork and tent architecture as explorations of their relationship with nature. Some of the outcomes of these workshops resembled asylum seeker refuges, entangling the romantic Rousseau-like notions of childhood with the impossibility of romantic childhood in the Anthropocene, which is marked out by children being born and dying in refugee camps. Children's architectures of empathy model a kind of citizenship without adults, entangled with children's relationships with their more-than-human environments. The chapter shows the relationality of children's sense of citizenship as they collectively reconfigure their environments through processes of habitation, sensing, moving, enacting, thinking, making and talking about connections with place. These processes are open. They shift human conditions of value and practices of othering and remake the delineation of matter as 'human' and 'non-human'.

In chapter 8 we discover the pathways to becoming a citizen are not straightforward. Global transience and migration means that children directly or indirectly experience discontinuous connections to place, and this impacts the development of their sense of civic connection and legal status. During Scaling the City, children created dance and mapping responses to the Godwit/Kuaka, a migratory bird that settles each year on the Te Atatu Peninsula in New Zealand, to refuel before beginning its return journey north to the Arctic. The birds habitually visit the same spot each year, so by connecting Scaling to City to the visitation, the children were able to use dance and mapping to critically think about belongings, community, reciprocal connection and individual rights of access. This iteration of the project data sparks discussion on cosmopolitical theories of collectivity and civic agency. We consider how the notions of the human citizen and civic rights are historic concepts that do not acknowledge the cosmopolitical force of the more-than-human urban dweller. In extending the humanist political realm to the cosmopolitical, how might rights, civics and citizenship become a hopeful and possible democratic idea again?

In chapter 9 we outline the contributions of the book to theorising children's posthuman civics and publics in the Anthropocene. We argue for the rethinking of urban environments and examine how urban environments are designed for different civic and public use, arguing that children navigate these assemblages of human and the more-than-human as they constitute civic participation in the Anthropocene. We theorise the posthuman child as a political subject and citizen, forming posthuman civics and publics during the great social and environmental upheaval of the climate crisis. We argue these posthuman civics must be based on an ethics of care for the more-than-human of urban environments, acknowledging the cosmopolitical force of the more-than-human urban dwellers in children's formation of posthuman citizenship. Finally, we conceptualise posthuman publics and civics in relation to family, education and play arguing that multimodal forms of expression through art and sensuous mapping allow children to articulate the complexities of their posthuman civics, and to call publics to attention in response to the Anthropocene.

Chapter 2

Posthuman Publics

Like so many others before us we have discovered a lie. It wasn't independent, free men being called to attention in the agora, it was those men who were supported by their wives, pleasured by boys, men who had eaten the local animals and who had brought these seemingly delicious animals with money earned through exchanging land. Men, who by arriving and saying they spoke for themselves, were already many, were already speaking with their wives, their animals, their land. Yet the lie that they could 'stand alone' famously sold. Habermas, and indeed Socrates before him, made the Agora seem like a *place for men and a place of men.* For Habermas, the agora offers a model of 'The Public Sphere' as a democratic space that fosters debate amongst its members on topics concerned with the advancement of public 'good'. For example, Habermas (1991) quotes Bergasse saying 'you know, it is only through public opinion that you can acquire any power to promote the good' (99). Drawing on Greek configurations of public and private spaces and modes of social operation, Habermas (1991) characterises the public sphere as a space in which 'citizens . . . interacted as equals with equals' (4). While this space of citizenship is signposted as a bourgeois arena, Habermas characterises debate within the public sphere as socially inclusive, 'a realm of freedom' (4). It is a space that, due to its access to economic and social resources, is separated from the power of the church and the government. It comprises:

Merchants, bankers, entrepreneurs, and manufacturers [who] . . . belonged to that group of the 'bourgeois' who, like the new category of scholars, were not really 'burghers' [comfortable members of the middle class] in the traditional sense. This stratum of 'bourgeois' was the real carrier of the public. (23)

21

Habermas goes on to qualify that the texts the public read, or those which engage the public, are not necessarily 'scholarly'. Indeed, he now famously introduces the concept of the public sphere by discussing an actor performing for his audience. Habermas considers the ways different kinds of texts gather divergent publics by drawing a 'distinction between the public that gathered as a crowd around a speaker or an actor in a public place, and the *Lesewelt* (world of readers). Both were instances of a "critical *(richtend)* public"' (26). The attention of the audience and the constitution of audience are crucial to the definition of a public, then. Sites of performance and display — be they distributed or localised, constitute publics as long as they draw audiences to attention. While *The Structural Transformation of the Public Sphere* maintains an ongoing discussion of the relationship between different viewing publics and textual forms, children are never positioned as authors of the texts that call publics to attention, and textual forms remain conservatively conceived: newspapers, orations, plays. The posthuman publics we write about are children's attempts at calling audiences to attention, through engaging with practices of making and the more-than-human world. The posthuman publics with which we are concerned are a long way from Habermas's adult, masculine public sphere. However, in order to deconstruct this model we must further introduce it.

THE ADULT, MASCULINE PUBLIC SPHERE

Feminist scholarship on the public sphere has long critiqued the gendered and (hetero)sexed nature of the public sphere discourses. In *States of Injury,* Wendy Brown (2020) outlines how the rhetoric of a crisis in masculinity functions as a cipher for much larger governmental anxiety about the public sphere, the family and men's place within the family. In critiquing the public sphere Brown focuses on contemporary forms of liberal democracy and their enmeshment with late capitalism. She is concerned with the modes of governmentality to which the 'family' and 'liberal democracy' give rise; that is, with the effect they have on our capacity to think of ourselves as politically, socially and economically 'free' subjects. Brown asks how we can think of ourselves as liberated political subjects, as politically 'free', when the terms of political discourse, of political engagement, are so highly structured by the liberal democratic structures within which we live. Brown begins by noting the paradox of feminist appeals to state power, for example, in appeals for maternity leave or equal representation of women in federal and state parliaments. These are paradoxical because, as Brown goes on to show in considerable detail, the very model of liberal democracy, its structures and modes of exercising power, are masculinist. Brown asks:

What are the perils of pursuing emancipatory political aims within largely repressive, regulatory, and depoliticising institutions that themselves carry elements of the regime (e.g. masculine dominance) whose subversion is being sought? (ix)

In other words, Brown is suggesting that there is something counterintuitive about appealing to the state for gender justice, when the state's disciplinary and biopolitical apparatuses retain the power to both define what counts as justice, what counts as gender and also to restrict access to such normative definitions. Put more simply, Brown thinks it is daft for women's groups to ask governments for greater rights because governments exercise power in masculine ways.

Brown is concerned with how we practice politics, or more precisely with the effects of those practices on how we live. She argues that governmental practices are shaped by the state's biopolitical and disciplinary powers, especially how these powers encode freedom. Brown argues that the state enables freedom, but that this freedom is differently enjoyed. Some people are enabled to enjoy their freedom more than others. For example, changes to family benefit payments were sold by the Australian government as enabling parents to 'choose' to send – and pay for – their pre-school-aged kids to childcare. In effect, these changes require one parent to be earning a very good wage to financially cover for the other parent spending all their time on childcare. It does enable a 'freedom', but not one accessible to many people.

Broadly, Brown sees such governmental practices as masculinist. Masculinism here is conceived at a discursive level. She isn't concerned with numerical statistics about the relative numbers of men and women in parliament or state bureaucracies. Rather, Brown is critically interested in how the exercise of power is masculinised, something she defines as powers put to work in the pursuit of continued male dominance:

The elements of the state identifiable as masculinist correspond not to some property contained within men but to the conventions of power and privilege constitutive of gender within an order of male dominance. (166–167)

In other words, state power is exercised in a 'masculine' way, and in ways that privilege masculine experiences. Brown's argument is that power and privilege are repeated according to the conventions which govern their performance. Brown asks two questions about this codification of White masculine power:

i) How is masculinity installed, recited if you like, as the unspoken norm of political, legal, and economic discourse? And;

ii) What are the implications of the state's masculinism for oppositional politics?

This critique is useful for our work here for two reasons. Firstly, the critiques Brown (2020) advances of the state are absolutely applicable to the public sphere constituted Habermas:

> *The public sphere was coextensive with public authority . . . . The public sphere in the political realm evolved from the public sphere in the world of letters; through the vehicle of public opinion it put the state in touch with the needs of society.* (31)

The public sphere, in other words, was a vehicle by and through which men governed men, women and children according to the needs of men. While our posthuman critique and re-imagining of the public sphere responds to Brown's argument about the gendered nature of state power and, indeed, the construction of the state through rendering Habermas's masculinist public sphere void and enlivening our own posthuman public, this contemporary model for thinking about civics is a form of oppositional politics. Responding directly to Brown's second question above, posthuman publics are a form of oppositional politicking because they are children's alternatives to adult, masculine publics. Posthuman publics are children's more-than-human communities: the collectives to which they belong, which include animals, plants, the built environment, rubbish, weather and (crucially) possibilities for change.

The defining features of Habermas's public sphere are democratic space that fosters debate about public good, equality between those occupying the sphere, specific relationships between texts and audiences and calling a public to attention or holding attention. While these characteristics change in response to our critiques of their conceptualisation, some aspect of their utility and intent remains in the final iteration of our posthuman public. We contend that just as 'we have never been modern' (Latour 1993, 1), men have never really been men. The Greek Agora modelled a culture of masculine exchange and political debate, a space that specifically excluded women and presented animals (and women and children) as property. Since 7000 BCE, changing ways of thinking have transformed how European, capitalist thought perceives trade, culture, society and 'man'. We have never been modern or, indeed human; we are, and always have been, much more-than-human. As a noun, *the posthuman* expresses the more-than-human nature of everyday life and the posthuman condition, it names the 'everything else' that the supposedly solo man (who enjoys being 'free' among his equally 'solo male' companions) relies on to survive. Through a posthuman lens, the agora, the place of 'men's' trading, needs to be rethought. The Agora was originally positioned by Habermas (1991) as a model of thinking about public life. He explains:

We are dealing with categories of Greek origin transmitted to us bearing the Roman stamp. In the fully developed Greek city-state the sphere of the polis, which was common (koine) to the free citizens, was strictly separated from the sphere of the oikos; in the sphere of the oikos, each individual is in his own realm (idia). The public life, bios politikos, went on in the market place (agora), but of course this did not mean that it occurred necessarily only in a specific locale. (3)

'Public life' is the heart of the public sphere, and while this is originally presented as mobile, it was also clearly framed as an adult man's world. However, if men were actually always more than men, if they were the women, children and animals that fold in to constitute who they are, then the Agora was obviously about more than men trading and talking politics. It was also about the male control of women and children, animals and land. If we were to take a posthuman approach to considering the Agora as fora for engaging publics, perhaps we could include the smells as agents of engagement? Sounds? The items sold? The things relied on in order for the Agora to exist? If we are to take Rosi Braidotti's (2013) theory of the posthuman seriously, then we have to expand the concept of the human or the agent/actor to encompass the material assemblages surrounding them. Braidotti (2013) explains:

The human of Humanism is neither an ideal nor a statistical average or middle ground. It rather spells out a systematic standard of recognizability – of Sameness – by which all the others can be assessed, regulated and allotted into a designated social location. The human is a normative convention, which does not make it inherently negative just highly regulatory and hence instrumental to practices of exclusion and descrimination. The human norm stands for normality, normalcy, normativity. It functions by transposing a specific mode of being human into a generalized standard, which acquires transcendent values as the human: from male to masculine and onto human as the universalised format of humanity. This standard is posited as categorically and qualitatively distinct from the racialized, naturalised others and also in opposition to the technological artefact. The human is a historical construct that became a social conventional about 'human nature'. (26)

The invention of 'standards' based on men occurred absolutely to make them appear the norm, rather than a result of needing a norm. Travelling back to this invention of 'man', the agora/polis, and publics as a collection of men, one can already begin to see all the Others who are there with the men. These others include children and the more-than-human. The 'reasonable adult' of the public that is drawn to attention in Habermas's ideas, is not the embodied child, or animal. The reasonable adult figure of the audience positioned as a focus of Habermas's is an adult male who is also assumed to be the owner, and leader of public life.

Despite this bias, Habermas (1991) characterises debate within the public sphere as socially inclusive, 'as a realm of freedom' (4), although clearly a realm of freedom for men. It is a space that, due to its access to economic and social resources, is separated from the power of the church and the government, as it is composed of capitalists.

Habermas qualifies the fact that the texts the public read are not 'scholarly', and considers the ways disparate texts gather dissimilar publics, so even from earlier discussions of this concept, the audience and the agency of the audience is important. Sites of performance or display – be they distributed or localised, constitute little publics (Hickey-Moody 2013) as long as they draw audiences to attention. However Habermas's ongoing discussion of the relationship between different viewing publics and textual forms remains centred on adults. While this line of inquiry later inspired a scholarly field on media and their publics, including Butsch's[1] influential collection *Media and Public Spheres* (2007) and *The Citizen Audience* (2008), it has only been more recently that we have seen an inclusion of children and child-focused texts in such discussions (Hickey-Moody 2013).

According to Habermas, a 'public', such as one assembled to watch a performance of Hamlet, might be localised and quite small. Different textual forms (newspapers, journals, performance and so on) thus operate as 'public organs' (Habermas 1991, 2) that configure distinct critical publics. A constitutive feature of any given public is a concern with advancing a common good, a concern:

> t[T]ranscending the confines of private domestic authority and becoming a subject of public interest, that zone of continuous administrative contact became 'critical' also in the sense that it provoked the critical judgment of a public making use of its reason. (Habermas 1991, 24)

This point about provoking the critical judgement of a public making use of its reason is significant, and is one to which we respond through considering child publics developing their own forms of unreason, of wildness and collectively mobilising this wildness and unreason. Suffice to say, an investment in some iteration of democratic ideals and thinking about society is a constitutive feature of a 'public'. Such investments remain implicit in the different ways that the human remains enmeshed in uses of the public sphere. We continue this investment through thinking about how children collectively conceive of things other than themselves: adults, animals, things.

A body of work exists (including Bennett 2010; Butsch 2000, 2008; Bruns et al. 2011) that examines the Habermasian public sphere in expansive, although not posthuman, ways. These texts offer a contemporary perspective on the fact that through calling an audience to attention, media texts create 'affective and emergent publics' (Bruns et al. 2011, 9) which are 'structured by affect as much as by rational-critical debate. Such engagement can occur in and through popular culture . . . and everyday communication . . . . By decentering more formalized spaces of rational debate' (Bruns et al. 2011, 9). We might also think of a children's performance, painting or the playing through of a forest scene as calling an audience to attention. Affective and emergent publics of bird calls, children's expressive art and animal territories are other possible uses for this concept that do not require the centring of the adult male. The most useful text in this space, for our purposes, is Jennifer Barrett's (2012) book *Museums and the public sphere*. Barrett builds on critiques of Habermas's public sphere 'based exclusively on rationality' (165). To investigate the spatial and visual discourses of museums as cultural and aesthetic, Barrett argues we need to introduce visuality and spatiality to Habermas's public sphere. She aims to rework Habermas's 'public sphere' as a cultural public sphere to reveal the significance of 'the cultural' in understanding the public realm. Barrett highlights that while Habermas argued access to the public sphere was a basic right of all citizens, his focus on the proper modes of rational communication made citizenship in the public sphere 'conditional upon the public *use* of reason' (21, emphasis added). Habermas was concerned primarily with the discourses that constituted the public sphere, and was largely silent on the spatiality and materiality of the public sphere. 'Public spaces' are simply sites where 'public discourse' occurs (20), and art and aesthetics was not the site of the rational discourse that was required for participation in the public sphere. Habermas, Barrett argues, views the public sphere as constituted by a 'world of letters' – literature, manuscripts, media, letters, pamphlets, newspapers – the 'technical and cultural context in which the bourgeois public sphere was constituted' (21). Habermas excluded visuality, aesthetics, and art because it is 'the (uncertain) science of the senses' (Barrett 2012, 21). Habermas considers the literary as public, but other 'culture' as private, because it is subjective, personal and therefore supposedly unreliable and irrational. This means Habermas views art and aesthetics as essentially apolitical, because art does not communicate issues that are 'of public concern'. Art is 'too subjective and too particular' and 'lacks the necessary respect for reason and rationality' (Barrett 2012, 30): 'Sentiment, for Habermas, is too personal, irrational and particular' (21).

Habermas's focus on 'rationality' limited the forms, modes and places of participation that were allowed to form the public sphere. Access to this world of letters is a right of citizens as they are narrowly defined by Habermas, and is therefore subject to the same limitations and exclusions that citizenship holds that is, a citizen is White, male, land-owning, educated elite and so on. But furthermore, the designation of discourse that operates outside the public sphere as private, subjective and sentimental, further excludes women, children, (then) slaves, people of colour and the non-human, from the definition of the rational, objective citizen of the public sphere. Barrett (2012) offers the museum – constituted of spatial and visual elements – as a non-normative mode of communication, making the public sphere accessible to more individuals and modes of expression than Habermas's rational, civilised, bourgeois public sphere.

Barrett (2012) also critiques the universality of Habermas's public sphere, arguing for the inclusion of 'subaltern publics' that have historically been made up of working-class, popular or peasant populations. We might position a posthuman public within Barrett's offered possibilities of non-universal publics that are characterised by 'situated reason' (34). This would draw posthuman subjectivities to the fore.

Barrett (2012) argues that these multiple publics are constituted in no small part by what is defined as public space, such as a museum: 'being a citizen in the museum constitutes the public' (17). The inclusion of a more cultural understanding of the public sphere, Barrett argues, involves acknowledging cultural differences, and 'the multiple ways in which different publics articulate their "publicness" and the spaces in which they present themselves' (37). Acknowledging these differences undermines the supposed universality of Habermas's public sphere. The models for thinking about public culture and the collective voice that we advance in this book certainly draw on an expansive approach to thinking about texts and citizenship, the non-universal public and the relationality of public and private, culture and politics.

If, as we maintain, publics have also always been posthuman, or more-than-human, we need to modify the constitutive features of public spheres in response. What, for example, constitutes 'the reflexive circulation of discourse' (Warner 2002, 90)? Through a posthuman lens, patterns, sounds, body language or echolocations can be seen as forms of discourse. The Agora needs to be seen as the circles of stones upon which men sat and traded, as the geographic location in the heart of the acropolis, as the animals and coins that generated so much debate, as the men holding the debate themselves. We are certainly not the first to begin discussions of posthuman publics, and in so doing, we mobilise a very specific genealogy (or 'wild disorder' (Halberstam 2020)) that is somewhat different from that employed by others working on posthuman publics. We devote time and space to explicating the genealogy of thought that informs our work here and for centring children as a part of this conversation.

A WILD DISORDER OF POSTHUMAN PUBLICS

We are inspired by Jack Halberstam's (2020) *Wild Things* to make the suggestion that a 'wild disorder' might be considered a collective noun. Halberstam suggests that when considering an order of things or composing a genealogy, *'a disorder of things* . . . emerges and takes its ghastly shape in the shadows cast by the very project that discerns, desires, and demands order in the first place' (12). In many ways, the concept of posthuman public can be seen as the ghastly shape in the shadows cast by Habermas's public sphere. Existing scholarship on posthuman publics is eclectic, diverse and brings with it different theoretical emphases depending on the approach taken to employing the concept. The first record we can find of the term 'posthuman public' being used, which may not necessarily be the very first, is Daniel Richards's 2019 paper on Dewey and the possibility of a posthuman public. This publication takes up Dewey's Habermasian reading of the public sphere and asks: 'To what extent does Dewey grant or attribute agency to nonhuman things?' (373). Richards's intent here is to explore the possibilities and implications of 'more attentiveness to the bodies and ecologies up to this point ignored by [. . .] respective contemporary public theorists', to 'reconstitute what constitutes a public' (386). We also look to reconstitute a public, both in terms of who is allowed to belong to a public sphere and where public spheres might be located. As we go on to show, posthuman publics populate spaces such as parks, art galleries, church building balconies and city squares. They comprise children, animals, art, foliage, tents, sounds and smells.

Richards utilises Jane Bennett's (2010) interrogation of Dewey's publics as constituted by *both* human and non-human bodies. Bennett hypothesises that 'Dewey, given the language, would have been amenable to the possibility of a distinctly posthuman public' (in Richards 2019, 392). Thus, while not quite arguing that publics are 'always-already posthuman', Richards contends that Dewey's work actually 'anticipat[ed] in some ways the work of contemporary posthumanists and new materialists' (366), including Bennett and Latour. Richards argues that Dewey hinted at 'an ontological framework attributing potentiality to all "things" in his version of nature, including not only those that are experienced or not experienced but also those that can be construed as nonhuman, nonliving entities' (375). This, Richards suggests changes the ways we can apply a Deweyan vision of publics to extend beyond people only as the 'actors'.

Richards offers an answer to Allen's (2011) question: 'Can we share our democracy with them, the nonhuman objects?':

I don't argue that we bring them into our politics; I argue that they are our publics – they co-constitute public spaces in influential, persuasive ways. They are already and perhaps always have been part of our posthuman publics.
(Richards 2019, 393, emphasis added)

We agree. Richards acknowledges the more-than-human world on which humans rely and presents the possibility that Dewy's 'publics'' might be constituted by both the human and the non-human. In what Richards characterises as anticipation of Barad's (2007) 'agential realism' (33) and 'onto-epistemology' (409) and Latour's 'missing masses' (1992) of materiality – 'Dewey wanted philosophy to tilt down at the dirty blistered hands in front of our eyes' (Richards 2019, 370) – Richards offers Dewey's philosophy as one that refuses to centre 'man' in 'the complex network of ecological and material relationships' (369). He embraces Hamardstrom's argument that Karen Barad's 'agential realism' 'shares and . . . radicalises Dewey's trans-actional idea of the entanglement of the organism-in-environment-as-a-whole' (in Richards 2019, 372). Here, a posthuman public is a collection of materials, not even necessarily organic materials, just responsive materials. Objects that react, respond, diffract are citizens in such a posthuman public.

Following along these lines, Bennett's (2010) formulation of a posthuman public hinges on the distribution of political responsibility across human and non-human agents. This idea is useful for our work as it changes how we can value the connections between human children and non-human agents. Bennett's model of accountability is networked, and involves sets of intra-acting things. She calls researchers to think about questions of scale, actants, systems and the wild. She states:

Even if a convincing case is made for worms as active members of, say, the ecosystem of a rainforest, can worms be considered members of a public? What is the difference between an ecosystem and a political system? Are they analogs? Two names for the same system at different scales? What is the difference between an actant and a political actor? Is there a clear difference? Does an action count as political by virtue of its having taken place 'in' a public? Are there nonhuman members of a public? What, in sum, are the implications of a (meta)physics of vibrant materiality for political theory? [. . .] What, if anything, does the claim that worms and trees and aluminum are participants in an ecosystem say about political participation? (94–100)

Clearly, a change in the nature of what political participation might be is embedded in the project of thinking about animal-human and, indeed, aluminium-human interactions and the other examples Bennett offers. Richards like Bennett argues that Dewey 'wants us to recognize that humans are but one bond in this long sequential series of translations marked by continuity, and at times are playing second fiddle' (383). Richards links Bennett's dispersed model of agency with Dewey's 'conjoint action', arguing that some of these actions can originate from both human and non-human actors. Dewey's most basic idea of power refers to making differences through what he calls 'conjoint action' within a social medium. Dewey contends that only when effective social practices are absent is it possible to identify power as interactional instances of conflict between wills, structures or expertise. Richards builds on this idea, thorough characterizing conjoined action as sociological:

> *The field of political action is in many ways ecological, with no one body solely responsible for action as each body is conjoined with another, clustered together as they respond to harm, and then re-acting from this formation into new trans-actions and new groups (or 'swarms') to be affected – and publics (re)emerge ad infinitum.* (390).

Dewey and Bennett's conceptions of political responsibility are relational and, to a certain extent, distributed. Greta Tunberg calling for climate action and living a low carbon lifestyle and changes in animal behaviour, spending more time in burrows to avoid the rising heat caused by climate change are two examples of what such conjoined action might look like. Both rely on the more-than-human, or, in Dewey's case, the human in context. What matters for us here is that political responsibility is part of how acting agents are conceived. If they are analogs, ecosystems and political systems must both have a politic and an ecology. It is also useful to think about Stengers's cosmopolitics (2010) here, and her work on the frustration of disruption by the 'idiotic' – a term she employs not an ableist slur, but rather as a celebration of things that disrupt the status quo and keep politics foregrounded for people. The agency of *the disruption*, which might be caused by non-human bodies and things, helps to think about how posthuman politics operate: sometimes they communicate diagonally, unexpectedly, through disorganization. Other times they run regular migration patterns that follow the same route for hundreds of years. They are both traditional and radical in non-human ways.

In addition to the imperative to recognize the political responsibility of distributed actants, the posthuman public sphere calls us to think about collectives and collectivities: how clusters of different things move, communicate, create and respond. The collective is an actant. For example, the idea of the public as a swarm:

Deleuze and Guattari are theorists of the swarm, the pack, the multiple and the multiplier. These collective nouns express different kinds of publics – they offer means of thinking through animal publics, human publics, human-non-human aggregated publics. Deleuze and Guattari always think in terms of the (public) aggregate, or the private collective. They think and model relationality in publics. They explain the multiplicity of the unconscious as 'A multiplicity of pores, or blackheads, of little scars or stitches. Breasts, babies, and rods. A multiplicity of bees, soccer players, or Tuareg. A multiplicity of wolves or jackals . . . . All of these things are irreducible but bring us to a certain status of the formations of the unconscious'. (Hickey-Moody 2016, p. 536)

The idea of the public as a swarm has been written about by Hickey-Moody (2016), where she takes up these visions of the multiple as a method for understanding public culture. In developing the idea of conjoined action as a more-than-human network of responsive, active agents, we build on Hickey-Moody's earlier identification of the public as a pack or swarm, thinking partly in terms of possibilities afforded by collective nouns, both existing and becoming. Posthuman publics take many forms and speak through action and through sound. We have examined the construction of masculine, adult publics and the more contemporary affordances of posthuman publics. Yet little of this literature addresses children, and, for our interests, the roles that children play in the construction and constitution of posthuman publics. It is to this issue we now turn.

POSTHUMAN CONNECTIONS

In this section of the chapter we dig down into our suggestion that *connections between* objects and people are the active agents within a posthuman framework. The ideas we have presented thus far examine the fact that masculine subjects are valued by 'humanist' principles and frameworks (such as Habermas's public sphere). We have collected and developed some critiques of this concept with a view to activating and extending them, and here we begin to apply these ideas to the act of thinking about the posthuman children we introduce above. Children and the connections they make in the world can be seen as an alternative 'guiding pathway for the conduct of encounters, relations, and organisation' (Bignall 2020, 4) of an assemblage like a society or public. Posthumanism offers an alternative way to orchestrate or regulate relations between the human and non-human actants in the assembly of a public. Speaking specifically of a decolonial approach to societies, Bignall suggests that posthumanism can regulate 'collaborative and consensual modes of interaction as the basis for a transformed political system, predicated on respectful communication between differences' (3).

To draw out the particularities of a posthuman public, Bignall (2020) positions the humanist figure of 'the human' against the disaggregated posthuman subject. The human is defined by 'properties essential to Man [. . .] his natural autonomy, rationality, competitiveness, possessive individualism, and so forth' (3). Posthuman subjects, on the other hand, have their character defined by the affects and the assemblages to which they belong: they are defined by the impact or affect they have or are part of making, rather than the matter from which they are composed. We propose throughout this book that it is problematic to make such easy distinctions between the Human subject and the non-human subject because the boundaries around these bodies are porous and are constantly breached: water is now full of oil, aluminium and microplastics, and human bodies are currently trying to avoid being breached by a virus pandemic. Nancy Fraser's (1990) now-famous critique of the Habermasian public sphere, where she particularly dismissed the assertion that the public sphere is (or could be) 'universal' is humanist, does not necessarily align with our posthuman perspectives. However, her (1998) essay on Alain Locke famously worked to open out the 'white' canon of pragmatist thinkers to include more African American scholarship, and this political de-centring of the White male is significant.

Fraser (1990) argues that marginalised social groups are excluded from any possibility of a 'universal' public sphere. She contests the suggestion that such a space, as it currently exists, is – or has ever been – actually inclusive. A posthuman approach to public spheres and citizenship offers a new way forward. Yet for Fraser, marginalised groups form their own publics: 'subaltern counterpublics' or just 'counterpublics'. These groups speak back to, or critique, social investments which further the interests of the bourgeois, who Fraser characterises as 'masculinist', stating that: '[w]e can no longer assume that the bourgeois conception of the public sphere was simply an unrealized utopian ideal: it was also a masculinist ideological notion that functioned to legitimate an emergent form of class rule' (62). For Fraser, the notion of independent 'citizens' is masculinist because in order to function in the public sphere one must rely on a certain level of domestic (private, usually female, often exploitative) labour. Fraser advances this critique through arguing that there are problematic assumptions on which the notion of the public sphere is built:

1. *The assumption that it is possible for interlocutors in a public sphere to bracket status differentials and to deliberate 'as if' they were social equals; the assumption, therefore, that societal equality is not a necessary condition for political democracy;*
2. *The assumption that the proliferation of a multiplicity of competing publics is necessarily a step away from, rather than toward, greater*

democracy, and that a single, comprehensive public sphere is always preferable to a nexus of multiple publics;

3. *The assumption that discourse in public spheres should be restricted to deliberation about the common good, and that the appearance of 'private interests' and 'private issues' is always undesirable;*

4. *The assumption that a functioning democratic public sphere requires a sharp separation between civil society and the state.* (62–63)

The imagined separation between civil society and the state and the associated 'split' between public and private present some of the problems that arise from a humanist (masculinist) frame. Fraser continues, explaining that:

Women of all classes and ethnicities were excluded from official political participation precisely on the basis of ascribed gender status while plebeian men were formally excluded by property qualifications. Moreover, in many cases, women and men of racialized ethnicities of all classes were excluded on racial grounds. (63)

These are what Deleuze and Guattari (1987) would call 'molar' categories, large, socially visible, aggregate ways of understanding people: gender, race, class. In contrast, a posthuman approach looks at what makes up the molar categories, what they 'do' and talks about their constitution in terms of the 'molecular' (Deleuze and Guattari 1987), in terms of the agency of the smaller parts that are read as the larger aggregate. Deleuze and Guattari explain that: 'we find becomings-elementary, – cellular – molecular, and even imperceptible' (248). Tiny changes are the beginning of much larger shifts, and in this book we perceive such changes in things like children connecting to the outdoors, engaging responsively with matter, working collaboratively and inventively, birds migrating, objects changing people's feelings, all constitute different kinds of posthuman pubics and are significant sites of minor activism.

Drawing this micro-political approach to thinking about children and civics together with Bignall's (2020) offering of the posthuman subject as a way of countering the humanist public comprised of the self-contained, rational, 'bounded' man, we might think through Fraser's critique of Habermas as paving the way for our posthuman approach. For example, Fraser calls for the inclusion of the *assemblages* that accompany and, indeed, make up 'independent', rational, masculinist 'citizens' that then participate in the public sphere: the private, unpaid, usually female labour is absolutely central to men's capacity to inhabit the public sphere — and thinking though assemblages, we can see that the 'public' and the 'private' spheres are part of the same assemblage and are intimately entwined: every extension in the public sphere requires support from the private sphere. Bignall, Fraser (1990) and

Richards (critiques of Habermas) each discussed at different points above, can be seen as being somewhat in line with the ideas of assemblage, affect and partial objects that we present as a way of identifying how publics are constituted, called to attention and what an 'active agent' is. We explore these ideas in greater detail now as a way of setting up the theoretical framework for the work undertaken in the book.

We Are All Assemblages

Deleuze and Guattari, argue that our world is made up of assemblages. This is an ontological as well as a material position; they are making a physical as well as conceptual argument. In Deleuze and Guattari's early work (1977) they describe an ontology of machines: 'machines driving other machines, machines being driven by other machines, with all the necessary couplings and connections. An organ-machine is plugged into an energy-source-machine: the one produces a flow that the other interrupts. The breast is a machine that produces milk, and the mouth machine coupled to it' (8). This connectedness of matter to meaning, this functional ontology, becomes rendered as assemblage in their later work (1987, 1994). The ontological proposition being relied upon is that nothing stands alone, that the one is more than the sum of its parts as connections make up how things are able to perform in context.

In *A Thousand Plateaus*, Deleuze and Guattari (1987) explain how they think about differences between conceptual and material assemblages; to use their words 'machinic assemblages' (physical things) and 'assemblages of enunciation' (ideas). The two intersect in complicated ways. Material assemblages (things and connections between things) are machinic assemblages:

We may draw some general conclusions on the nature of Assemblages .... On a first, horizontal axis, an assemblage comprises two segments, one of content, the other of expression. On the one hand it is a machinic assemblage of bodies, of actions and passions, an intermingling of bodies reacting to one another; on the other hand it is a collective assemblage of enunciation, of acts and statements, of incorporeal transformations attributed to bodies. (88)

The machinic assemblage of bodies, of actions and passions and 'intermingling of bodies reacting to one another' is part of the material world. Yet the ways in which we come to understand the material world through collective assemblages of enunciation shape the affective capacities of that world. Deleuze and Guattari describe assemblages of enunciation:

Collective assemblages of enunciation function directly within machinic assemblages; it is not impossible to make a radical break between regimes of signs and

their objects. Even when linguistics claims to confine itself to what is explicit and
to make no presuppositions about language, it is still in the sphere of a discourse
implying particular modes of assemblage and types of social power. (7)

Birds and tents don't communicate through language, for example. Later on
in the same text, examining how the conceptual and the material intersect,
Deleuze and Guattari explain:

[T]here are no individual statements, only statement-producing machinic
assemblages. We say that the assemblage is fundamentally libidinal and uncon-
scious. It is the unconscious in person. Assemblages have elements (or multi-
plicities) of several kinds: human, social, and technical machines, organized
molar machines; molecular machines with their particles of becoming-inhuman
. . . . We can no longer speak of distinct machines, only of types of interpenetrat-
ing multiplicities that at any given moment form a single machinic assemblage,
the faceless figure of the libido. (36)

Desire is a product of context. The 'faceless figure of the libido' is a force, not
a person, but is made up from all the capacities and the wills of the contexts
that produce it. We want things partly because they are positioned as desir-
able in our context.

One of many possible ways for advancing assemblage thinking that
Deleuze and Guattari (1987) offer in *A Thousand Plateaus* is thinking about
swarms and packs. Indeed, building on the collective thinking we introduced
above as a way of expressing being more than singular, we contend that
swarms and packs are posthuman publics. Deleuze and Guattari specifically
differentiate swarms and packs from 'crowds' or groups of humans:

Among the characteristics of a mass . . . we should note large quantity, divis-
ibility and equality of the members, concentration, sociability of the aggregate
as a whole, one-way hierarchy, organization of territoriality or territorializa-
tion, and emission of signs. Among the characteristics of a pack are small or
restricted numbers, dispersion, nondecomposable variable distances, qualita-
tive metamorphoses, inequalities as remainders or crossings, impossibility of a
fixed totalization or hierarchization. (33)

Packs, small collectives, speak through affect, they communicate through
extending or decreasing a given body's (or collectives') capacity to act.
Affecting a body is changing the relations of speed and slowness in a body,
changing what it can or cannot do. Affects are the changes that create feelings,
they move people but they are more than people: they include the contexts in
which people are moved. Affects are a channel of communication: they are

one way that audiences are called to attention. Affects are the primary way in which children communicate, particularly before they are verbal.

CHILDREN IN POSTHUMAN PUBLICS

While children are a part of all publics, although not necessarily recognised as such, they also create their own posthuman publics. Within their own and other posthuman publics, children's agency is relational. Engaging seriously with the relational ontologies of children, Karen Murris (2016) argues that learning occurs in the space in between the child and the material world – between the hand and the paper, the clay, the chairs, the walls of a classroom. Murris draws heavily on Barad to develop an ontology where things *are* because they *relate*, using Barad's (2007) term 'intra-action'. Intra-action 'does not presuppose individualised existence – not only of subjects, but also of objects "in" the world' (Murris 2016, 12). These points of connection between the child and their learning materials reveal the agency of matter that is produced through acts of doing and in specific agentic contexts; agency can be found in the interaction between – or the points of connection between – the child and the classroom, the stones of the agora, the walls and atmospheres of an art gallery. Murris's critical philosophy of education moves across the dualism of mind/body, in/out, nature/culture and so on, arguing that children constantly engage in relational and dynamic intra-actions:

> [T]he ontological inclusion of the material and the materiality of bodies (including nonhuman bodies) requires a philosophy of education that disrupts the mind/ body thesis, and therefore, the Nature/Culture dichotomy that depends on it. (6)

Like Deleuze and Guattari (1987), Murris conceptualises the posthuman child under a monistic onto-epistemology. Here, the child's subjectivity, their unbounded bodymindmatter, is an intra-active part of the world, rather than 'in' it. Murris's posthuman child is an entanglement of material forces, elements that intra-act and lose their boundaries. A child operating in a posthuman public is therefore 'an unbound mangle' in a process of becoming. This ontology, or theory of being, is relational, material, inclusive and non-othering:

> [the] [p]osthuman child is relational. There is no prior existence of individuals with properties, competencies, a voice, agency, etc. Individuals materialise and come into being through relationships; and so does meaning. (84)

Murris engages only tangentially with civics and publics; she does so specifically in relation to justice. She argues that children's learning processes, from a material relationist perspective, are ways of being part of the world, rather than acting *upon* it. The 'Anthropocentric gaze' as constructed by Murris, very much echoes the Agora/polis constructed by Habermas (1991) populated by 'masters of households' (3). The Anthropocentric gaze therefore poses a problem for justice. The 'deep dualism' in Western metaphysics is an instrument of Othering, and supports an individualism that is at the heart of discrimination. We can see this play out in the typical exclusion of children from traditional conceptualisations of the public sphere.

Including the child in a public sphere becomes much more possible when we conceive the public sphere as always-already posthuman and humans – including children – as not necessarily at the centre, but part of a distributed network. Murris (2016) sees the Anthropocentric focus of traditional approaches to education as furthering ageist discrimination, excluding children from the citizenship and civic participation that is afforded to adults. She argues that this cannot be remedied by simply assigning children the 'same rights as adults', such as those set out by the UN Convention on the Rights of the Child, because this still positions the child as the 'not-yet-formed', the 'almost adult'. The adult remains a 'transcendental signifier' (Murris 2016, 89), the goal towards which children must strive and against which they are 'measured'. What is needed, Murris argues, is this radical shift away from Anthropocentrism that re-configures the child as a 'rich, resilient and resourceful child (e)merging through material discursive relationships' (36). We agree, yet shift our focus slightly to think of the child-in-relation, the partial objects of connection between the child and the other actants in its network. The child is part of the assemblage, not the centre.

Throughout this book, we adopt just such an approach to thinking about and writing with children, maintaining our emphasis on the points of live connection between children and things. Similar to Murris's relational approach, we see civic participation occurring in the points of connection between children, what they make, and their environment as agents, what Deleuze and Guattari, drawing on Melanie Klien, term 'partial objects' (1987, 13). Kleinian partial objects are things that connect the interior of the body and the psyche and exterior world such as the breast, the faeces, the phallus as an imaginary object and urinary flow. Or, in the examples from our fieldwork, partial objects could be intersections between children and the pastels they use to draw with, children and the atmospheres of the galleries in which their work is displayed, the child's memories brought to life with paint on canvas. Drawing on Deleuze and Guattari's generous interpretation of this term, we consider partial objects as the connections between things, connections that bring subjectivity into contact with something 'outside' its interior fold and thus transform it in some way. Partial objects are live, connected, contextually specific and constitute civic participation. Their politic is embedded and we look to bring this out and emphasise the live politics of partial objects in our conceptualisation of the publics formed by the children in our research.

CONCLUSION

Through our wild disorder of posthuman publics, we have shown that the public sphere was actually first conceived not as a place for coming together 'as equals with equals' (Habermas 1991, 4), but as a space of participation that had been carved out for a very specific group: male, human, Western, members of the 'free' capitalist market. Thus, the public sphere began as an instrument of inherently humanist, masculinist and indeed classist thought. However, building on, and extending changes made by theorists such as Fraser (1999), Barrett (2012), Richards (2019) and Bignall (2020), we have shown how we might formulate a public sphere as always-already posthuman, already made up of assemblages that accompany and make up men, as well as their children and wives, and the livestock, women, slaves, paving stones and breeze that constitutes the agora – the human and the more-than-human. This not only means turning a critical eye to the exclusion of groups and subcultures from the public sphere: to explicitly centre and include the indigenous communities, women, children, queer peoples, animals and plants left out of Habermas's vision. It also means expanding our theoretical lens to appreciate the fact that the public sphere has always been posthuman. Richards and Bennett's (2019) refreshed readings of Dewey (Dewey and Rogers 2012[1927]) offer the possibility of a public sphere in which political and civic participation are not defined by an agent's humanity but by one's ability to make change, to have an affect. We look to centre non-human planet dwellers through the lens of Deleuze and Gutarri's (1987) concept of the assemblage, viewing the posthuman public as made up of assemblages of 'points of connection'. To this we introduced the agent of the de-centred and networked child, first conceived as 'the last savage', those 'other planet dwellers', and once held outside the public sphere and thus constructions of citizenship. Considering children as entangled in these truly posthuman publics, as made up of these complex assemblages of points of connection, expands the possibilities of considering their public and civic participation. It is this conception we take into our discussion of citizenship practices.

Chapter 3

Posthuman Civics

In this chapter we focus on critical theories of citizenship, participation and belonging and the ways they inform our concepts of a posthuman civics. Departing from chapter 2 and the historical and theoretical underpinnings we discuss with respect to posthuman publics, we now consider how critical theorisations of citizenship, which discusses who, how and what is a citizen, expand notions of civics beyond the voting, human individual to encompass other pulsing bodies, other material bodies and elemental forms. Much of the literature we include here is contextualised within the extraordinary times in which we live and the impacts of environmental, social and political global changes on contemporary conceptions of civics. We are interested in how social belonging and participation occur within urban spaces enduring extreme conditions. The task of developing a capacious notion of citizenship that includes the more-than-human is fraught, because the rights of the human have been hard won by minority groups. We approach this conversation wanting to bring together the human and more-than-human in ways that maintain the rights of minoritarian subjects and cultivate care for, and engagement with, the more-than-human world.

Posthumanism and posthuman civics is not a Western concept. Ideas and concepts of the more-than-human world have been long-held in many world cultures, and so the recent posthuman 'turn' should be understood as emerging from colonial practices that 'systematically sought to discredit and dismember non-Western ways of knowing' (Noorani and Brigstocke 2018, 15). Colonial practices have not only impacted on human cultures and societies, more-than-human animal, plant, water, and critter citizens also constitute a civic presence and history that predates the contemporary cityscape. These diverse bodies are a reminder that cities have colonised spaces that were already social and civic spaces for collectives comprising elements, matters, critters, and Indigenous peoples. The claiming of land as *terra nullius* (as declared by James Cook after he landed in Australia in 1770), as being 'nobody's land' is not only an act of erasure of Indigenous people, it erases the presence and rights of other, more-than-human bodies too. And in both cases the colonial overwriting pays no heed to the social and civic systems already in place. We see that a big responsibility of posthuman theories and especially posthuman civics theories is around reparation, and doing the political work needed to support reconciliation. There is no point in being excited by theories and approaches that uphold not only humanist interests, but that uphold colonialism and White supremacy. Those of us who describe ourselves as White scholars would do well to look around and learn from examples of reconciliatory civics projects.

CIVICS AND THE CITIZEN

Discussions on 'what counts' as citizenship are influenced by contemporary scholarship such as Jouni Häkli's (2018) examination of the citizen subject and the possibilities for a posthuman civil society. Häkli considers the implications of posthuman thought on the concept of citizenship and human ethical agency in the discipline of political geography. Chris Hables Gray's (2000) examination of posthuman politics presents the citizen as cyborgian, and Mel Y Chen (2012) approaches concepts of the citizen through the lens of biopolitics. Ai-Ling Lai (2012) also takes up the cyborg trope in her exploration of self-identity and citizenship within the context of emerging transplant technologies. Lai examines cultural constructions of citizenship, identity and humanity in relation to transplant technology, as a way of theorizing posthumanism in consumer research. Lai (2012) takes Gray's (2000) concept of the cyborg citizen: 'political bodies, whose corporeal status dictates the extent to which they are granted civil rights, protection, equalities and freedom in a democratic posthuman society' (386) and applies it to several interviews with the British public about transplant technologies. This includes narratives regarding 'restorative transplantation (i.e. the rejuvenation of lost bodily functions through organ replacements derived from xenotransplantation1 and artificial organs) [and] regenerative medicine (e.g. the engineering of organs through stem cell therapy and cloning' (Lai 2012, 386). Hultgren (2017) examines how the political production of bodies and technologies generates three posthuman constructions of citizenship: structures of citizenship, subjects of citizenship and voices of citizenship. Hultgren outlines how posthuman concepts of citizenship might address certain facets of traditional approaches to citizenship (including Marxist, feminist and post-colonial approaches), such as the blurred lines between practices of power in public and private spheres; the impacts of power relations on social identities; conceptions of citizenship outside state-based definitions around a global 'public good' that nonetheless excludes Others; and the anthropocentrism of citizenship. Hultgren also explores environmental citizenship that includes non-humans and deterritorialises citizenship from the nation state.

We also examine posthuman concepts of civic relations. We draw upon contemporary scholarship and particularly on Tsing and Yanagisko's (1983) kinship theory, in which they examine how relationships between humans and the more-than-human emerge as lines of connection, reciprocity and entangled care when formulating a posthuman civics through a new materialist and posthuman lens. We also explore more-than-human civic relationships in Watson's (2019) examination of the role of water in the formation and regulation of connectedness with and in the world. Finally, Flanagan's (2013) examination of dystopian future young adult (YA) fiction supports our discussions of the relationship between childhood, national identity and citizenship, arguing that these relations provide the opportunity for the construction of posthuman child citizenships.

It is important to consider how historic concepts of civic rights were tied to the human citizen, understood through a Cartesian framing which posited the human mind as distinct from the body (and, thus, perceived as superior) to other living things because the human mind was seen to possess the discrete capacity for rational thought (i.e., being self-aware, having the capacity to think independently of other bodies and things around it). This is a simplistic description of course, and it doesn't address the ways in which humans were and continue to be hierarchised and dehumanised with respect to gender, race, disability, sexuality, and so on. We understand, for example, how, historically, slavery enabled colonisers to treat colonised human bodies as tradeable commodities (Dalrymple-Smith 2019; Hunt 2018), and we are aware that colonisers often considered First Nations peoples as 'savages' and also treated them as useable and tradeable commodities (Lydon 2021; Warren 2016). Although a deep discussion on the topic of slavery falls outside the remit of our book, it is important for us to acknowledge that although slavery has 'officially' been abolished, contemporary versions of it continue to thrive globally, in both developed and developing countries in the form of sweatshop labour, bonded labour, human trafficking and child labour (Campbell et al. 2011; Murphy 2019; Nolan and Boersma 2019). We briefly mention slavery here because early constructions of civic belonging and citizen rights were deeply entwined with tiered social systems which afforded unequal rights and freedoms to some people over others – but within these inequalities however, was a unifying notion that civics and citizenship was humanist. Civic rights, in contrast to the spiritual and animist cosmologies of different world cultures, have not acknowledged the civic rights of the more-than-human urban dweller. It is this cosmopolitical, civic force of different biologic, material kinds of urban dwellers that we are interested in exploring in this chapter.

The historic reasons for awarding civic rights and responsibilities to (certain types of) humans, is because, as Hultgren (2017) argues, the structures of citizenship – who or what is considered a citizen – stem from ideas and beliefs about the things that distinguish us and make us human; our very humanness, in contrast to the rest of the living world. This distinction is described by Hultgren (2017) as 'the capacity of humans to participate in political communities' and that, the conditions for being a citizen 'going back to Aristotle at least, stems from "our" difference with animals' (187). Distinguishing our human biological and cognitive capacities as wholly different to all other lives and beings is what conceptually underpins traditionally masculinist liberal constructs of citizenship. Liberal constructions of citizenship are built upon not just human/non-human difference, but additionally and within humanity, on foundations of inclusion and exclusion: 'the very condition of possibility for citizenship is the reduction of some Other (or some set of Others) to non-human or quasi-human status' (Hultgren 2017, 188). Having civic rights to speak about, vote and shape the society one lives in was inherently tied to tiered and hierarchical systems of status that were bound up in race, gender, wealth and a host of other physical and cognitive components. Whilst posthumanism blurs these boundaries, Hultgren (2017) cautions that trying to ignore the distinctions between human and non-human and essentially trying to liberate citizenship from its hierarchies must not result in turning attention away from global inequalities and the marginalisation and persecution of individuals and groups through modern forms of slavery. For Hultgren, seeing citizenship as inherently humanist highlights and exposes the distinctions between human and non-human beings and entities, and this distinction is a reminder that citizenship is not a neutral status but is never dislocated from conditions of marginalisation and persecution.

POSTHUMAN CITIZENS

So, although we certainly do advocate for the abolition of marginalisation, persecution and modern forms of slavery, we are interested to critically examine civics and citizenship in a wider cosmopolitical frame, and part of that work is to think more widely about 'how' is a human citizen. To put this another way, we explore and critically examine assumptions about citizen bodies and whether they only can be human, or more-than-human. Contemporary civics scholarship has shifted ground in terms of understanding how the human citizen might be composed, and exactly just how human that 'human' citizen is. Kezia Barker (2010) for example, sees 'the political space' of citizenship as where active civic actions intersect with more-than-human biological and ecological components, and that these agglomerations formulate a kind of 'symbiotic individuality', or, a chimeric bio-citizen that is connected to and intertwined with the rise in biosecure citizenship (351). Barker (2010) points out that this form of biosecure citizenship is 'forged relationally between individuals, states and territories, and between public and private realms' (352), and this co-constituted relationship is especially exposed since the advent of the COVID-19 pandemic. The notion of 'symbiotic individuality' is one in which the relations between different kinds of host and parasitic bodies co-constitute a posthuman citizen. This symbiotic citizen thus participates in a civics that enacts as well as being somewhat determined by 'the mobility of pathogens, viruses and invasive species' (Barker 2010, 350). Since the global outbreak of COVID-19 in early 2020 this enacting/determination is particularly evident via the closing of borders, and the snap controlling of communities through sudden lockdowns, quarantines and isolations, hospitalisations, mass vaccinations, medical failures and death in public spaces (see India, North America). In addition to bio-citizenry, forms of 'new citizen' emerge through the technologic. Aside from the (rightful) critiques of the rise in surveillance culture (Dalley 2020; Clarke et al. 2021) on vulnerable communities technologies can enact more subtle and broader-scope controls on citizenship and subjectivities, Victoria Flanagan (2013) observes how new kinds of citizenship are now facilitated by technology, and pays attention particularly to the technologic civics of online activist communities and how these multi-age, transnational groups exercise their rights. Flanagan (2013) is especially interested in whether young users can enact their civic rights in this space, and argues 'although children may not be able to exercise their rights as citizens in the real world', it is certainly the case that 'virtual reality provides a more utopian space in which they can actively participate in political activities' (253). So the technologic citizen can simultaneously be surveilled while also gaining status irrespective of their age, location or social standing. Flanagan describes how a technologic civics therefore:

> [U]ses the virtual world of an online game to advocate on behalf of child subjects, constructing an alternate reality in which adolescents belong to a political community, use their membership as a form of identity, and act as 'political agents' (to use Leydet's phrase) within this community. (251)

These more-than-human, biochemical and technologic participants infiltrate, permeate and complicate the simplistic image of the human citizen, and consequently, the civics that transpires. Hultgren (2017) outlines how the subject 'body' of citizenship is both a radically interdependent cyborg and a 'multiplicity of actants' (189) composed of other living bodies as well as chemicals and also inert materials. They argue that this multiplicity has direct implications on the body politic: 'If the body is itself not only one but many – co-constituted by a diversity of varied actants and forces – then a plural, multidimensional, body politic might be necessary' (190). Hultgren then considers ethical obligations and responsibilities of posthuman citizenship, in that it refuses an ethics based on a single subject. Instead the authors advocate for an ecological, intra-connected ethics that embraces multiplicity, suggesting the question 'if "we" were not fully "we", how would "we" relate to the myriad "theys" in the world?' (190). The questions asked by Hultgren highlight that the historic laws, policies and rights around citizenship are much harder to stick to when we complicate the determinants for identifying 'how' is a citizen. Hultgren clearly indicates that the 'human' is no longer simply that.

Gray (2000) explores ideas of cyborgian citizens and posthuman civics through a dystopian, sci-fi framing by speculating on possible futures where the earth is populated with a subclass of half-humans. Published in the year 2000 and at a time when advances in CRISPR[1] and gene-editing technologies were becoming publicly known[2] Gray's book *Cyborg Citizen* imagines the subclass as humanoid clones, 'grown' especially for the harvesting and transplant of vital organs. Gray's book taps into public anxiety over the then, little-known science of gene editing and Gray evokes this in his descriptions of 'a divided cyborgian society, which is made up of the underprivileged "technopeasants" and the privileged "technocrats"' (2000, 392). This dystopian image, which heavily references Aldous Huxley's (2007[1932]) *Brave New World* returns to visions of a highly tiered and classed society, presents conceptualisations of citizenship as founded on practices of exclusion, and that draw boundaries around the 'human' at the expense of the Other. Lai (2012) challenges Gray's interpretation, arguing that Gray's (2000) vision of posthuman citizenship is 'grounded in our embodiment' (392) meaning that, despite the shift to a cyborgian being, the frames of reference Gray uses are anchored in historic and linear humanist power structures. Lai (2012) offers an expansion on this social structure and suggests that emerging gene editing and transplant technologies offer 'a challenge to Western understanding of the "integrated self", which is predicated on the ideal of the "bounded body"' (392). To participate in posthuman citizenship, Lai (2012) argues, Western society must:

contemplate embodying a permeable body, where boundaries are continuously shifting, collapsing, regenerating and fusing with collective 'others'. . . [individuals] must come to terms with their joint kinship with machines, animals and their clones, and be comfortable with embracing the partiality of 'fractured identities'. (392)

Lai offers an expanded vision of the human citizen as cyborgian, as being more than a single body. This shifting, collective image not only expands definitions of 'the human' outwards; this more-than-human body also expands definitions of the citizen outwards to acknowledge the collectivity of the others that make up the human. This posthuman citizen in all its collective assemblage enacts a posthuman civics to maintain and support the thriving of its collectivity.

What might be a term for describing the peculiar ways that cyborgian bodies are active citizens? Beyond the cyborgian human, how does any other 'more-than-' body energetically participate in the public sphere of urban life, affecting or enacting civic participation? Chen (2012) uses the term 'animacies' and puts the concept to work in his book of the same name. For Chen, animacy is a concept that has great applicability because it can describe the diverse forms of agency 'expressed' by different types of bodies (and by different, we mean cyborgian bodies, but also those bodies that fall within different classifications, such as biologic, geologic, plastic, atmospheric bodies and so on). Taking up Chen's use of animacy provides us with a term for describing the different capacities of different bodies: cyborgian, and more-than-human, and different forms of matter to create change, and for these different bodies, through their various capacities to create and affect posthuman civics. Animacy offers a conceptual referent for explaining capacity and thus it is also a useful term for dispersing widely held beliefs about who or what can act, and what is acted upon. Chen suggests that thinking with animacy helps expose how humanist cosmologies ascribe animate hierarchies, and an order of things in which humans (and animals), sit atop the hierarchy with their agency to act, and objects sit below, in their subject position, to be acted upon. For Chen, animacy is a liberatory concept because it exposes deeply embedded social microfacisms:

> *What if nonhuman animals, or humans stereotyped as passive, such as people with cognitive or physical disabilities, enter the calculus of animacy: what happens then?* (3)

What Chen challenges here is our commitment to posthuman theory – in practice. Essentially, Chen is asking: Just how willing are we to forego our human exceptionalist power structures and prioritise the lively agency of other bodies and things over ourselves? If we want different kinds of civics that work to alternate systems of rights, how prepared are we to work with different citizen classification stratas?

CIVICS AND CITIZENSHIP IN AN EXPANDED FIELD

The cosmopolitical theories of collectivity and civic agency articulated in the chapter by Chen (2012), Lai (2012) and Hultgren (2017) inform our thinking about the ways animated bodies as citizens, whether they be cyborbian humanoids or more-than-human bodies that collectively enact a posthuman civics which bears little resemblance to the tiered linearity of classist, humanist systems. We propose that there is no single, alternative definition of a posthuman civics but some details of it can include the ways trash animals (Fredricks 2018; Nagy and Johnson II 2013) such as pigeons, rats, bats and insects participate in urban life to such an extent that their activities and presences result in the establishment of civic by-laws and acts, such as placing spikes on building ledges, timely collection of garbage, the use of baits and poisons near food outlets. The branches of trees favoured by fruit bats must be pruned to not overhang pathways and allow bat droppings and saliva to fall on other citizens walking under the branches. The molecular stability of buildings prompts preservation laws that maintain that stability or the building must be removed. Elements and matter such as water, wind and seismic movements contribute to urban architecture and planning laws. Elements occasionally break their boundaries and cause enormous infrastructural damage, forcing the diversion of traffic, the evacuation of neighbourhoods and the reconstruction of buildings. These short descriptions extend a humanist civics out to a cosmopolitical, posthuman civics and prompt thinking about whose rights are we addressing in our current systems and laws.

We propose that posthuman civics challenges the colonial and patriarchal prejudices of humanist understandings of citizenship and its democratic basis of the rights of the individual to vote, participate, dwell and occupy space in the public sphere. To embrace posthuman civics, we need to challenge our concepts and ideas of democratic rights – not to do away with them but to consider them in more expansive terms and in relation to more-than-human bodies and lives. As we have discussed above, posthuman theorisations of cyborgian, technologic bodies help to broaden the definitions of political community to include the active, democratic participation of more-than-humans. This political broadening must also directly involve how we can think about the institutional fora through which citizenship is carried out. Hultgren (2017) points to Latour's 'parliament of things' and Deleuze's 'idiot' in the abstract and Gray's (2000) 'Cyborg Bill of Rights' in practice as ways of 'opening up spaces where the non-human could be listened to in different, more attentive ways' (p. 191). Hultgren (2017) agrees to Gray's proposal in principle but see it as human-centric, and instead argues for a more collective, ecological conceptualisation of a posthuman citizen voice. He suggests:

Focusing on the variable ways that 'we' inhabit and perceive the socio-natural world does not mean that 'we' give up individual rights, but that discussions of individual rights are embedded in a broader, more critical discussion of our own indelible foreignness, interconnectedness and positionality. (193)

Sophie Watson (2019) also calls for a generative critique of the persistence of the individual at the heart of traditional conceptualisations of civics and citizenship, instead of proposing a possible civics characterised by deep connectivity, empathy and kinship, which crosses and indeed blurs boundaries between the human and non-human. Watson's call for recognising 'we have soft boundaries' is echoed by Erin Manning (2013) who proposes that 'there is no stable identity that emerges once and for all. Becoming-human is expressed singularly and repeatedly in the multi-phasing passage from the feeling of content to the content of feeling, a shift from the force of divergent flows to a systematic integration' (4). Manning explores how dance and movement play and experiment with transversal encounters and interactions. Both Watson and Manning see that civics and citizenship is spongy and builds from collations of interior and exterior aspects, and not all of these are human. Guattari (2014) also indicates the potential of collectivity, proposing that our willingness to traverse transversal and subjective boundaries is crucial for countering homogeneity. The relational sets of referents across what he terms the three ecologies: environment, social relations and human subjectivity (see chapter 6 for a detailed discussion of Guattari's three ecologies) each have their own 'expressive subsets that have broken out of their totalising frame and have begun to work on their own account' (Guattari 2014, 29). Expressive subsets permeate humans in ways that contribute to building richly complex subjects, and this constantly changes as time and movement pass. Thinking of citizen subjects as clusters of collectivity across the three ecologies promotes a civics from heterogeneity. Guattari indirectly promotes the potential of civic collectivity because these 'ecological praxes strive to scout out the potential vectors of subjectification and singularization at each partial existential locus' (Guattari 2014, 30), meaning collectivity is constantly concerned with social connection. We have discussed above how the human body is not a distinct separate entity; Guattari's ecological and multi-referential praxes propose that human subjectivity must also be considered beyond a self-contained whole to understand how it is composed from continually changing codings and semiotic signs of surfaces, buildings, spaces, other bodies, affects and many other things.

Although we wholly support the posthuman civic citizen, we also acknowledge that concepts of porosity, whether in relation to bodies or to subjects, need to be carefully thought, and that many have concerns about the implications on our thinking about humanity and society. Häkli (2018), for example, is cautious about blindly promoting the possibilities of posthuman subjectivities and citizenships. He identifies an 'ontological inconsistency' in posthumanism, in that he feels posthuman theorists 'construe analytical propositions that are consistent with the adopted posthumanist ontology, yet . . . communicate how they push forward research on issues and events identified as important in more conventional terms' (169). Häkli finds inconsistency, for example, in Bennett's (2010) dispersal of political agency and responsibility across assemblages, and argues it has potentially detrimental implications for how these concepts relate to citizenship. We discussed these debates in chapter 1 and now in chapter 3, and suggest that Bennett's networked accountability is generative, affording agency and therefore civic responsibility to the more-than-human, but not through a narrow scope of concerns that primarily serve human interests. Bennett frames her discussion around the agency and desires of garbage, for example, and how the objects of detritus are certainly not acting for human good as the ways they occupy water sources makes the water serve the needs of the garbage but makes it polluted and toxic to humans. As we discussed in chapter 2, Bennet draws upon Dewey's 'conjoint actions' to think of activities carried out by citizens of these publics in posthuman terms. In chapter 2 we discuss Bennett's defence of Dewey as being open to posthuman theory because she argues Dewey would likely have expanded his definitions of citizens to include the more-than-human. By considering all actions as transactional, Bennett proposes that Dewey's view of publics could be expanded to include all the things with which we interact in our civic activity and all the things that interact to create change, or what Bennett and Latour call *actants*. It is these actants that we encompass in our definitions of *citizenry*; the assemblages of actors that make change, participate in civic activities and are citizens of urban spaces. This digression in the discussion is useful because it helps to suggest that, although more-than-human ontologies and cosmologies have been central to Indigenous world cultures for millenia, the spread of these ideas into non-Indigenous scholarship is quite recent and is highly generative and potent. Scholarship in this space is not necessarily holding on to persistent humanist agendas, but is working through them piece by piece as different facets of society are examined and critiqued.

Hakli is not the only one with questions. Flanagan (2013) too attends to her concerns in her exploration of the state of abjection that results in a complete loss of agency, attributed to the loss of the status of citizen. In her study of young adult fiction narratives that explore posthuman and citizenship themes, Flanagan suggests that the technological advancements in these texts result in their protagonists becoming not so much non-citizens, or those outside citizenship, but 'a slave or a prisoner: a subject whose rights have been forfeited" (255). One protagonist in particular lacks agency *because* he lacks a status as a citizen *and* because he is a child, suggesting (although not explicitly

stating) that citizenship draws its legitimacy from agency, which technological advancements can both enhance and restrict. Posthuman citizenship, on
the other hand, proscribes this agency to all subjectivities, including children,
although this is not explored in depth by Flanagan. Flanagan touches on the
implication this hyper-techologisation has on notions of subjectivities. In particular, she examines the construction of a kind of collective feminist citizenship enabled by the internet in one short story that centres on the protagonist
drawing bridges between her 'real' and 'virtual' subjectivities, her online self
and her body. Lai (2012) also addresses potential issues to do with bodily and
subjective porosity through three main themes emerging from in her research
fieldwork data: 1, emerging transplant technologies have the potential to 'vio-
late the purity of humanness and self-identity'; 2, the danger of objectifying
the 'cyborg-body as a medical commodity'; and 3, the potential of these technologies to bring about 'inclusion/exclusion of these posthuman cyborgs"
(388). This last theme is the most relevant to the project of posthuman citizenships because it encompasses the tendencies to see porosity not as an enrichment – to achieve an 'ecosophic' life in Guattarian terms, but as some form
of dilution. The porosity is seen as an invasion that takes something away or
that infiltrates and tarnishes. This is one of the biggest challenges we face in
shifting our mindset about cyborgian human citizens, because until we make
the shift it is difficult to consider different conceptions of posthuman civics.

The issue with this reluctance is the blindness we have to the posthuman civics already taking place. Claudia Rankine's (2014) *Citizen, an
American lyric,* offers a collection of affecting, microcosmic moments
that convey something of what it is to be a citizen of colour in the United
States today. Rankine's almost mundane observations and recollections of
everyday life belie the violence of continuous microaggressions inflicted on
Black Americans by every corner of society including friends, shopkeep-
ers, colleagues, school parents and sports professionals. Not only do Black
Americans endure these microaggressions through the words and behaviours
of other people, they also experience them through the more-than-human:
through the validity of a credit card being questioned, through knocking at
a front door in a particular neighbourhood, through the racial prejudice of
an umpire declaring tennis balls being 'out', through the naming of a street
and the sign that records it and through the zoning of seats in an airplane.
Rankine's prose shows how civics is never only human, it is experienced by
subjects who are bodily and subjectively porous, being multiply inscribed
through semiotic codes and whose civic participation is shaped by and
through objects, spaces and surfaces.

Thinking about a posthuman civics, then, requires a posthuman reading
of citizenship which extends beyond a 'pure' human citizen. It requires
us to support and embrace the experimental and ongoing refinement of

contemporary posthuman scholarship in its drive to challenge long-held beliefs about aspects of society and culture. This means persisting with speculative scholarship and thinking carefully about its weak spots, such as seeing how, despite the title, Flanagan's (2013) analysis of children's citizenship in a posthuman era remains bogged down in humanist perspectives on the relationship between humans and the rest of the world in terms of citizenship. Much of Flanagan's analysis is concerned with the relationship between humans and technology, investigating instances where humans are being oppressed and abjected through technology, and instances where these same humans 'use' technology to achieve their goals and have the technology 'work' for them to keep them safe. Flanagan draws out the co-constitutive relationship between the protagonists in her analysis texts and their technology but does not really interrogate it: technology is both a tool of oppression and a tool of liberation, but it remains a tool. This demonstrates the extent to which it isn't easy to be in this space and shrug off all our normative, humanist ideas. Häkli (2018) offers Plessner's concept of 'positionality' as a way of extending 'the notions of civil society and citizenship by moving beyond the humanism/posthumanism controversy, towards "humanizing posthumanism"' (173). Deleuze and Guattari (1987) talk about not supplanting one theory for another but to encourage theoretical and conceptual multiplicity. Plessner's ontology, Häkli (2018) argues, might open up new ways of thinking because it offers the possibility of a citizenship that is not forced to choose between humanist or posthumanist stances on human ethical agency but is something other again. Multiplicity is what we need in the world. The damage caused by hierarchical thinking has left us in a state of environmental disaster and it is no longer possible to blinker ourselves against climate change, nor against the anthropocentric approaches that might lead to new ways forward. Manning (2013) proposes that fixed inscriptions which emerge from narrow conceptual framings bring about 'singular points of identification', or reductive and normalised ideas of bodies and beings. These narrowly defined subjects have a subsequent impact on what in the world is deemed as important to care for. Manning declares that the subject will 'always remain mired within the complex forces of their prearticulation' (5). Manning proposes that the energies and forces taking place around us are far more than we imagine so we therefore need a more expansive mindset – and 'bodyset' – to extend our awareness. We might not immediately see the value of seriously taking up a posthuman concept of civics and citizenship but this is because, as Manning explains 'prearticulation', which is the event before thought, and before action occurs: 'not strictly as the before of articulation but the witness of the unutterable, the ineffable' (5) is full of these different energies and forces that are impacting us even if we cannot recognise that. Just as we don't walk about consciously thinking every two minutes 'this is how I am being a citizen' but are living as a citizen, so posthuman notions of civics and citizenship help us to live-otherwise, as Donna Haraway (2016) describes, by following 'lines of inventive connection as a practice of learning to live and die well with each other in a thick present' (1). Expanding our conceptual frame outwards can help us acknowledge there are other bodies and things around us contributing in different ways to the civic space.

We understand through our living, through these civics, that all the things in the urban milieu are citizens and, collectively, we all constitute a posthuman civics. We understand that we can no longer exploit the more-than-human things around us for our sole human benefit (and historically, only for certain humans); we need to form new civic relations, or what Haraway (2016) calls 'kin': 'a wild category' (2) of neighbours that have occupation rights too. As mentioned above, urban matter participates in the civics of a city; what we might consider 'inanimate' matter such as concrete, water, earth, plastic, bricks and pollutants can break boundaries, cause large-scale change, force human diversions, evacuation of neighbourhoods and reconstruction of buildings. Watson's (2019) encounters with water are encounters of connection, always already embodying a networked relationally between humans and the ecological and technological citizens of cities: dams, reservoirs, systems of plumbing, precipitation, wetland ecosystems that form around catchments and treatment plants, rust and pressure and hot and cold showers. 'Water stretches and flows across human–non-human networks' (Watson 2019, 2). Watson (2019) embraces, as we do, Neimanis's (2017) 'wet ontologies' as a way of facilitating a specific kind of relationally and interconnectedness. Watson's and Neimanis's watery relations challenge the individualism that remains at the heart of liberal concepts on civics and citizenship, conceiving instead civics defined by entangled bodies and becomings beyond the confines of human and non-human. Water participates, in short, in the urban civics in which human and non-human animals are a part and continue to form, reform and negotiate.

Haraway (2016) provides an example project between migrant and Black children in Washington, D.C., and the city pigeons. The project, in which two different, outsider civic communities came into contact offered 'space for recuperation across despised cross species categories of city-dwellers' (24). Haraway saw how the encounters fostered an uneasy reconciliation:

City kids, overwhelmingly from 'minority' groups, learn to see despised birds as valuable and interesting city residents, as worth notice. . . . The kids transmute from bird hecklers and sometimes physical abusers to astute observers and advocates of beings whose they had not known how to see or respect. . . . Perhaps, because pigeons have long histories of affective and cognitive relations with people, the pigeons looked back at the kids too. (24–25)

Haraway works with the concept of 'kin' to think about interelationalities, and mutually reliant, symbiotic civic communities. These kin are multi-body, multi-species families but they require and rely upon each other to enact their respective responsibilities to thrive and survive. Tsing and Tanagisko (1983) examine the relationships between gender and kinship, and in particular how specific cultural systems construct gender and how this impacts the boundaries of kinship. Tsing and Tanagisko particularly investigate gender and kinship in relation to feminist philosophy and politics:

> *[F]eminists have changed the meaning of the political. No longer does it seem useful to equate politics with 'public' institutions, statuses, and social groups previously considered a predominantly male 'domain'; instead, politics should be seen as a system of power relationships and value hierarchies, which necessarily includes both men and women.* (511)

Interrogating these social gendered constructions can reveal possibilities for different relational models of sociality and collectivity. By broadening what 'counts' as political in the social and public sphere, feminist approaches to civics can engage the relationality between humans and the more-than-human and engage them as inherently *political*. These examples advocate for new conceptual and methodological approaches to commit to dismantling existing systems of power and exclusion, Hultgren (2017) also makes this call, proposing that studies of posthuman intersections with citizenship must critically evaluate the historical political structures that have actively supported and produced, or implicitly condoned, normative constructions of citizenship. They request we turn to ecological sciences and Indigenous communities to meaningfully learn about their experiences in the dissolution of the boundaries between the human and non-human and to pay our dues to these as posthuman ideas of civics are explored.

Collectivity is a concept that facilitates critiques of humanist civic relationalities, colonial and masculinist centring and autonomous childhoods and citizenships. A posthuman reading of civics not only opens up practices and approaches for reconciliation and social equity, it also pushes forward new conceptual ideas of collectivity at a time of global environmental fragility, indeed at an ecological tipping point. Posthuman civic collectivity particularly supports the open critique of extractivist interests that simultaneously reveres the rarity and capacity of metals, minerals, biology and water on the earth while reducing its materialities to nothing more than commodified resources to be mined, processed and manufactured. Having concepts to think through posthuman civics is particularly pertinent therefore when thinking about more-than-human thriving in relation to Braidotti's (2019) zoe-centred justice during what Braidotti identifies as the Fourth Industrial Revolution and Sixth Extinction:

> *The Fourth Industrial Revolution involves the convergence of advanced technologies, such as robotics, artificial intelligence, nanotechnology, biotechnology and the Internet of Things. This means that digital, physical and biological boundaries get blurred (Schwab 2015). The Sixth Extinction refers to the dying out of species during the present geological era as the result of human activity.* (2)

The practices and legislation of biosecure citizenship provide a significant implication of forms of posthuman civics, and demonstrate the politicisation of our relations with non-human matter and agency. Barker (2010) explores concepts of biosecure citizenship and how the political constructions of biological threat create symbiotic relationships between the perceived threat and the perceived security. Barker examines this in the New Zealand context, and how the biosecurity regimes in New Zealand can be thought of as instances of a posthuman citizenship. Barker (2010) argues that this citizenship is inherently posthuman: rather than pre-determined citizen values, the obligations of biosecure citizenship are now built around 'the relational assumption of continued human-nonhuman mobility and symbiotic individuality', which 'undercuts traditional notions of individual human agency deeply woven into Western understandings of citizenship' (353). Barker draws on Rose's 'biological citizenship' and Dobson's 'ecological citizenship' and their shared focus on the material-relationality of the citizen and its importance to the formation of citizenship identity, rights and responsibilities (353). For Barker, the awareness of and regulation of symbiotic relationships between humans and other *biota* form the basis of 'good' biosecure citizenship in New Zealand. Barker argues that biosecure citizenship reframes political space in three ways:

> *[T]hrough the symbolic recentring of national native nature with the simultaneous embodiment and deterritorialisation of the national border; through an extension of state political powers from acting on the body-surface of the bounded human citizen to our symbiotic associations with co-constitutive non-humans; and through the state penetration of the private sphere of the home and body.* (351)

The politicisation of the symbiotic relationship between humans and non-humans has incorporated non-humans into the domains of citizenship by recognising and acting on human–non-human relationality.

Collectivity should not be a byword for unity. In the posthuman context the social cohesion of a civics that takes place can be uneven, and through a collectivity of uneasy interaction. As Barker's (2010) study exemplifies, different bodies, things and elements can be symbiotically interconnected in difficult or complex ways, and this is partly because of the situation we are in, politically and environmentally. The ethical standards of posthuman civic collectives are likely to be quite imbalanced. It is possible there is a reluctance to acknowledge the scholarly validity of posthuman theory and posthuman theorisations of publics and civics because of an equivalent reluctance to dislodge the centrality of the human. Häkli (2018) displays this reluctance by picking up on the issue of the ethical capacities of non-human things and suggesting that researchers will have a tendency to assume that a unified ethics 'pertain to all phenomena, irrespectively of what their status is when evaluated in moral terms' (172). Häkli argues 'A world where objects rather than subjects transform objects' (172) would remove moral and ethical responsibility of human subjectivity from notions of citizenship in civil society. Häkli presumes that humans would think they are held accountable in only a material sense, not a moral one:

> For considering acts of citizenship, embedded in a moral landscape of constant
> negotiation, [the posthumanist] view presents immanent problems . . . without
> the possibility to link intuitive or intentional acts of citizenship to normatively
> charged situations it is difficult to account for the political dynamism that
> results from human attentiveness towards felt injustice and harm, and willing-
> ness to act towards correcting them. (172)

These uncertainties stem from long-held, classicist beliefs about citizenship that we discussed in chapter 2, where the rights of the citizen are inherently tied to originally masculine capacities to vote, debate, agree and move freely. As we discussed in chapter 1, these are part of the lie of citizenship – if these were the conditions of being a human citizen, then slaves could not be regarded as human (which of course, they weren't for centuries). Häkli's concerns highlight not so much problems with posthuman concepts of civics, but the need to let go of outdated, humanist concepts of agency and rights.

CONCLUSION

In this chapter we have extended a discussion of civics beyond the humanist political realm and into the cosmopolitical. We have asked how might rights, civics, and citizenship become a hopeful and possible democratic idea again? In her essay 'Political Ecologies', Bennett (2010) explores the *political* capacities of the actants of assemblages. Through this chapter we have explored and investigated the civic potentiality and agency of the more-than-human, and we have considered the implications of the vibrant materiality of these posthuman citizens, and what kind of impact such a radical rescaling of political agency might have on political theory.

We have addressed the concerns and reluctances of scholars to consider posthuman theorisations of citizenship and civics, and have proposed that the basis of these concerns connect with a reluctance to dismiss theories that uphold humanist interests. We discussed how reluctance is disguised, such as in the characters in young adult literature who address 'an anxiety about the cost of such technological developments to human subjectivity' (Flanagan 2013, 248). We have made a call for scholars to check their prejudice and work towards reconciliation and liberatory agendas, identified by Seppala et al. (2021) as 'creating alternative theories, methodologies and epistemological inquiries to open new, less Eurocentric forms of knowing and inquiry to support the perspectives and political projects of the colonised and/or subaltern layers of the society' (4).

Committing to new agendas is not only about being committed to new political and social worlds, it requires new concepts of 'how' is a citizen. This means thinking deeply about Chen's (2012) proposition of turning to 'matter that is considered insensate, immobile, deathly, or otherwise "wrong"' (2) and asking how it animates cultural life and creates political consequences, and the stringent and ongoing policing of the boundaries between animate and inanimate. We have suggested this is not easy work, but as Häkli (2018) argues, posthumanism invites us to reconsider the normative underpinnings of agency in citizenship, civil society and political agency. He argues that posthuman thinking has placed a 'strain' on human political, ethical and moral agency as it exists in civil societies, specifically the dissolution of human subjectivity and the distribution of human (political) agency. Häkli argues that the dissolution of human subjectivity has called the concept of responsibility in acts of citizenship into question and this is sorely needed in our current times.

We have argued for change to a posthuman reading of civics to halt an underground, global disaster that is modern slavery. Flanagan (2013) explores the state of abjection that results in a complete loss of agency, attributed to the loss of the status of citizen and that 'non-citizens', or those 'outside' citizenship, become 'a slave or a prisoner: a subject whose rights have been forfeited' (255). The observations Flanagan makes, from young adult fiction where a protagonist lacks agency *because* he lacks a status as a citizen *and* because he is a child, suggest (although do not explicitly state) that citizenship draws its legitimacy from agency, which technological advancements can both enhance and restrict. Posthuman citizenship, on the other hand, proscribes this agency to all subjectivities, including children.

We finish this chapter with a proposition from Erin Manning (2013) who, in her work with autistic people, thinks about worlding differently: 'When the skin becomes not a container but a multidimensioned topological surface that folds in, through, and across spacetimes of experience, what emerges is not a self but the dynamic form of a worlding . . . what emerges is relation' (12). Worlding is a *practice* of citizenship, it is a practice of relating and it is a practice that bodies, things and elements can do. We feel it is time to take seriously the civic participation of all things in our world.

Chapter 4

Methods

Enacting Publics and Civics

Children's knowledge matters, and for children, matter seems to matter.
(Aslanian 2017, 424)

Conceptual methodologies for critical engagements with publics and civics have been developed through the work of North American theorists such as Micheal Warner (2002), Lauren Berlant (2008, 2011) and Wendy Brown (2020, 2015), and the Australian postcolonial scholar Simone Bignall (2020). These approaches are modes of thinking rather than ideas for acting, or ways of acting. In this chapter, we discuss material practices of making, research creation, creative methods as different, although related and significant means of undertaking empirical research with children. Making art and movement through creative approaches to research are methods that centre on youth voice, while decentring the human. Children express themselves in relation to, and through relations with, the more-than-human. In exploring these approaches, we bring together the two substantial empirical projects that inform our arguments in this book and we examine the original methods developed in these projects as performances of posthuman publics and civics. As outlined in the introduction to this book, these research projects are the Interfaith Childhoods project and the Scaling the City project. The Interfaith Childhoods project looks for everyday stories and experiences of belonging, and invites these to be expressed through images, words, memory, allegory and collaborative exchanges. The project has developed an approach to research and data collection that is concerned with making space to recognise subjugated, non-mainstream knowledges and is a decolonialising approach to a feminist, new materialist methodology concerned with the agency of experience and the agency of places, matter and things. Similarly, the Scaling the City project was a multi-sited research-creation project in Australia and New

Zealand that investigated how children use creative practices to move through city spaces and build their civic connection as urban citizens. Scaling the City is methodologically aligned with participatory art. Through the project, children created experimental and emergent movement works and gestural mapping responses to urban space. These movement works were then captured through visual, photographic and video 'data'. Movement and gestural responses allowed for different forms of presence in and intervention on the space, with many different traces and imprints left remaining.

The two approaches are both centred around the agency of matter and intra-active experiences for children. They explored relationships between creativity and experience, and the emergent data sets both projects created acknowledge the centrality and importance of vernacular culture in making meaning and informing civic practices. Indeed, both sets of data present civic practices as ways of responding to the agency of matter and of political landscapes. Our methodologies recognise that meaning and communication are often non-verbal and are constituted in the vital present in ways that are shaped by complex political, social and cultural histories.

A posthuman reading of participation might be conceptually difficult for some to accept. Those not immersed or familiar with posthuman theories might hold detrimental views about the experimental nature of more-than-human participatory research, but this exposes the coloniality of research itself, with its focus on extracting and distilling information for the benefit of particular interests and to uphold particular worldviews (Parker 2016; Rogers Stanton 2014; Tuck and McKenzie 2015). Although conceptually challenging, the experimental nature of the approach is what is interesting about it, and makes it of value to researchers using posthuman concepts and theories and who want to do more than work only with human communities (Bastian 2017). Posthuman researchers are interested in using methodologies that are purposefully experimental. Participatory research offers this, facilitating practical and theoretical exploration of 'broader questions of ethics, voice, knowledge and power' (Bastian 2017, 19) beyond human concerns. More-than-human participatory research methods embrace experimental ways for exploring 'ethical relationality, the problem of representation, of exchange across different perceptual worlds and anthropocentrism' (Bastian 2017, 19), intentionally experimenting with speculative ideas and concepts; not just of the world, but of the ways for inquiring into these ideas and concepts. Posthuman participatory arts explores through practices how different bodies and things come together, how 'knowledge comes in diverse forms, and is collected for the purpose of change [. . .] participating as a body, being present as a body and thinking of ways through which I can practice change as a body' (Hast 2021, 46). In her participatory arts research with women and girls in a refugee camp, Hast considers how bodies are always in relation to the affects, politics and materialities that are also present. Likewise, Bastian (2017) found that experimenting with more-than-human participatory research methods enabled the foregrounding and questioning of 'the power relationships between humans and nonhumans' (27) when we are open to thinking with human bodies and more in an expanded relational field. On the one hand, conceptually accepting the posthuman in an expanded field might seem highly provocative and experimental; however, we already embed posthuman and more-than-human perspectives in our everyday thinking. For example, we go to the beach to experience the more-than-human: to see the sand and sea, rockpools, crabs, feel the wind, sun and salty spray. Similarly, when hiking or walking in nature (called bushwalking in Australia) we cognisantly wish to experience the impacts of topologies, of different natural surfaces so that we can walk easily or climb rock, we wish to smell the smell of nature and feel the outdoors. Effectively we already accept the expanded relational field but we tend not to theorise this through a posthuman conceptual frame, even though we might no longer accept the human/nature binary, even though we might understand 'the Anthropocene' and our role in that, even though we are more aware that creatures in the animal kingdom display capacities to possess emotion, kinship bonds and cross-species communication skills. We acknowledge the affective agency of the more-than-human, but we are more resistant to acknowledging how the conditions and events for living on this planet impact the more-than-human as well as each of us, and make us all chimeric neighbours and cyborgian posthuman citizens.

In developing our original methods for enacting posthuman publics and civics through different projects and contexts, we identify clear meta-textual principles of practice and ethologies of engagement. Conceptually speaking, the first two chapters of this book can be considered a methodology; a philosophy of action. They offer a way of understanding the more-than-human world and new approaches to thinking about both children's and the nonhuman's role in creating community. Building on these philosophical-methodological approaches, in this chapter we examine forms of enactment as modes of performing ideas, and this exploration also gives insight into the inventive ways we, as researchers, need to animate ideas. The aliveness of relationships between ideas and things is dynamic that research methods need to embrace and this chapter offers some examples of how we have animated the ideas we have introduced previously.

RESPONDING TO THE AGENCY OF MATTER

Conceptually and practically, our methods are designed to respond to the agency of matter. They are organised intra-actions. Karen Barad (2007) explains this by suggesting that:

intra-action . . . represents a profound conceptual shift in our traditional under-
standing of causality, we argue that it is through specific agental intra-actions
that the boundaries and properties of the 'components' of phenomena become
determinate and that particular material articulations of the world become
meaningful. A specific intra-action (involving a specific material configuration
of the 'apparatus') enacts an agental cut (in contrast to the Cartesian cut-an
inherent-distinction between subject and object), effecting a separation between
'subject' and 'object'. That is, the agental cut enacts a resolution within the
phenomenon of the inherent ontological (and semantic) indeterminacy. In other
words, relata [sic] do not preexist relations; rather, relata-within-phenomena
emerge through specific intra-actions. (333–334)

The two approaches and the resultant data sets acknowledge the centrality
and importance of matter and also of vernacular culture in the construction
of meaning. Our methods are a means of responding to the agency of matter and political landscapes. Broadly speaking, posthuman methods foster
a certain attentiveness to 'how humans, nature, and materialities are not
separate, but actively emerge through entanglements and in co-constitutive
relation with one another' (Taylor and Ulman 202, 7). Such an approach is a
direct contestation of the often masculinist and progressivist narratives that
have characterised much research with children (Hickey-Moody et al. 2021).
Our methods problematise developmental narratives with an approach that is
keenly attuned to children's positions in complex assemblages of actors, both
human and non-human.

To begin with, both projects draw on methodologies that are focussed on
making 'research data' not gathered *from* children but made with them, as 'co-
researchers' (Luny et al. 2011) or as 'Knowledge Holders' (Lenette 2019).
Posthuman participatory methods allow for an opening in regards to 'who has
the capacity to know' (Ulmer 2017, 832). Such methods also allow insights
into different ways of producing knowledge and draw attention to ways of
producing different *kinds* of knowledge. In different ways, knowledge is
understood as always being 'situated, material, interconnected, processual,
and affirmative' (Ulman 2017, 836). Our methodologies therefore recognise
that meaning and communication are often non-verbal and are constituted
in the vital present in ways that are shaped by complex political, social and
cultural histories. Ulman (2017) argues, 'language – whether it be in the
forms of texts, sounds, or images – insufficiently represents the inter- actions
among society, culture, geology, and ecology' (834). Through their focus on
non-discursive forms of expression, both the Interfaith Childhoods project
and the Scaling the City project work to draw out knowledges that lie beyond
discursive constraints and language. Through drawing, movement, digital art,
dance, collage and sculpture, the projects draw forth knowledge that has often

been constrained because it does not take the form of mainstream knowledge and expression. Multimodal means of expression are engendered by the projects' capacity to allow for entry points for non-mainstream knowledge, which may be expressed in languages other than English, or else in non-linguistic forms all together (Knight et al. 2015). As well as foregrounding the voices of marginalised communities, these methods also often rend the inexpressible expressible – traumatic knowledges, for example, or stories of migration, displacement, violence or difficulty. Multimodal forms of expression are a key form through which children communicate complex ideas (Wolfe and Flewitt 2010). The methods outlined below are therefore key when researchers are working to foreground the voices of communities who are historically marginalised and removed from mainstream forms of expression.

As a form of dance, mapping as movement moves the body in relation to spaces and surfaces. Surfaces are figuratively and literally touched, by feet and hands, parts of the body and by tools such as chalks and brushes. The movements of the children's bodies engage different decisions and corporeal arrangements, creating new forms of what Guattari (2014) calls 'ecological practices' that 'articulate themselves on these many tangled and heterogeneous fronts...to processually activate isolated and repressed singularities' (34). Our methods are therefore deeply attuned to the relations between bodies, materials, metaphysical objects and subjects that emerge through the children's participation in the projects. Hackett and Somerville (2017) consider movement as a mode of communication characterised by an explicit entanglement of the more-than-human with human bodies, and children's dance as a form of emergent literacy practice. Methods that focus on movement, such as those employed in the Scaling the City project and, to a lesser extent, the Interfaith Childhoods project, are posthuman because of their focus on the interconnections between bodies, the children's bodies, those of the godwit birds or the body of the city. Hackett and Somerville see movement as 'young children's emergent language and literacy practices [. . .] generated directly and spontaneously through multiple bodies coming into being in the world (rather than children's being in the world providing inspiration for thoughts that may then lead to literacy practices)' (388). Our project methods practically support this multi-relationality, and Interfaith Childhoods and Scaling the City each 'offer the children a way of putting themselves into relational space as architects of these enviro-art assemblages to express their kinship with other parts of the world and to make sense of their continuous co-mingling' (Hickey-Moody et al. 2021, 101). These methods are crafted specifically to respond to the agency of non-human and more-than-human matter. A method that is animated by posthumanism and new materialism 'situates, processes, and affirms knowledge in interconnected and material contexts' (Ulmer 2017, 832). While methods that centre the voice of the child still have the potential to centre the human, Aslanian (2017) argues that a posthuman methodology is key to the full incorporation of the child's voice into a research methodology. This is because posthuman methodologies specifically support the inclusion of children's perspectives, centring them as knowledge producers. Posthuman methods with children are key to moving beyond more developmental theories of childhood to centre the child as she interacts and intra-acts with the world. 'Children's conceptions of the world are children's knowledge' argues Aslainain (2017), 'they are the concepts through which children make meaning in the world and as such are more than preconceptions or misconceptions' (424).

Aslanian (2017) also identifies the resonances between posthumanism as an expanded sense of actors and actants and some children's existing views of the world. Similar to our argument in chapter 2, namely that childrens' publics are always already posthuman, we highlight in chapter 5 that children always already seem entangled with the world around them; *of* the world, not in it, as Barad (2007) argues. A posthuman method is therefore about centring not the human child's body per se, but the child's perceptions of the world, which are always already posthuman: they are always already connecting with and in relation to the more-than-human. These posthuman perspectives enable children's knowledge to guide research, blurring the traditional empirical divisions between 'researcher' and 'subject' or 'participant'. Aslanian argues that children's concepts of the world hold potential for addressing children's issues in education research, and therefore posthuman perspectives 'enable *children's knowledge* to guide research, rather than knowledge *about* children' (423, original emphasis).

Our methods focus, therefore, not only on the child-as-researcher but on the sets of relations that emerge through their interactions with the nonhuman world – the points of connection (Deleuze and Guattari 1987) from chapter 1 or the space in between the child and the materials of education mentioned in chapter 5. At first glance posthuman methods might seem to run counter to the normative requirements of empirical research methods and data, or what Murris and Haynes (2018) identify as the normative split between observer and observed, researcher and participant. Murris and Haynes approach this empirical issue as an ethical one, querying the human ethics of creating a research methodology that was truly posthuman. They ask: How did the presence of cameras, microphones or adult researchers observe children in their entangled processes of becoming? How does an awareness of networks and objects foreground the agency and power relations of the children and their material surroundings? These ethical concerns were valid, and Murris and Haynes state that their research team 'sat with' the discomfort they provoked. But turning to Barad, the cameras and facilitators and recorders are apparatuses that are active parts of the networked assemblage of relations in which the children are positioned, and which posthuman methods are aimed at investigating; 'Like anything else, research is a material-discursive practice and part of the world in its differential becoming' (Barad 2007, 89). Ulmer (2017) argues:

> *Posthumanists do not seek to study phenomena – social or otherwise – in isolation. Rather, phenomena are multiple, subjective, and produced from a series of complex relations. In moving away from empirical models of science that seek to determine causality, reliability, and validity, posthuman knowledges move toward material ways of thinking and being.* (836, emphasis added)

In the Interfaith Childhoods and Scaling the City projects, facilitators moved, created, talked and experienced the projects *with* the children. They played the same games, made the same jokes, ate the same food and were covered in the same pastels, chalk and glue as the children. The cameras and recording equipment were similarly entangled, being swept up in the techno-social processes of becoming that characterised each project, literally swept along and imbricated in movement sessions or seized and controlled by the children, becoming part of their processes of making art, mapping the city and entangling themselves with the non-human. Murris and Haynes (2017) write:

> *In posthuman research, the question 'Who/what is observing who/what?' is always part of the analysis. The apparatus (including the technology) is part of the phenomena studied and the cameras and adults in the room causally intra-act with and are part of the knowledge produced. The shift in thinking is to give up the idea that educational research can observe (either directly or with recording apparatus) humans in isolation ('objective' 'pure', 'given' in perception) without taking into account the relational material and discursive networks they are always already part of.* (66)

These methods also specifically engaged in the process of creation, more than the 'end result'. 'Process, which I oppose here to system or to structure', argues Guattari (2014), 'strives to capture existence in the very act of its constitution, definition and deterritorialization' (29). The civics and publics that were formed in the below methods were established around and through the processes of dance, collaboration, inhabiting space, interaction with and responding to the materiality of space and place and the process of making art or mapping the city. 'It is important not to homogenize various levels of practice', argues Guattari (2014), 'but instead to engage them in processes of *heterogenesis*' (34). Guattari defines heterogenesis as the way by which new singularities continually emerge. Each of our projects has experimented with new ways of connecting bodies with spaces and materials, and contesting bodily norms in terms of subjectivities, citizenships and rights, and through practices that purposefully contest creativity and expression norms (which we have done through art, digital stories, movement, mapping).

The two projects discussed here were both international empirical projects: the Interfaith Childhoods project ran in six cities and two countries and engaged eighteen partner organisations in its research. Scaling the City ran in three cities and two countries, with three partner organisations. These two transnational, multi-sited empirical projects were also linked by the fact that they choreographed expansive and creative ways for young people to realise, or materialise, their ethical engagements with society and to think about what society, broadly, might be seen as being. Through these creative engagements children were invited to explore their relationships with the more-than-human world as part of answering bigger questions about social belonging, what their place in the world is and what civic participation is, not just for humans but also for birds, forests and living non-human things. Noorani and Brigstocke (2018) highlight that methodologically, 'participatory research is a research practice that is dedicated to empowering stakeholders in the research', although they declare 'What empowerment might mean in relation to non-human animals, however, remains unclear and contested' (29). Posthuman research is not about anthropomorphically inscribing all bodies and agencies. Practically, posthuman research is interested in creative and fertile methodologies that record how 'components are interdependent and rely upon one another' (Noorani and Brigstocke 2018, 34) to maintain the animacy of the milieu. It is this reciprocity that we are interested in and committed to exploring.

INTERFAITH CHILDHOODS

The Interfaith Childhoods project was a multi-sited ethnography (Marcus 2016) that employed arts-based methods to facilitate the communication of complex information from mobile groups often left out of mainstream narratives (Hage 2005), including youth and new migrants (Hickey-Moody 2013; Capous-Desyllas and Morgaine 2018; Lenette 2019). The ethnographies took place in twelve locations across six cities and two countries. In contrast to studying 'mobility' and moving cultures, Interfaith Childhoods undertook a multi-sited ethnography of similarities, investigating multiple experiences of religion, of belonging, of fear of climate change and hopelessness and of feeling different.

The site locations in Australia included primary schools in Fitzroy and Noble Park, Melbourne; a church and a mosque in Norwood and Marion, Adelaide; a mosque and a settlement services organisation in Auburn, Sydney; and a primary school in Weston, Canberra. In the United Kingdom, the sites were three primary schools in Moss Side, Levenshulme and Hulme, Manchester, and two primary schools in South East London – one in Charlton and the other in Isle of Dogs. We explore some of the 'thisness' or haeccity (Deleuze and Guattari 1987) of these places in chapters 5 and 7. For our purposes here we are noting the diversity of places that constituted our multiple sites and across which resonances circulate. In each of these locations, we looked for everyday stories, media and experiences of belonging, as expressed through images, words, memory, allegory and collaborative exchanges. These collaborative exchanges took the form of conversations (individual interviews and focus groups) and arts workshops, in which children and young people worked together to visually and creatively explore 'what really matters' to them. Additionally, the project had a quantitative component that benchmarked the rich qualitative data through providing statistical profiles of the areas' responses to research questions which were then explored through qualitative methods in arts workshops and focus groups. These diverse ways of communicating provided us with different forms of knowledge and a range of stories about the same topics in places that are linked by their (de)colonial history. This is not at all to say the places in which we worked were the same, nor the people were the same, but it shows resonance, similarity and what we go on to theorise as togetherness. As Rosi Braidotti (2020) so accurately describes, in our global contemporary 'we are all in this together but we are not one and the same' (52). Multi-sited ethnography shows the togetherness of diverse communities across very different contexts. We are all so different and resonances across this difference matter even more because they survive our differences.

The Interfaith Childhoods project aimed to develop reflexive and critical faith beliefs, build interfaith community relationships and foster long-term aims of a more inclusive and equitable society. Through a longitudinal series of workshops and focus groups, the project explored the everyday stories and experiences of children's belonging, often expressed through images, words, memory, allegory and collaborative exchanges (for a more detailed exploration of the methods of the Interfaith Childhoods project, see Hickey-Moody et al. 2021). The project employed an arts-based, multi-sited, transnational empirical research approach grounded in a feminist, new materialist methodology, which took the form of on-site ethnography, arts workshops, one on one interviews and focus groups. These methods uncovered marginalised, subjugated and non-mainstream knowledges on a range of issues regarding intercultural understanding, belonging, migration and so on. Making art with children is a fantastic way of having insight into their worlds and was also contextualised alongside the insights of parents and family members.

Anna Hickey-Moody began the project in 2016 with funding from the University of Sydney. She started recruitment in Western Sydney and developed research questions and new research methods with children aged five to twelve through piloting methods of data collection at a settlement services organisation in Western Sydney. Across three workshops, different forms of making and modes of asking questions to provoke the making were explored. This led to the establishment of the arts-based methods for working with children that were used for the duration of the project (Hickey-Moody et al. 2021). These methods included answering, or responding to, questions about belonging and faith through textile collage, paper-mache, installation, painting, drawing and mixed media collaboration on canvas. The project grew over four years to encompass sixteen fieldwork sites that included schools, community centres, religious centres such as churches and mosques and community arts and outreach centres. Through a longitudinal series of arts workshops and focus groups, the project worked to collect stories and experiences of 'what really matters' in the lives of children and adult community members living in some of the most disadvantaged areas of the United Kingdom and Australia, culminating in over 400 participants in 2020.

The empirical data from the Interfaith Childhoods project is much larger than the data that informs this book, which is drawn solely from the arts workshops with children. This visual and ethnographic data was collected from sites across six cities in Australia and the United Kingdom, including primary schools, community centres and religious institutions. The arts-based data collection workshops were for children aged three to fifteen and, as noted above, asked children to answer or respond to questions through two-dimensional art, such as drawing and painting, three-dimensional art such as papier-mâché, making and decorating small tents and digital art, such as the making of animated identity stories. Through the series of workshops, the children explored the overall theme of 'what really matters', through activities such as drawing self-portraits, depicting emotions and values on paper, creating and decorating refuges, imagining future cities and creating self-narrated animations about themselves.

The workshops contained both individual visual and three-dimensional art tasks and collaborative group projects, and supported children in thinking about and expressing their opinions and experiences both individually and as part of a group, community and, as we have suggested and shall show, as citizens and members of a public. Each workshop began with a short introduction, followed by a group discussion in which Anna led the children through an exploration of their responses to and existing knowledge of the subject of the workshop. After the group discussion, Anna wrote up the children's main ideas on a whiteboard or large sheet of paper, which was then drawn on as a resource for inspiration and ideas throughout the course of the workshop. The children then created their art, explaining and discussing their process as they did so, and discussing their work with their peers and co-researchers at the end of the workshop. The arts-making workshops were structured in blocks, with each three-to-four-day consecutive block focusing on a particular media (digital animations, paper-mâché, quilting, collage) and associated outcomes (animations, quilts, canvases exhibited in galleries and schools). The analysis chapters in this book that are directly concerned with data from the Interfaith Childhoods project engage with two different making methods and materials. These are explained in detail in chapters 5 and 7, respectively, and in order to situate the reader we offer a brief overview of these methods here.

Chapter 5 examines collaboratively produced future cities that children made with mixed media (crayons, pastels, felt tip pen, material, fabric, paint) on large canvases. The process of scaffolding the children's collaboration took three hours, with children working individually, in pairs and then in groups of four to six on a canvas. Throughout this process, children were encouraged to visually express what really matters to them for the future. This process of exploration culminated in a large canvas of a future city that depicts everything that 'really matters' to the children as a small group. As we discuss in chapter 5, these canvasses were exhibited in galleries and they were also exhibited in schools. In chapter 5 we draw on the movement of the children's art out of the classroom, community centre or religious building and into art galleries and spaces in which they are often excluded. The Interfaith Childhoods project exhibited much of the art created in the workshops and also held several workshops in art galleries, moving the complex negotiations of self, values, the future and communities into very public civic engagements with their communities. Chapter 5 draws on these exhibitions as an example of children calling a public to attention and forming their own, inherently posthuman publics. Chapter 7 explores some of the ways children voiced their concerns about the Anthropocene through working with, and responding to, the agency of art materials. Children made mobiles that they decorated with symbols of 'what really matters' for the future and expressions of things in which they take refuge. Anna Hickey-Moody facilitated workshop discussions about things that made participants feel safe, using a range of visual art materials such as cardboard, felt pens, glitter, pipe cleaners, fabric, glue, crayons, pastels and buttons. These materials both inspired ways of making – for example, through patterns on the material or colour schemes – and also aligned with children's visions for expressing safety and refuge. Once decorated, the children's refuge tents became ideal playspaces and both in workshops and exhibitions children enjoyed playing make-believe games in the decorated tents.

As we explore above, the conditions in which the children produced their artwork – and the relationships between the people involved – affect the 'outcome', or art-making, as well as the interactions and intra-actions that are enacted and observed through the process. Chapter 5 discusses how these complex assemblages of power relations between the children, their art and their surroundings formed new ecologies of learning in which the children learned from each other and from the non-human world as well. The geographic and cultural/class contexts from which the children come, in particular the kinds of urbanity in which they are embedded, directly informed their artwork and the processes of making the artwork, and we discuss this relationship in the following chapters. The methods of the Interfaith Childhoods project and, as we go on to show, the Scaling the City project, are finely attuned to these contexts, recording not only the 'end product' of the artwork but also the complex processes of discussion, negotiation and enactment in which the children participate as part of the workshops. The *processes* through which children created art emerged as a central form of 'data', as much as the 'end result' of the workshops. A method that was attuned to these processes – through informal interviewing, discussion, participation and ethnographic observation – drew out deeper understandings of the complex stories underlying the artwork. Such a method posits that these processes, as intra-actions between human and the agentic non-human, are as important as the 'outcome' of the arts workshops themselves. As such, the empirical insights generated through the art-making workshops often arose from observing discussions with children and recording children's explanations of their artwork, alongside their complex and negotiated processes of creating and recreating their artwork. The children's discussions, negotiations, presentations and explanations of their artwork were therefore documented in detail to draw out the ideas, thoughts and processes behind the work, as were their interactions with the material and spatial elements of the art-making processes.

As mentioned above, and in keeping with Lundy and colleagues (2011) and Lenette (2019), children of the Interfaith Childhoods project were not research subjects or even participants. Working with children as they created self-portraits, decorated tent refuges and narrated their identity animations, positions the child not as a research subject but as a 'co-researcher'. While the focus of our methodology is on the relationships between the human and the more-than-human, we need to acknowledge that this focus occurs in a research context that positions children and young people as co-researchers, collaborators and research activators. There is a significant body of knowledge on youth as co-researchers (see for example Honkanen et al. 2018; Jacquez et al. 2020; Smit 2013; Luchtenberg et al. 2020). This work is grounded in the agency of children; their contributions as co-researchers to research processes are incredibly significant and child and youth participants can be seen as co-producers in the research assemblage, or research process. The positioning of children as co-researchers was a key way in which our research methods were designed to recognise the affective agency of children as they create and learn. Children used their art as a way to negotiate and express complex ideas and issues surrounding their identity, their belonging, their concerns and hopes for the future, and our methods centred their voices within the conversaticn through creating multiple opportunities to express an opinion – physically, visually, verbally, collaboratively; this list could continue.

At the same time, the methods of Interfaith Childhoods and Scaling the City were carefully attuned to the more-than-human elements that were at work in the workshops. As discussed elsewhere (Hickey-Moody 2019a), matter is part of any given research conversation and has agency. When working with creative methods, the nature of matter's contribution is not necessarily any more significant than working with science, or engineering: all research methods are ways of casting 'planes over chaos' (Deleuze and Guattari 1994, 202). Indeed, different disciplinary methodologies 'advance by crises or shocks in different ways, and in each case their succession makes it possible to speak of "progress". It is as if the *struggle against chaos* does not take place without an affinity with the enemy, because another struggle develops and takes on more importance – the *struggle against opinion,* which claims to protect us from chaos itself' (Deleuze and Guattari, 1994, 203). The chaos of matter is sectioned by art, science and philosophy in different ways, but different disciplines are united in their organizing relationship to chaos. Across this process of organising, matter speaks back: it resists, reshapes and informs processes of construction.

Matter has many ways of resisting, fighting back and inspiring children to relate to it materially in totally unexpected ways. A result of this is that research can produce unexpected outcomes. Figures 4.1 and 4.2 are examples of unexpected data. A workshop participant in South East London was clearly enamoured with the technical gear: digital cameras and iPads were used to record the research workshops, and, as the images suggest, the blue blocks held his attention and captured something in his imagination.

Rather than making future cities with his peers, this boy spent most of one morning of the arts workshop photographing these blue blocks. This is an example of what we could call material agency: the blocks captured the boy's imagination and inspired him to engage with them, capture them and mediated versions of the blocks became his artwork. Other examples of the agency of matter can be found in Hickey-Moody's writings about paper-mache (2018). Material agency was also a key focus of the methods in the Scaling the City project.

SCALING THE CITY

Scaling the City was a participatory movement and visual art (creative mapping) project undertaken with children and young people across three urban sites in Australia and New Zealand. The project investigated the ways

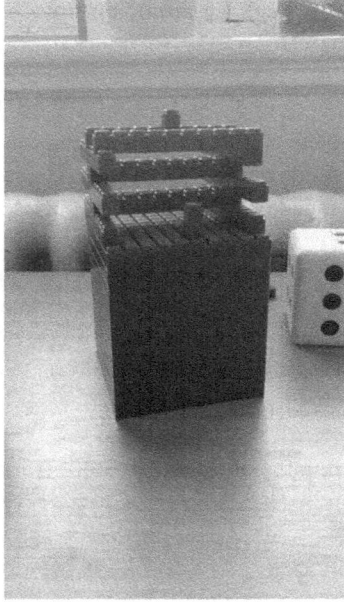

Figure 4.1   Block Toys. Photographed by a child during a workshop, Claremont Primary School, Manchester.

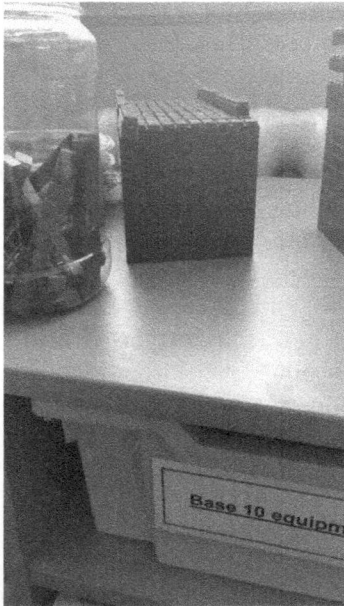

Figure 4.2   Block Toys. Photographed by a child during a workshop, Claremont Primary School, Manchester.

children build and perform civics and citizenship through their movements in and across cities, and how their creative movements through the city build their sense of belonging. The first iteration of the project worked with a dance group made up of boys aged eight to eleven in Auckland called the Urban Activators. Researchers and the group mapped and charted the city using movement, pavement, chalk, brushes and water. Moving into an Australian context, the project then worked through a similar mapping and choreographing process with children recruited in Brisbane. Several mapping and movement workshops were held in public spaces such as parks and playgrounds in the city, in which children mapped their experiences of urban space through movement and chalk markings. The sessions were held in the early mornings to avoid the infamous tropical heat of Brisbane that increased as the day progressed. All workshops mapped the children's movement across the urban space as a form of expression of their citizenship and belonging.

In each workshop the children thought about citizenship and civics and we considered different kinds of citizens, such as animals and plants, the weather, swings, stones and so on. We discussed the possible answers to these questions and explored our different ideas of citizenship. The children thought expansively about what was included in ideas of citizenships, drawing in the unrefined and unmanufactured parts of the world – the trees, grass, water, birds, insects – the manufactured elements, including the concrete and rubber of the playground, glass windows of neighbouring buildings, their clothing and footwear and the materiality of the music player that often accompanied the sessions and the atmospheric elements, including the sun and the wind of tropical Brisbane, the shadows cast across the concrete and the colour of the sky.

Finally, the project was then expanded in New Zealand, at a primary school on the estuary in one of the shorelines of the islands, the subsidiary areas around the city of Auckland. The project, called Godwit Neighbours, used a participatory approach informed by Knight's (2018, 2020, 2021) research methods whereby creative and artistic practices attune to the non-representational in a research event. Knight's previous participatory projects include collaborating with adults with disabilities to design and create costume wearables responsive to their individual physical and intellectual needs. The wearables disguised the adults as giant insects, and were worn as they participated in a large-scale street carnival (Knight 2019). In another project Knight collaborated with her (then) young daughter, intergenerationally and collectively creating hybrid creatures based on their ideas about possible childhoods (Knight 2016; Knight and Rayner 2015). In these projects a participatory arts approach enabled voices and ideas to come forward in ways (Wake and Birdsall 2016), which carried through the duration of the project, providing meaningful connection for everybody involved.

The ethical intentions of participatory research, which usually has a focus on collective human actions, choices and behaviours in social projects, can be taken up conceptually to expand out and consider frameworks of more-than-human participation (Bastian 2017; Noorani and Brigstocke 2018; Akama et al. 2020; Heitlinger et al. 2018). The Godwit Neighbours project incorporated the godwit birds and their migratory patterns through conceiving the birds as posthuman citizens, and the civics around having these citizens arrive periodically each year. Through visiting the shoreline and observing the birds feeding, the researchers worked extensively with the children to get them to think about civics and citizenship in relation to their relationship with the migratory bird citizens. Expanding on the science-based investigations students had done in class on the godwits and working in close collaboration with the Urban Activators dance group, children and researchers worked in large multi-age clusters to map the birds' civics and citizenship through chalk lines, movement and music. This included mapping the migratory patterns on the floor of the school hall in chalk, mirroring the scaling of the city with the birds' scaling of migrations. Outside in the school grounds, string and grasses were used to work through cartographic movements and creatively construct the migration patterns of the godwits. Participatory approaches enable critical work into the ways community building relates to belonging, reciprocal connection and rights of access. The participatory approaches used in Godwit Neighbours were channelled through creative movement and mapping, and this embodied practice helped centralise the posthuman community-building aims of the project as well as critically evaluate what participation is (Bala 2018) for different bodies and things. This does not mean we naively assume because we used participatory approaches, that the project was automatically 'good' or ethical. The critique of the inclusivity of participatory research over other methodologies (Cleaver 2001) raises important points about whether participation simply repackages the usual power imbalances in a socially focused fieldwork; concerns that are especially pertinent in posthuman attempts to conduct participatory research with diverse bodies and things. These concerns should not dissuade researchers from experimenting, because to do so is to avoid asking creative and speculative research questions and 'close off the option of tackling macro issues' (Bastian 2017, 32).

'Scaling' refers to all the ways in which children chart the city, through movement, through choreography, through mark-making and mapping and through inscribing the surfaces. The Scaling the City project asked children to think through their relationship with the city as a way of critically conceptualising being a citizen. The mapping used choreography and movement to expand the question of who 'counts' as a citizen, and to include the non-human beings of birds, concrete and chalk as beings that held affect and rights with the collective, community urban space. But the project also developed

children's sense of citizenship by increasing their connection with their surroundings. Scripting and inscribing surfaces with chalk, water, brushes and
their body manifests as a way of 'leaving a mark', enhancing their sense of
confidence and belonging to an urban space. The project understood that
children need to be in the space to build relations and build their citizenship.
It doesn't happen conceptually, but practically and physically.

At the heart of the Scaling the City is movement. The children incorporated
choreography and movement into the processes of mapping – they were not
held separately. In the urban settings, the children enacted their relationship
with the urban spaces through dance and movement. These points of encounter were dramatically different to those of adults. Guattari (2014) argues that
'at the heart of all ecological praxes there is an a-signifying rupture' (30), and
the children moving differently through mapping meant that materials and
affects took on different significations and significance. Footpaths and walls
shed their conventional semiologic significations and become something else
for our participant children. The children rarely walked; they rolled. They
stood on their hands. They jumped and tried to touch ceilings. They hung off
things. They ran and hopped and skipped and gambled, and worked together
to build towers out of their bodies. Their action in relation to their surfaces
created unique points of encounter, out of which their form of civics and their
position in a posthuman public emerged.

CONCLUSION

In this chapter we present two projects that co-researched with children and
young people. As noted in our introduction to this chapter, if the second and
third chapters in this book outline our methodology, this chapter has opened
the door to some of our research *methods*. As our analysis unfolds across this
volume we give further insight into the practical means of engagement and
material entanglement that our methods provided. Both projects worked with
an emphasis on distributed agency and situate the human child in relation
to the more-than-human world. We see the human child as always already
a collective, a more-than-human actant in a network of material others. The
methods we employed to engage young collaborators and co-participants
through the Interfaith Childhoods and Scaling the City projects both worked
with young imaginations and bodies intra-actively to create data.

At their core, both methods of the Interfaith Childhoods and Scaling the
City projects leaned into the participatory nature of arts as method. For
instance, including movement in creative arts practices is incredibly important for posthuman approaches because, as Hast (2021) states' 'through
our presence as bodies in movement, we can make participatory research

embodied. Movement work is not automatically ethical, but we can think about the ethics of research' (56). The corporeal basis of creative moment and gestural mapping is a way of thinking in, of and through movement, and is immersed in relational encounters which prompt further, relational movements. Participatory arts approaches like those employed by our two projects, are, at their core, continually asking 'to what can the emergence of a participatory aesthetic be seen as responding?' (Bala 2018, 14) Participatory arts approaches can only continue within cycles of encounter, reflecting and response. In that sense, and as Ianelli and Marelli (2019) observed in their project, the fact that 'participatory public art constitutes one of the multiple ways of doing citizenship and taking political agency in contemporary democracy' (642) because corporeal movements are created through collective effort between different bodies in social contexts. While only one of the projects worked specifically with movement as a research method, both projects created a space in which children and young people were able to build and articulate their subjectivity through creative, intra-active and relational methods. Guattari (2014) explains the significance of creative processes such as this, explicating they operate:

> . . . *through the promotion of innovatory practices, the expansion of alternative experiences centred around a respect for singularity, and through the continuous production of an autonomizing subjectivity that can articulate itself appropriately in relation to the rest of society.* (40)

In other words, creative participatory research makes contexts in which children and young people come to know themselves in relation to others and can find non-verbal ways of expressing themselves that highlight the uniqueness of their experience. Furthermore, both projects opened out onto social questions, spaces and practices, and in doing so supported children and young people in new forms of sociality. The methods we developed involved different materials and directives but are brought together by a responsive and collaborative ethos of working with children and young people as coresearchers. This approach to research is a social and political practice, which we see as in line with, and expressive of, Guattari's (2014) suggestion that it is 'essential to organize new micropolitical and microsocial practices, new solidarities, a new gentleness, together with new aesthetic and new analytic practices' (34). Interfaith Childhoods and Scaling the City are ways of creating new micro social practices and forming emergent solidarities.

Finally, these research projects also created new aesthetic forms and extended our work in developing new ways to think about publics and civics. The posthuman subjects and indeed communities in our research both extend our existing posthuman analytics and pave the way for our analysis in the ensuing chapters. Responding to, and extending, the children and young people's work in the chapters to come, we examine the creation of new urban publics that call expanded audiences to witness young people's visions of the future, posthuman civic practices of engaging with animals and the built environment, responses to climate change and the shifting parameters of what childhood might mean and practices of participatory community building with transnational others. Across these individual areas of focus, the children and young people's voices and imaginations show us visions and practices for a more sustainable future.

Chapter 5

Urban Publics

The second arts workshop of the Interfaith Childhoods project asked children to collaboratively design a future city that contained 'what really matters'. Coleman (2020) suggests that collaborative and creative making is a useful way in which young people can 'invent ways for actualising futures' (63). The cities that participants created were made on large canvases after a discussion about what makes a city work, what will be needed in the cities of the future and how a city can engender important values (values that had been identified in previous sessions of the workshops). Through these large, collaborative, vibrant, messy and innovative pieces of art, the children consistently conceived of a posthuman city and posthuman urban life. While the collaboratively produced canvases were often chaotic, and featured fanciful and imaginative objects – such as flying ice-cream machines, dragons, pineapple houses, flying cars, mermaids, monkeys, camels and a flying cat that breathes fire – they were also populated with familiar features in urban landscapes: football fields, Tescos, schools, hospitals, mosques, churches, synagogues, Hindu temples, shops, museums, parks and people. Consistent across these fanciful and everyday elements was a distinctive entanglement of human and non-human life and matter, striving towards a posthuman public sphere characterised by an ethics of care and a posthuman civics.

In this chapter we explore these collaborative imaginings of a shared future as a call to attention for the publics that the children formed around and in response to their art. The elements of these cities called to attention a wide public, often in the form of a call to action to be more caring and more environmentally friendly. When prompted with questions of 'values' and 'what really matters', children begin crafting future cities that are characterised by an ethics of care, an ethics entangled with non-human life and matter of the city. What's more, the urban scapes that spring to life on these canvases are direct calls to action, calling on the world of adults to create futures in which the urban and the non-human are deeply entwined, and which are characterised by a thoroughly collective and caring civics. If we embrace publics as a call to attention and as necessarily formed around a problem or 'concern', then the posthuman urban scapes that are defined by values of care and collectivity can be seen as a direct call to action: care for one another, become entangled in a relationship of care and community with animals, water, green spaces and dragons.

We begin this chapter by investigating the ecologies of learning in which these future cities were made, and detailing the elements that children used to construct their imagined urban futures. Drawing on theories of ecologies of learning and spaces of pedagogies, we then engage the interactions of the children with the materiality of their urban surroundings, classrooms, the paint and pastels of the artwork and the more-than-human elements of their environments as swept up in this posthuman assemblage around which a public was formed. The children, embedded as they were in their familiar, urban and somewhat stratified cultural and physical geographies, drew on this enmeshment when formulating their future cities and calling a public to action around their imagined futures. We explore how these and other more-than-human (and even supernatural) conceptions of the children's relations with the world inform their sense of publics and civics in a posthuman world.

These future cities then became part of art exhibitions that took the children's work into new and different socioeconomic contexts where the artwork served as a form of cultural capital. From superdiverse and often under-resourced communities, the children's artwork made its way into galleries at prestigious art and culture universities and museums, calling new and expanded publics to attention with an imagination of a posthuman future civics. The second part of this chapter turns to examine how these future cities, the public spheres created by children to be inhabited by the more-than-human, activate the public spaces of art galleries and call expanded publics to attention. At several galleries and exhibitions across a range of cultural, class and geographic contexts, the public spheres on the canvas were brought into a very real and present public. The children use their imagined futures – filled with the more-than-human, the supernatural and a determined ethics of care – to call an expanded public to attention in the form of an art exhibition. We might look to these exhibits as a form of communication around which these posthuman publics might form.

ECOLOGIES OF LEARNING

Harwood and colleagues (2016) developed a theory of 'ecologies of learning' to account for the existing cultures of education that contribute to exclusion in education, or 'educational foreclosure' (6). Their aim is to draw feelings back into conversations around widening participation in education. Specifically, the authors seek to include 'the feelings and educational views of the marginalized youth that [widening participation efforts] seek to include' (7) in efforts and theory on educational inclusion. These feelings, as well as cultural politics, construct ecologies through which 'the university is constructed as impossible' (14) for growing strata of young people. By incorporating these feelings, Harwood and colleagues argue, ecologies of learning can attend to 'the influence of the affective domain on young people and how this impacts their conceptualization of educational futures' (7). Focussing on emotions in relation to young people's engagement in higher education, they find that enduring feelings towards place, belonging, self and young people's family and peers form a significant part of the ecologies of learning through which they view their education futures and/or foreclosures. Widening capabilities, Harwood and colleagues argue, lies in drawing links between higher education pathways and these ecologies of learning – the 'existing skill sets that young people have and the cultural values and practices embedded within them' (187). For instance, they find that the numerous ways that disadvantaged young people have been abjected from higher education has created an emotional cost at the heart of the ecologies of learning which these young people then need to negotiate when approaching the pathway to university. It is only through centring the young person, and their lived experiences of the ecologies of learning, that the enduring impacts of this abjection can be countered and participation can be widened.

The below analysis does therefore not approach the children's interaction with higher education institutions and 'high art' galleries as a site at which the children are 'allowed' into spaces from which they have previously been excluded. Rather, by centring the child and their complex set of relations with their worlds, the arts workshops creating future cities probe the complex assemblages that make up the child and their attitudes and pathways towards education, but also their attitudes and concepts of their place in or *of* the world (Barad 2007). Children's ideas of their entanglement with the world – which we have argued is always-already posthuman – form the ecologies of learning in which they form and negotiate their relationship with non-human matter. We examine this alongside theories of pedagogical spaces such as those of Ellsworth (2005) in which the material spaces where learning 'happens' are considered as swept up in the relational assemblage of children learning – both the classroom, paints, canvases as well as the other children they created the art with and the galleries, universities, projections, light beams and parents through which they displayed their art. As we shall see below, imagining their urban futures reveals children's posthuman conceptualisations of their publics and civics, their position in the world as inextricably entangled with that of the human and non-human fellow planet dwellers. Both the children's neighbourhoods and classrooms and the art galleries and museums become entwined in these ecologies of learning.

Most significantly, the Interfaith Childhoods project brought children's art into museums and art galleries, introducing their posthuman conceptualisations of publics and civics to a specific set of spatial, social and cultural relations that accompany these spaces. McRae and colleagues (2018) apply Murris's (2016) notion of the posthuman child to reconceptualise children's learning and apply this specifically to the learning that occurs in museums. They argue that reconceptualising the child as posthuman not only repositions the child and their learning *within* museums as an assemblage of vibrant materials with agency, but it also repositions the researcher in their quest to make 'meaning' out of data. 'By taking the non-human more seriously', the authors argue, 'this approach gives agency to the data itself, so that data can "speak back"' (508). Drawing on non-representational theory, the methods of the Interfaith Childhoods project problematise questions such as 'What do these canvases of future cities mean?' or 'What does it mean to have a child *in* an art gallery?' Instead we draw attention 'to that which is beyond representation' (McRae et al. 2018, 507); specifically, the interactions between the children and their classroom, pastels, school shoes, stretched canvas, air conditioning, all of which has some kind of agency or the ability to affect change. By conceptualising both the child in a classroom and the child in an art gallery as posthuman, meaning 'emerges from diffuse and diverse relationships between human and non-human' (McRae et al. 2018, 507):

> *Understanding some of the ways in which children play with objects as autotelic removes the need to find a verbal, rational explanation for why a child does something and what this could mean. Thus, children carrying stones in their pockets, or [a particular research participant] rolling a tiny ball of clay with his fingers, are examples of thought-in-action, or non-representational aspects of children's experiences in museums.* (McRae et al. 2018, 510)

McRae and colleagues' study specifically argues the utility of reconceptualising the relationship between museums and visitors in terms of understanding their 'meaning', especially when those visitors are children. Similarly, we might approach children both making and exhibiting their future cities in both classrooms and art galleries as 'deeply entangled' with 'different and unique kinds of objects, spaces, sensations, architectures (McRae et al. 2018, 513), and this entanglement is a large part of children learning and calling publics to attention. Viewing meaning 'not as separate representations of the world, but as thought-in-action' (McRae et al. 2018, 514) is a move to anticipate and place greater emphasis on unexpected connections formed through human (child) and non-human encounters in the classroom. As we shall see below, the children's learning and forming of posthuman publics evolves through their interactions with the materiality of both their classrooms and the art galleries.

Posthuman Learning 'in' the Public Sphere

Like McRae and colleagues, Barrett (2012) offers the museum as a site of the public sphere. The museum – constituted of spatial and visual elements – is a non-normative mode of communication, making the public sphere accessible to more individuals and modes of expression than Habermas's rational, civilised, bourgeois, public sphere. Museum and art galleries are cultural institutions that are inherently public, Barrett argues, but have a deep history of being part of that Habermasian, rational, civilised, bourgeois public sphere we critique in chapter 1. Galleries are public in that to be in them or at them is to be 'in public', 'to be outside of, or apart from, one's private realm, and to be engaged in social relations with others' (Barrett 2012, 22). We have established how this concept of the public sphere necessarily excludes large swathes of planet dwellers, both human and non-human, and how this exclusion hinges largely on the perceived divide between public and private: 'To be private is to be with oneself, to be an individual, to be particular. The private sphere is also more often feminized, because it also connotes the domestic familial sphere' (Barrett 2012, 22). Once again this shifts when we consider the public sphere through the lens of posthuman subjectivities, wherein we accept that these supposedly exclusive, rational, masculinist public spheres were always-already posthuman, in that they are assemblages of the women, the slaves, the children, the animas, the cobblestones of the Agora.

When applied specifically to learning that can occur at, in or through art galleries and museums, the problems of a traditional characterisation of 'public space' become increasingly apparent. When we approach the public sphere as a realm of participation in representation – such as making and displaying art – normative models of the public sphere are insufficient to include the very real calls to attention that can be found in the children's future cities:

Access to the public sphere of representation came to be considered a basic right of citizens, but for Habermas, representation in the public realm was conditional upon the public use of reason. Sentiment, for Habermas, is too personal, irrational and particular in this model. . . . According to Habermas, then, new problems arose historically, as different sectors of society demanded access to the public sphere as a 'basic right', without necessarily understanding the rational form of discussion that was required for democracy to work. (Barrett 2012, 21)

Under a Habermasian public sphere, the collaborative artworks of children depicting their future cities – cities full of flying cars to reduce emissions, flying hospitals and mosques and ice-cream machines (to make sure everyone can access the important things) and housing estates to ensure everyone has a home – have no position in the 'rational form of discussion that [is] required for democracy to work'. This view of the public sits alongside humanist models that we critiqued in chapter 1 and is used to exclude specific groups from the public sphere, as Nancy Fraser established. When we look at the role of a Habermasian public sphere specifically in relation to institutions such as museums and art galleries, however, the children's emotional, sentimental and often irrational art taking up a place within these public institutions becomes all the more impactful as instances of posthuman publics being formed and called to attention.

To illustrate this, we might look more closely at the children's art being displayed in art galleries in light of Barrett's (2012) exploration of the museum as a site of public spheres. Despite being 'public institutions', Barrett argues, museums and galleries have historically not been 'for' the public. Recent pivots towards universal accessibility come on the tail of a solid history of exclusion of specific publics, or rather groups that have been traditionally perceived as outside 'The Public Sphere'. But the pivot towards universal accessibility has resulted in what Barrett calls 'competing notions of the public within the museum' (8): in one notion, the focus is on drawing as many visitors to the museum as possible, and often results in efforts to discover why certain groups do or do not attend museums. In the other, visitors are considered as already having knowledge when they walk through the door, and thus their visit to the museum becomes a process of mutual 'knowledge creation'. We might therefore approach our co-researchers – the children – and their presence in the galleries as acts of knowledge creation, a mutual process in which they simultaneously form their own 'little public spheres' (Hickey-Moody 2013) and call an expanded, posthuman public to attention. In their act of occupying the spaces of galleries and museums with their collaborative art, of drawing on the agental matter of the gallery and the classroom to create their future cities, the children draw a public around a Dewean 'concern' or problem – that of the continuing humanist approach to futures and urban citizenship.

We also approach children's artistic rendering of future urbanity as inherently political; it is caught up in the affective assemblages of accountability that disperse political responsibility across networks of agentic actors, including non-humans, in the spirit of Bennett (2010), Latour and Deleuze and Guattari. Habermas, on the other hand, '[did] not see art as intrinsically communicating and debating issues of public concern' (Barrett 2012, 29) – the art speaking to a post-climate crisis city would therefore be considered outside the public sphere, under Habermas's model. The prevalence of the 'issues of public concern' in the children's future cities cannot be overstated: as we will see the children expressed concern about climate change, over-population, deforestation, rising ethnic and religious tensions, gun violence, environmental degradation, species extinction and homelessness. We have written elsewhere of the potential of art and art-making as a form of expression for children to discuss complex ideas beyond verbal forms of expression (Hickey-Moody et al. 2021), and our posthuman publics as seen in the children's art displays are evidently sites of children working through deeply complex issues of public concern.

To deal with this, Barrett (2012) offers art as a way to 'take into account the multiple ways in which different publics articulate their "publicness" and the spaces in which they present themselves' (37). Barrett offers the physical space of the museum as one of these sites of articulation, but in this chapter we expand this to consider the interaction and intra-action of children *making* art as sites of forming and participating in the posthuman public sphere, a sphere that therefore includes children as well as chalk, canvas, gallery walls, atmospheres, paint and more. As ecologies of learning, children's art *and* the acts of making and displaying their art might offer 'viable alternatives to the centrality of the literary public sphere' (Barrett 2012, 37). Thinking of the children's art in exhibitions as examples of posthuman publics engages the inherent agentic materiality of both the art and the gallery spaces, a materiality that is bound up with a public sphere that centres around 'areas of public concern'.

We turn now to these areas of concern that were depicted in both the making of and the 'end product' of the future cities arts workshops. Above all the canvases demonstrate how the children imagined explicitly posthuman urban futures, characterised by a civics grounded in care across boundaries of human and non-human, and around the concept of a posthuman public.

FUTURE CITIES

Urban Nature

The environment is through it all. – Future cities workshop facilitator.

As they discussed the elements of a future city, the children were evidently familiar with both the richness and mundanity of modern cities. In the early brainstorming stages, they present the parts of the city that are, on the surface, everyday: 'buildings for work', 'lots of cars on the roads', 'monumental structures', 'people entertaining other people', houses, schools, mosques and shops. The discussion was also framed around values, so many canvases featured hospitals as sites 'where caring happens'. One hospital had large windows, through which one can see a doctor, beds with flowers next to them, stairs and a bathroom. Religious buildings also often featured in the canvases, as they are frequently identified as sites of 'values' or 'what really matters'. Play spaces are also common, as are shops and 'work buildings'.

But once the children's discussion and focus moved to the actual space of the blank canvas, these mundane elements of urbanity became deeply entangled with the natural and the supernatural. Animals, water and green space consistently and persistently invaded these imagined future cities (Figures 5.1, 5.2 and 5.3), merging and enmeshing with the more mundane, functional – and likely familiar – elements of a city. The 'building for work' stands next to a giant duck and is being climbed by giant monkeys. Cars share the roads with camels, or else fly through the sky while people parachute out of them back to the ground. One of the 'monumental structures', which one child suggested was like the Eiffel Tower or 'statues', became an immense monument to and symbol of the city made of gold and crowned with fire. The houses are made of pineapples, and have ice-cream machines and slides in them, and the shops and museums are topped with trees and cars and a flying, fire-breathing cat. There are flying dolphins, flying cars, flying trains, even

Figure 5.1 A Future City Canvas Made in Workshops, Claremont Primary School, Manchester. Photograph by Anna Hickey-Moody.

Figure 5.2   A Future City Canvas Made in Workshops, Claremont Primary Manchester. Photograph by Anna Hickey-Moody.

Figure 5.3   A Future City Canvas Made in Workshops, Claremont Primary School, Manchester. Photograph by Anna Hickey-Moody.

a flying road and a donut for a sun. In one canvas, a mosque, a church and a synagogue are all combined into one building, allowing all people to access them at once and at will. One child created a building shaped like a pinecone, because 'in the future we will probably be bored of rectangular buildings'.

This entanglement of the mundane and human with the fanciful and (super) natural is an example of how children imagine futures as posthuman. These images show animals and supernatural creatures as active participants in urban life, citizens of a public sphere characterised by care and responsibility that is shared across all urban inhabitants regardless of their humanity. The cats, cars, trains and dolphins must all *share* the flying road equally, and in fact the flying road has been built specifically to cater to these flying citizens. The monkeys climbing in the work building reveal a playfulness that the children have already established as necessary to counterbalance the serious- ness of 'work', which sits alongside the comment about future urban citizens probably being 'bored of rectangular buildings'. The monkeys climbing the work building also displays an awareness that even in our office buildings we remain inextricable from nature. One might even consider the monkeys as *attending* the office building to carry out their own work; these non-human urban citizens actively participating in the hum-drum but essential activities of urban life. The combined mosque-church-synagogue provides a demo- cratic approach to different faith cultures as they are embedded in the urban fabric, imagining and indeed demanding an egalitarian public sphere in which these faith cultures and communities are enmeshed with everyday urban life. These shared and collective values are also found in the flying appliances; flying seems to assure universal accessibility to essentials such as healthcare, ice-cream and a space to practice faith, denoting an urban civics that can cater to *all* citizens, human or otherwise, without the restrictions of geography.

Despite common assumptions of a 'divide' between the urban landscapes in which these children spent most of their time and more 'natural' spaces such as parklands, forests or national parks (Malone 2018), when imagining an ideal future city, this separation was nowhere to be found. Roads made of water ran past urban football fields, monkeys climbed over drab brown and mundane office buildings, while zoos were populated with animals that took care of humans. These imagined urbanities were constructed by children who lived and moved through urban spaces on an everyday basis. The natural world was central to the children's imagination and they did not want it to be confined to pockets of green space, parks, zoos or lakes. Nature and the urban are so thoroughly entwined in these pieces that there is no boundary between them.

This blurring between the 'natural' and the 'constructed' exists because, as Malone (2018) argues, children's concepts of the world are always-already posthuman. Malone offers the figure of the posthuman child as a way to reimagine humans' relationship with the planet and the more-than-human. 'We have much to learn from children', Malone argues, 'about the differences in everyday encounters they have in their cities and those other humans they co-inhabit these environments, namely adults' (24). Children's encounters with nature 'are central to how they learn what it means to be human, a human who is in relation with other humans and the non-human world' (85). Malone argues that listening to children therefore offers a *model* through which we might rethink what it means to be a human in relation to the non-human world: 'a reimagining of the transitional potential for a posthumanist theorizing of children and sustainability' can reveal 'the entangled complexity of human–non-human relations' (23).

Far from a disconnect of urban children from 'nature' or 'natural spaces', Malone (2018) suggests that children in Anthropocene cities live in 'ecological collectives'; their relationships with the other objects entangled with their lives. The children's encounters with these other planet dwellers, both as they make their way to school and as they depict them on the page, are encounters in which children 'come to recognize as beings in common, they are not exempt or exceptional to the ecology of the planet' (Malone 2018, 85). Malone continues:

> *The capacities of children to be open and aware of the fluidity of 'timespacemattering' with and through 'other' beings and objects who they are intra-acting with, and adapting alongside them in the aftermath of disasters and disastrous situations, are unique.* (249)

Malone argues that the intra-relations between children, nature and the city – such as those that play out across these canvases – can reconfigure human-nature encounters that are built around normative anthropocentric environmentalism that maintains a strict nature/culture divide. The urban futures that unfold in our art workshops move beyond divides of 'urban/natural' to demonstrate the children's feeling of kinship between all planet dwellers. Taking our cue from children, and indeed heeding their calls to action that are expressed through these canvases, we might continue to imagine our relationality to the more-than-human world through a lens of relational, ethical citizenship.

Water Roads – Care and Collectivity with 'Nature'

The large canvases depicting future cities were not only an exercise in collaborative world building, but a deliberate, concentrated call to attention to a specifically formed public: the world of adults. An emerging theme of these future cities is a future characterised by collective benefit, care and sharing.

The children identified 'becoming friends', 'opening up communities' and 'sharing things with other people' as values that would feature in their future cities. These values are characterised by relationality, a reliance on socialisation and cultural activities, existing only in relation to others. Below we explore the prevalence of water roads in these cities as an example of the children's sense of civic responsibility to other residents of the urban landscape.

Water roads, or 'roads made out of water', were a persistent feature in the future cities across several fieldwork sites. They were often offered as an 'environmentally friendly' alternative to roads, allowing fish and water creatures – including mermaids – to move freely about the city. One child explained she wanted roads specifically for animals to bring animals into closer contact with the city and the urban life she and her fellow city engineers had designed. At some level, the presence of water roads might speak to the largely urban, working-class cultures of the children and their urbanised 'distance' from nature. The children often spoke of the roads as bringing nature into closer contact with humans, literally entwining them into the fabric of the cities. But the water roads also suggest a form of civics characterised by an entanglement of the human and non-human, a civics that is characterised by a sense of collectivity and kinship across the human-non-human divide. Water roads in the future cities necessitated the invention of underwater or floating cars, busses and trains. Green spaces and water were almost always placed in the centre of the city: 'a town square', 'full of things that kids like', 'a park, a water park, a playground, and a skate park'. We might look to the water roads as persistent insistence on the deep integration of not only nature but non-human actors into the urban fabric of the future cities.

Watson (2019) writes of how water enables and assembles publics in cities, as a cultural and political object around which these publics can form – a type of Habermasian 'matter of concern'. The presence of water in cities could be expected in children's art given the potency of water in news and debates about the climate crises, either in relation to water scarcity or to rising sea levels and increasingly inclement weather. However, the children's concern for water in the normative sense – about rising sea levels, water scarcity, all the other related crises of water that go hand in hand with climate change – is difficult to find in their future cities. Indeed, a sense of crisis seems to be largely absent from these cities all together. Rather than water scarcity, there is an abundance of water – blue and green dominate many of the canvases. And yet, this abundance is not necessarily framed in terms of flood or rising tides, a common cultural motif (not to mention a reality) of climate change with which the children would be undoubtedly familiar. The water roads might instead point more to a city engineered to deal with climate change, an acceptance of the reality of rising tides that will undoubtedly characterise these children's futures. The water roads, viewed through a more cynical lens, might be the children's acceptance of rising sea levels, and perhaps an embrace of the closeness this would cause between humans and nature. The water roads speak to a deep entanglement that is not always hopeful or positive – see for example Braidotti's (2020) essay on the COVID-19 crisis as a posthuman crisis, brought about by the forceful entanglement of humans and animals through the encroachment of humans and humanism into the habitats of bats. The deep entanglement of humans with the more-than-human in these cities shows an acknowledgement of the realities of our Anthropocene future, a somewhat cynical acceptance of this closeness and the dangers or inconveniences it might entail.

However, the blue roads that wind through these cities are not *flooded*; they are made *of* water, engineered and designed specifically to allow for a closer entanglement of cities and marine life. This is in contrast to initiatives of various governments to raise city areas or build sea walls, like the UK Water Partnership (in Watson 2019); initiatives aimed less at embracing and incorporating the natural world and more about remaining stalwart against the encroaching threat of the sea. The children's interest in making roads of water must of course be read alongside the very real threat of rising water levels that are already displacing thousands and creating 'climate refugees', but it is interesting to note how the children's future imaginaries are not only accepting of water within and through their cities, but embracing of it.

Water roads might therefore be a further emphasis of the always-already posthuman lifeworlds of children:

> Water lies at the very heart of the interconnectedness and entanglements of humans with our environment and reveals, arguably more than any other substance, the impossibility of thinking of ourselves as separate from nature. (Watson 2019, 2)

By entwining their cities with water, and by fashioning them as forms of civic infrastructure, the children introduce a sense of deep interconnectedness to their future civics. Watson draws on Astrid Neimanis (2016) and her 'wet ontologies' when emphasising the interconnectedness of water and watery bodies like the water roads. Neimanis offers thinking of humans as *bodies of water* as a direct challenge to the discrete individualism of Western and humanist philosophy:

> For us humans, the flow and flush of waters sustain our own bodies, but also connect them to other bodies, to other worlds beyond our human selves. Indeed, bodies of water undo the idea that bodies are necessarily or only human. . . . Our watery relations within (or more accurately: as) a more-than-human

hydrocommons thus present a challenge to anthropocentrism, and the privileg-
ing of the human as the sole or primary site of embodiment. (2)

In particular, both Watson and Neimanis identify how thinking of ourselves
as watery bodies is a specific way of understanding ourselves in relation
to others. Watery bodies challenge individualism, Neimanis (2016) argues,
and 'are gestational milieus for another, and for others often not like us' (3).
We can see the water roads of the children's canvases offer a form of civic
participation specifically geared towards the Other, the 'not at all like us',
the bodies and becomings of the other bodies that make up a future city. The
water in many of these pictures is a road, shared between cars and people
and mermaids and marine life, as they all move through their interconnected
processes of becoming. These relational, more-than-human, watery roads
are an essential part of civic life, an inextricable part of a posthuman civics
in these future cities. Watson (2019) points out how encounters with water
are inherently encounters of connection, whether connection to ecological
systems of evaporation and precipitation or 'the vast technological shrines
of the dams and reservoirs, often distances away', (6) to which we become
connected when we turn on our kitchen tap. The water roads re-emphasise
this sense of connection, offering water as both a symbol and a material of
human-environmental interdependence and interconnectedness that operates
through networks of care (Neimanis 2016).

Watson engages water as a site around which publics form, but the water
roads of the children's future cities show water itself as a member of a public,
as well as the boats and fish and mermaids they bring into the city. Thus water
is not merely the site of a public, like the Agora; nor does it only enable a
public to form; in the children's posthuman cities, the water is a member of
the public, enacting a care-based civics by bringing humans into close contact
with animals, mermaids and the water itself. In their ability to enact change
and to have an effect, the water roads play a key role in the posthuman cities
and their posthuman civics.

As well as waterways, there was an emphasis on green places entwined
with the depicted urbanity (Figure 5.4). One canvas showed four rivers meeting in the centre around a tree; green spaces and water were both seen as
collective and connective:

The first addition to the canvas was a 'town square', upon which all the children
agreed. Inside the square was a campfire, and swings (spaces where people play
and come together). There was the suggestion to have 4 connecting roads run-
ning to each corner of the canvas. Houses were then added around the square,
a hospital, and Unitarian church.

– Fieldnotes, Unitarian's church, Adelaide

Figure 5.4 A Future City Canvas Made in Workshops, Cherry Orchard Primary School, London. Photograph by Anna Hickey-Moody.

These green spaces emerged as sites through which a sense of community and 'what really matters' could occur. These outdoor spaces appear to be a locus of collectivity, which is most often expressed by the children as sports or play. When prompted, the children tended to speak of these activities as spaces in which values can be enacted, such as sharing, care, support, friendship, helping and learning. These collective ideals were common in the discussion of the future – 'stop wars so that people don't get hurt', 'everyone is equal' and even simply 'showing kindness to other people'. But what is of interest is the ways that these green or wet and 'natural' spaces emerged as key sites through which these values might be enacted, not only by humans.

We, as well as others (Malone 2018), have written elsewhere on how children's sense of self and their position in the world is *relational*; how they repeatedly speak and depict themselves and their world as thoroughly intertwined, with an always-already posthuman concept of humans' position in and of the world (Hickey-Moody et al. 2021). Aslanian (2017) writes that 'posthuman perspectives offer an ethic of interconnectivity' (426), and these canvases show the children's imagined futures to be distinctly posthuman because of that connectivity. The presence of water roads speak to the children's sense that care and kinship are deeply imbricated with the more-than-human actors. The animals and 'nature' that populate the imagined worlds are distinctly *active*. One group spoke of a future in which animals use words and talk. While zoos were common depictions of sites of 'care for nature', one school group included a zoo in which animals care for humans. Animals were consistently framed in reciprocal relationships with humans: as well as the zoo, one girl specifically mentioned cats looking after their owners. Thus the children's sense of entanglement was also accompanied by a sense of reciprocity and mutual care. Nor was this entanglement limited to animals or to the 'natural' world. The children's futures included flying ice-cream machines that could feed the entire city, large buildings of apartments to house people who don't have a home and a mosque and a hospital that 'could fly around the world helping people'. Rather than being held separate to 'humans', a distinct world upon which humans can act, animals and the natural and urban world of the children's imagined cities are positioned in a world in which children, buildings, cars, planes and mosques all care for one another. These actors are deeply entangled, active and participatory, true *actants* in an affective assemblage, but one that is distinctly characterised and tuned towards *care*.

Within the relational assemblage of the art workshop, political responsibility for a safe and prosperous city, a city in which 'everyone has a home', becomes everyone's business. The children's work therefore resembles Bennett's (2010) dispersed network of accountability, a theory she developed specifically out of her efforts to engage Dewey's public sphere as posthuman (see chapter 1). If we embrace publics, such as those imagined in the future cities canvases, as a specific call to attention and as necessarily being formed around a problem or concern, then the children's posthuman publics that are defined by values of care can be seen as a direct call to action: care for one another, becomes entangled in a relationship of care and kinship with animals, water, flying mosques and dragons. As a call to attention, the deep entanglement of nature within the future cities can be read as an explicit politicisation of our relations with non-human matter and agency on the part of the children. Malone (2018) argues that posthuman children's agency to respond to the climate crisis 'will become a product of the assemblages, associations and relationships through which they are connected and attached to the more-than-human world' (84), and we can see this play out through a direct sense of kinship and entanglement with the more-than-human world in their imagined futures. If children's view on the world is always-already posthuman, how might the wider public, the adult world, take up their call to action that is found in their posthuman cities of care and kinship?

CRAFTING NEW ECOLOGIES OF LEARNING

As we mentioned in the introduction to this chapter, the Interfaith Childhoods project also held several art exhibitions and an art auction, in which the artworks made in the workshops were displayed to a wider public, as well as the children and their families. These took place at the St James Hatcham building on campus at Goldsmiths University in London, the Whitworth art gallery in Manchester (Figure 5.5), the P21 Gallery in London and Backroom at Project Space Gallery at RMIT University in Melbourne. At the art galleries, the children once again inhabited the cities they had been depicting on the canvas. Simultaneously, the children's call to attention that they placed on the canvas occupied sites that differed dramatically in geographical and class contexts from the sites in which the art was made, and in which the children are embedded.

While making the future cities, the children were embedded in environments that were a familiar part of their everyday life. As we outline above, the future cities reflect this, full of images of the familiar experience of urbanity: school, roads, work buildings, hospitals, playgrounds, churches, mosques. But the familiarity of their surroundings was also revealed in the way they

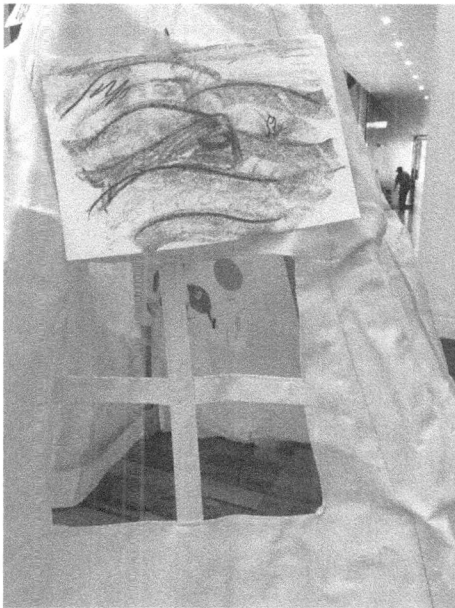

Figure 5.5   Children's Art on Display at the Whitworth Gallery, Manchester. Photograph by Anna Hickey-Moody

interacted with the space, each other, the art-making processes and the research facilitators in their classrooms and community centres where they made the art. The children were comfortable, they felt safe, they felt belonging. Sometimes this was reflected simply in the normal noise and chaos that accompany children in groups where they are at ease. At other times, this came through as a kind of ownership and leadership of the children, as they showed the facilitators proudly around their school or church, or instructed the newcomers as to the location of the bathrooms or drinking fountains.

In contrast, the exhibitions took the children's art and the children into social and cultural contexts that weren't part of their everyday lives. In particular, the exhibitions at P21, the Whitworth and RMIT galleries were ways of bringing children's art into unfamiliar contexts and calling new publics to attention. The exhibitions also allowed the children to call more expanded publics to attention to contemplate their valuation of city life in the Anthropocene. Many of the exhibitions were attended by the children's parents and teachers, and some by academics and members of the public. The children, whether in person or through their art, were allowed the opportunity to speak directly to adults on issues that concerned them in their own ways and through their own voices. What's more, the pictures on display spoke on behalf of an assemblage of children, and also brought children's worlds into social and cultural spaces which were not familiar to them or *with them.*

This had the added effect of bringing people who weren't previously engaging with the communities from which the children originated into direct contact with the children's experiences of the world. Gallery spaces are often frequented by particular social demographics who have everyday lives that are quite distinct from those of the communities in which we work. These communities are unlikely to visit art galleries, largely because they are seen as White, middle-class cultural institutions. Kids in Museums' study 'Hurdles to Participation' found that museum audiences tend to be from better educated and more affluent homes (Whitaker 2018). In one Australian study it was found that 'People born in a non-main English speaking country were less likely to attend [art galleries] than people born in Australia', and that 'People in the most disadvantaged areas (according to SEIFA) were less likely to attend [art galleries] than people in the "average" areas (or middle SEIFA quintile), who were in turn less likely to attend than people in the least disadvantaged areas' (Cultural Ministers Council 2006, 18). These results agree with Tony Bennett and colleagues' (1991) report *Art galleries: who goes?* which found that art gallery visitors are likely to come from households with above-average incomes (see also Farrell et al. 2010; Australia Council 2020).

Through our art exhibitions, gallery-going communities were able to build a sense of the children's posthuman lifeworlds and their imagined urban futures. This is an inherently political act, and the children's collective voices expressed in their artwork are characterised by their sense of kinship and relationality with the non-human world we explore above. We brought the children's civics of care for the more-than-human into expanded public spheres, calling expanded publics to attention with regard to humans' relationship with the planet.

In the latter half of this chapter, we explore how the spatial and cultural settings of both the arts workshops and the exhibitions influenced and were influenced by the art that was made by the children and the processes of the children making the art. We encapsulate these contexts into the assemblage of materiality and agency in which the children were caught up as they negotiated urban imaginaries and formulated posthuman publics. We begin by exploring the social and physical geographies in which these artworks were made, and examine how these geographies are caught up in, and reflected by, the art itself. We argue these differential forms of cultural capital and associated power relations were brought into sharp relief. The cultural contexts of the art galleries and universities, into which the children and their art were brought, expanded not only the publics to which they spoke, but those of which they were a part. We conclude by examining the children's art in these exhibition spaces as an inherently political act of calling an expanded public to attention and to *action* with regard to the climate crisis. Through their art, the children challenged their audiences to embrace a posthuman civics characterised by deep kinship with more-than-human elements of urban spaces and an ethics of care.

Geographies of Future Cities

The old school gates were out of the 1900's still, with a 'girl's' entrance and a 'boy's' entrance marked out in decorative red brick archways. The old entrances under the arches were walled off though, and the actual 'school gate' was a large, black metal grid that was electronically controlled and monitored by a camera. Everyone has to announce themselves to the camera, and then 'sign in' on the computer system in the foyer. The sign in machine prints everyone a barcode when they have signed in. I collect all of mine in my field notes book and watch my hair become increasingly frazzled and my face droop as the week continues and my enthusiasm gives way to exhaustion. The school hall still smells like school breakfast at 8am and both teachers and kids are hurrying down a slice of toast on their way to other things. I arrive in the staffroom to organize my materials and settle into a corner on the dark blue plastic couch before the morning staff meeting starts.

– Fieldnotes, Harbinger Primary School, Anna Hickey-Moody

We went through into a larger room (with a couch, a deep red patterned thick rug, a small ceremonial looking table with religious objects on top (a heavy metal elaborate candle holder, and a small metal bowl all sitting on a lace cloth) . . . a sunlit room that connected to the outside back area of the church, where there was a community garden. This room was the children's making/ activity room – there were cupboards with art/craft materials, the back wall had photographs of the children (most of whom were participating in the workshops) with their families at the church, there was art work made previously – a large figure and small fabric bunting with text on it. This was a room with community, history, materials. . . . The space is eclectic, warm, appears to be in frequent use, all the children knew their way around and appeared very comfortable in the (interior and exterior) spaces.

– Fieldnotes, Norwood Unitarian Church, Osmond Tce, Angelica Harris-Faull.

The room had no natural light in it, and was painted light grey with grey car-pet and neon overhead lights. The left hand wall was all glass and faced out onto an interior walkway through a disused mall, so the fawn coloured blinds were always drawn. The room was a long rectangle with folded furniture in the back right hand corner. Upon arrival, Mia and I would open up the tables and unstack the chairs and arrange the furniture into long making tables that allowed the children to work together. We would organize and display the art materials and pre-prepare snacks. It was relatively dark inside, in compari-son to the searing Western Sydney middle of summer sun melting the bitumen outside. We would turn the air conditioning on and off multiple times to try to get it working and then prop all the doors open with chairs. The first families always arrive 30 mins early, and once the children are in the space it completely changes. The bring such life, colour, noise, and energy. The depressed and dis-used community space becomes a learning environment.

– Fieldnotes, ADS community room in mall, Anna Hickey-Moody

In very different kinds of community centres, church group spaces, schools and mosques, collaborative art practices transformed the built environments and emerged as a form of world-making. Two of the future cities were created at an Adelaide church group fieldwork site; the canvas and the art materials were taken outside, and the children sat on the (fake) grass gathered around the large canvas and began adding elements. The facilitators helped the children begin on the canvases by sketching out their ideas, and the children introduced their own colours, animals, more ideas about how things might work and their conceptions of a future city. The canvases reflected the com-fort and the embedded nature of children's relationships with their urban (or occasionally rural) environments, but also, as we have seen above, showed a profound awareness of the importance of 'natural' or more- -than-human elements. This speaks in no small part to the entanglements of material space that are caught up in pedagogy and which we explore above, but we also wish to incorporate the intimate and familiar geographies that played a part in calling publics to attention through the imagined future cities – whether through making, collaboration or display.

As well as depicting a worldview that was deeply entangled with the more-than-human, the collaborative canvases of the future cities can be seen as the material manifestations of enmeshed and entangled processes of making and becoming. The canvases were produced through sessions in which the children became enmeshed with their surroundings and materials. Pastels covered the children's bodies as much as they did the canvases. One group used leaves, bark and wool from the surrounding grounds to depict the green spaces of their future city.

Webster school was an unusual fieldwork site in a number of respects. First, the children's relationship with the adults was quite different from those in other fieldwork sites: this school organised child behaviour through discipline and, as such, silence was rewarded. This is quite a difficult environment in which to make collaborative art, as children are accustomed to being told what to do rather than thinking about what they want to do. The school is built in a disused aircraft bunker originally built in the Second World War. The bunker was built from lead, to stop it from being detected by planes flying overhead. The contemporary impact of the lead bunker was that no mobile telephones worked inside or near the school. When phoning an interpreter or a taxi, one had to walk a few blocks away in order to get any reception. Inside, the largely White teachers controlled the largely Black student body with strict discipline routines that did not sit well alongside our collaborative approach to art production. The space-mattering of this place made it very difficult to inhabit but also made evident the relationality of place-making, or how we make and learn place. Like Page (2020) we approach place as relational, 'a process with its meanings continually made, performed, and learned' (2). Page like us argues that 'there can be no place without bodies and that through the practices of the body – perception (sensory, and memory) – with the socio-material, we make and learn place' (3). Both the processural fieldwork and the data that emerged from Webster were shaped through the embodied and material practices of relating with the classroom and schoolyard, as well as with each other, the staff and us as researchers.

Fieldnotes 12 June 2018
   WEBSTER PRIMARY
   This morning in the school we had been in the art room for 5 minutes when
a black boy about 8 years of age was dragged screaming through the art room

and curtained off in a makeshift cubicle made from green vinyl curtains. He was screaming at the top of his very loud lungs 'Get your hands off me' 'don't touch me' 'leave me alone' 'Let me back out there'. My team and I set up our materials and rearrange the furniture while the screaming continues.

We need to bring tables close together so students can share materials – with a view to providing the richest range of materials possible. We also have to be sure that the three students without ethical consent are not captured on camera. The art teacher is delighted to hand over to us for the afternoon and assures us that her Teaching Aide (TA) will be all we need. The TA is deeply distressed by how we have rearranged the space. Where will the students do their class registration? She asks. Can they not sit on the free half of the green mat I ask? No, they need the whole mat, that is what they are used to. She is adamant. We liberate the whole green mat and the students come in for registration. The screaming pupil is let go. Our workshop begins. We are told I have to seat the children. They are not to choose their own seat. I am to choose their seats for them.

I am encouraging to express themselves through colour. 'Use more colours' the teacher's aide says. That is really not what I am saying. Rainbows appear on pages. What colours express what feelings? I ask. 'Well everyone knows black is angry' the TA says.

'You're not green. Don't draw yourself in green' the TA says.

– Fieldnotes, Webster Primary School, Anna Hickey-Moody

The children's future cities at Webster were somewhat unrecognisable as cities or built environments, more just lots of coloured smudges and blobs on a page. We guessed the stress and control surrounding the children had blurred their thoughts into the whirring mess expressed on the page. Figures 5.6, 5.7 and 5.8 are future cities made by the children at Webster, each of which gestures towards shared life, civic participation and demonstrates human entanglement with the more-than-human. The images also express the children's stress and anxiety, resulting from their learning experiences being micromanaged in a lead bunker.

Elsewhere, we have written about how the always-already posthuman view of the world that children have draws significantly on their inherent entanglement with their environment (Hickey-Moody et al. 2021). As they play, make, refuse, fight, resist and learn, children are not separate from the materials with which they learn; instead they are caught up with them and co-produce their worldviews in collaboration with materials. As is evidenced in the differences in the artwork examined above, learning environments diffract through children's work and influence their ways of being, becoming and making in place.

Figure 5.6 A Future City Canvas Made in Workshops, Webster Primary School, Manchester. Photograph by Anna Hickey-Moody.

Figure 5.7 A Future City Canvas Made in Workshops, Webster Primary School, Manchester. Photograph by Anna Hickey-Moody.

Figure 5.8 A Future City Canvas Made in Workshops, Webster Primary School, Manchester. Photograph by Anna Hickey-Moody.

New Geographies of Civic Engagement

As mentioned above, the Interfaith Childhoods project displayed the children's art at Goldsmiths University in London, the Whitworth Art Gallery in Manchester, the P21 Gallery in London and Backroom at Project Space Gallery at RMIT University in Melbourne. As well as displaying the art, two of the galleries The Whitworth and P21 Gallery housed a workshop each, and the Goldsmiths exhibition had a small 'maker space' set aside in which visitors could try their hand at some of the activities that had created the art that was on display. The entanglements of space, material and children were therefore not confined to the classroom or community centres in which the future city canvases were made. At those sites, we worked with children to create 'refuges' or small, fabric and plywood tents in which they displayed things important to them, things that made them feel safe, things that made them feel at home. But there was a notable shift in the tone and results of the workshops when they moved out of the familiar spaces of the classrooms and community centres and into spaces that are normally quiet spaces of reflection and contemplation. As the workshops moved into unfamiliar territory for the children, the discussions, play and imaginings drew on the cultural and geographic spaces of the galleries and museums to create a different space in which children could call publics to attention through their art.

The cultural and geographic contexts of these sites played a significant part in the kinds of knowledges and learning ecologies that were formed there. Located in the cultural district of North West London, P21 is a prestigious art gallery displaying the latest artistic outputs from the international Arabic community. It has high cultural capital, a fact reinforced by its proximity to the National Library, the University of London, the British Museum and the Palace Theatre. In this space, the children's art became the main exhibition of P21 for a day, as well as an arts workshop. Four families of children and adults collaborated in deeply imaginative play and art-making around the themes of refuge and belonging. Two children imagined themselves as part of a public with many non-human citizens. By designing their 'refuge' or 'home', they ensured the incorporation of many non-human citizens. The 'view' out the window of their refuge was also significant to them; they made a vegetable patch and were careful to leave their shoes at the front door in neat rows.

At the same time, these girls occupied the gallery space in a radical deterritorialisation of the capitalist art market that is usually engaged by P21 gallery. They stuck their own art of whales, fish and dragons, to the walls, almost graffiti-like, explicitly bringing the more-than-human world that existed 'out there' into the main gallery of white space with extremely high cultural capital. Their deterritorialisation of this space – or rather their own re-territorialisation of their own space – had the effect of a direct call for a public sphere that was deeply entangled with the more-than-human, with the animal and with the supernatural. We explore this more below.

A similar workshop was held during the exhibition at the Whitworth in Manchester. Established in 1824, the Whitworth is a traditional institute of art, but one that is committed to inclusiveness. The Whitworth was billed as 'an inner city gallery' when it opened in 1889, with the aim of being a gallery 'for people of all special classes'. At the time this rang true, as it was situated in a largely working-class area of Manchester that would be later subject to slum clearing and gentrification. The Whitworth also holds an institutional commitment to drawing art across the traditional barriers between 'inside' and 'outside' the 'art world'. Known as 'the Tate of the North', the Whitworth has a section dedicated to Outsider art, and has previously held exhibitions that foreground the voices of children – see for example their exhibit *We are 11: Stanley Grove Primary Academy* in 2019. Elsewhere we have written about how we might consider children's art as outsider art – forms of pure creative and artistic expression formed outside the confines of the formal 'art world' (Hickey-Moody et al. 2021), and an inherently democratic art form. The Whitworth's dedication to outsider means that the children of the Interfaith Childhoods project are not the first from outside the art world to occupy the gallery space.

Like at P21, at The Whitworth we found how galleries engage a different kind of public from that of the classroom or community centre. The exhibitions facilitated the curation of newly connected publics, making space for collaborative family art making. The shared imagining of a future city or a refuge that was explored in the classroom became a collaboration between families. The Whitworth exhibition ran for a whole day, and an estimated 300 people moved through the space crawling, in prams, in wheelchairs and on walkers. Aged between one and sixty; making, talking, collaborating and imagining a shared future and shared experiences of refuge. The publics that were curated in these spaces – often little publics of families – explored entangled relationships with the world and relationships of care that were found in the children's future cities imagined in schools or community centres.

The Whitworth gallery is situated in Manchester's 'Knowledge Corridor' in Chorlton-on-Medlock and Victoria Park, a no-longer working-class neighbourhood now dominated by the nearby university, the Manchester Museum and various art galleries, theatres and creative spaces. Its proximity to the university means a large student population and the accompanying bars, cafes, shops and eateries. The Whitworth is also known for its expansive parklands, and recent renovations have made a concerted effort to bring the parkland inside. In the gallery in which the children's art was made and shown, large floor-to-ceiling windows cover an entire wall of the gallery, inviting the natural, green-tinged light of the surrounding parklands into the space to cover the children's art and the gallery's existing collection alike.

Perhaps because of this context of a high cultural capital and the light, airy space of the gallery, the workshops at the Whitworth were a much more subdued affair than those in the classrooms. The space had previously held several similar programmes around children's art, and yet the wildness, the messiness and chaos that had characterised the collaborations at the school-based fieldwork sites were replaced by a much more reverent, quiet and contemplative atmosphere. Much of this may have been due to the shift in the adult-to-child ratio – there were more parents and facilitators mixed with the children than in the schools – but much of this was also facilitated by the space of the gallery. The publics of the schools and their surrounds, the urban landscapes through which the children moved each day, have more non-human citizens with which the children could interact and so a more complex enmeshment of human and non-human could emerge. The children were less embedded in the Whitworth gallery than they were in their daily school spaces, and so were less enmeshed with any non-human citizenry. The gallery is a large, airy, refined space, with natural light and white walls. This kind of space perhaps facilitated more philosophical enquiries into 'what really matters' to the children and their parents, and what sustains them, as opposed to the mess and chaos and control and anger that were engendered by the children's classrooms.

Despite the deeply philosophical and almost reverent atmosphere of the workshops held at the Whitworth, the gallery still mostly attracts a White, middle-class and highly educated audience. The gallery tries to move past this, staging workshops in a similar style to that of the Interfaith Childhoods exhibition, and maintaining a dedication to outsider art and activism as a core philosophy. Just behind the parkland of Whitworth, although seemingly miles away from the towered facades of the gallery and the trendy shops filled with students, is Webster Primary School, one of the sites discussed above. Webster has a super diverse cohort of students. It is situated in Moss Side, a similarly super diverse, lower socioeconomic neighbourhood of Manchester. Moss Side has a high population density and large populations of Afro-Caribbean, Indian, Somali, Chinese and Eastern European communities. From Moss Side and Webster, it is a short walk to the Whitworth, but from Alma Park, the second Manchester site at which the future cities were made, it is a long hike into the city centre. While none of the students at these schools, the ones who created many of the future cities, attended the Whitworth's workshops of exhibitions, their work and their worlds were still introduced into a specific cultural environment from which they had historically excluded. By bringing the children's art and, more importantly, their *awareness* into these spaces, we were able to expand their ecologies of learning to include institutions such as art galleries and universities.

We have written before on the ways children express their being in space, negotiate space and relate to the spaces in which they spend their everyday lives (Hickey-Moody et al. 2021); we found that the complex spatial and embodied processes of children creating art are 'sites at which children form and navigate specific ways of being with and in relation to more-than-human entanglements' (Hickey-Moody et al. 2021, 82). The negotiations of the future, of refuge or 'what really matters' that took place at the Whitworth and at P21, were situated both within the bodies of the children and their parents and the environment in which they occurred – the point of connection between sensory perception and material contexts (Fors et al. 2013). Ellsworth (2005) speaks of pedagogical space, which draws on the material and sensory engagements of children with their physical environments of learning, as well as the social and cultural settings, like the high cultural capital and refined, reflective and even philosophical settings of the Whitworth and P21. We might expand these spaces to include the possibility of a posthuman space, where the more-than-human becomes swept up in the processes of making art and hearing children's voices, and caught up in philosophical questions about 'what really matters', 'where do you feel safe?' and 'what does it mean to belong?'

The Goldsmiths exhibition (Figures 5.9 and 5.10) was held in the St James Hatcham building on campus. The building is a former church, with a large round stained glass window and both lofty vaulted ceilings and low ceilings with exposed beams, covering small corners and dark alcoves. The exhibition contained examples of the objects created in the arts workshops, including large, printed decals of the future cities canvases, several 'geographies of belonging' quilts (see Hickey-Moody et al. 2021), and self-portraits. Several animations made by the children exploring the visible and invisible parts of their identities were projected on a wall. These were narrated by the children, and showed the process of them drawing, erasing and redrawing their identities, animated into short films. Finally, there was a maker-space in one section of the gallery, where visitors young and old could try their hand at making these objects, often alongside children.

The children who participated in the project had depicted 'what really matters' when it comes to being a citizen in the form of films, self-portraits and future cities. At Goldsmiths, the children who attended the exhibition were mainly from participating schools who then became part of these existing conversations around publics and civics, speaking *back to* the art and the assemblages of children that they represented. This occurred in a deeply embodied sense: one child used the projection of a child's animation about

Figure 5.9   Children's Art on Display at the Goldsmiths St James Hatchet Building, London. Photograph by Anna Hickey-Moody.

Figure 5.10   Children's Art on Display at the Goldsmiths St James Hatchet Building, London. Photograph by Anna Hickey-Moody.

themselves to create shadow puppets, and so an animated story about religion and food and belonging became a shadow puppet story about dinosaurs eating other dinosaurs. This child's engagement with the public, their enactment of a civics, was through light and shadow, their body, the technologies of animation applications and projectors. Elsewhere, children played in tents that had been constructed as refuges, transforming them into caves and schools and spaceships, and themselves into more-than-human actors. Through these assemblages of the non-human and the human, themselves and the other children who had made the art, the children at Goldsmiths were given a platform to become an animal, a dinosaur, a shadow – more-than-human.

However, we remain cognisant of the much wider spatial and cultural contexts in which these interactions occurred. The galleries and museums at which these exhibitions were held were more often than not in physical and cultural territories that were unfamiliar to the participants of the project.

Whilst the exhibitions of the Interfaith Childhoods project demonstrated the ongoing stratification of cultural institutions such as galleries and museums in terms of access and familiarity, the exhibitions also bought children and their art into new and unfamiliar cultural contexts. Harwood and colleagues' (2016) model of widening participation suggests that pathways into spaces such as higher education institutions or art galleries are often foreclosed by the complex set of influences on a young person's attitude towards these spaces – their ecologies of learning. The learning ecologies of the children involved in the Interfaith Childhoods projects seldom included imaginings of (or even access to) spaces like Goldsmiths or the Whitworth. Drawing the children and their collaborative urban futures into these spaces allowed for these imaginings to take place, incorporating the cultural, social and economic contexts of these spaces into the ways they approach cultural institutions, countering what Harwood and colleagues call the 'thick culture of educational pessimism that young people encounter' (2). In particular, drawing children and families into these spaces counters the assumption that children and their families do not *value* these educational and cultural spaces; on the contrary, 'parents from LSES backgrounds who have not experienced further education, and many of whom left schooling early, strongly value the role of schools and education' (Harwood et al. 2016, 3). Introducing children and their imagined futures into these spaces therefore turns instead to the ecology of emotions, imaginings and perceptions that form barriers to participation that face these families (Harwood et al., 2016).

A further example can be found at the exhibition held at Goldsmiths. Located in the south east of London, Goldsmiths is firmly embedded in a largely gentrified arts and culture neighbourhood, nourished by a student and artist population and Goldsmiths' focus on arts literature and cultural studies. Geographically, Goldsmiths is close to two of the fieldwork sites: Cherry Orchard Primary School in Greenwich and Harbinger Primary School on the Isle of Dogs. However, while both cohorts were invited to the event and while many of the children from Cherry Orchard attended the exhibition with their parents, the children from Harbinger did not. It is tempting to extrapolate that the class differences between the schools dictated their attendance or non-attendance at Goldsmiths. But if we take Harwood and colleagues' approach seriously, there is much more at play in the learning ecologies of the children from both Cherry Orchard and Harbinger and their relationship to universities. This apparent dichotomy between the schools raises questions in terms of the embeddedness of the children in geographies like liberal arts universities such as Goldsmiths or the politics of bringing children's art into these spaces. While Goldsmiths is relatively embedded in the geographies of the children, many had never set foot on a university campus before. More than one conversation was sparked between children and their parents at Goldsmiths about the possibilities of attending university in the future, and the parents' experiences of university in the past.

Harwood and colleagues' learning ecologies facilitates an interrogation of how existing attitudes to education regulate the imagining of going to university for young people and their families. Conversations between parents and children about the possibility of going to university are key examples of 'the relations of power that feed into and support the complexity of practices that impact engagement in schooling' (Harwood et al. 2016). Although not applying in this instance, these power relations often foreclose the possibility of attending or meaningfully engaging with higher education. This is despite, Harwood et al. are keen to point out, that these young people and their families *valuing* education immensely. As we can see with the exhibition at Goldsmiths, bringing children into higher education or art gallery spaces isn't necessarily bringing them into spaces that they do not 'want' to be in or do not value, but is instead tied up in a more complex set of power relations, in which young people's educational ecologies play a significant role, as well as wider cultural politics of belonging.

The exhibitions, intended as a way of bringing children's artwork into unfamiliar spaces, also served to bring the unfamiliar spaces into direct contact with the children and their families. We now turn to how the acts of display and explicit calls to attention, were often directed at highly specific publics that were rooted in the geographic and cultural contexts of the various sites. One of the final exhibitions of the children's art was at RMIT University's Backroom gallery in Melbourne. The exhibition was based around the idea of climate change and faith, and was aimed specifically at bringing the children's responses to the climate crisis into an explicitly academic environment. There were notably no children present at this exhibition. The art was viewed primarily by students, researchers and artists at RMIT. The public that was called to attention through this exhibition was quite specific, drawing on these groups who were specifically looking for child voices in discussions around posthuman and new materialist responses to the climate crisis.

The varying geographical and cultural contexts of the exhibitions brought several and varying publics to attention. The exhibitions at P21, the Whitworth and Goldsmiths were attended by a mix of child artists, their parents, academics and researchers and interested members of the public, while the RMIT backroom in Project Space gallery was by and large restricted to an academic-artistic audience. The project of widening participation remains an ongoing necessity with which cultural practitioners and academics need to engage.

CONCLUSION

In this chapter we have explored children imagining future cities as a way of creating a posthuman future, and as a way of activating the possibilities afforded by a posthuman conception of the city and urban life. The collaborative future imaginaries demonstrate the always-already posthuman lifeworlds of children, and acted as a direct call to action around which posthuman publics could form, starving for a similarly posthuman civics. As well as creating new ecologies of learning in which children learn from each other and from the non-human world, these posthuman imaginings established new ecologies of learning in professional gallery spaces and universities. By bringing these posthuman futures out of their classrooms and into art galleries and universities, the children created new publics, bringing a diverse group of people together around their visions for a posthuman urban future. The children's art called a range of quite different publics to attention, members of which many of the children will never meet but will have always changed. Beyond the walls of their schools and their brief encounters with art galleries, the children's call to attention – and their specific call to action – will live on. Deleuze and Guattari (1994) argue, art preserves, but that 'it is no less independent of the viewer or hearer, who only experience it after, if they have the strength for it' (164). The publics that children call to attention through their art and their exhibits are formed around an imagined possibility of a future defined by deep kinship and connection with the more-than-human, a posthuman public sphere ready for the Anthropocene.

Chapter 6

Urban Civics

Young urban children usually develop civic connections through movement with the spaces that they are permitted to encounter. Permissions might be sanctioned, such as the spaces they visit with adults, or illegal, such as the places they trespass. In each instance children develop their citizenship and civics in corporeal ways, by moving through, and, in relation with, the materialities and atmospheres of civic spaces. This creative movement with and in space enacts a change, leaving differently durational traces and residues. These traces and residues are civic belonging, formed from affective geographic cartographies of childish orientations. This chapter discusses how a research project: Scaling the City[1] which took place with young children in cities in New Zealand and Australia developed children's posthuman civics via experimentations in creative movement and visual mapping practices. In Scaling the City children creatively and expressively moved through the city, in choreographic and cartographic events that were co-designed and co-curated. The moving through was seen as a vital process for developing civics through movement with and among different materialities that initiated what Erin Manning (2013) describes as 'processual shiftings between strata that foreground and background modes of experience' (7). The encounter of, and response to different material surfaces and different, other, more-than-human bodies brings forth affective relations and experiential connections that lead to a civics and citizenry. In other words, children need to physically move through and with the city to develop their belonging to it. The terms: civics, politics, belonging and community aren't understood here as abstracted concepts; children build their knowledge and commitment to civics by physically being-in and moving in relation with material urban space.

Although focused on children in physical urban space, in this chapter we differentiate our work from scholarship concerned with child-friendly

111

cities. Scholarship into child-friendly cities identifies the impacts of diminishing demarcated play spaces in urban planning on children (Alexander and Frohlich 2019; Lai and Low 2019; Monbiot 2015), and the politics of play spaces in city zones with skyrocketing real estate value (Ekawati 2015; Gleeson and Sipe 2006; Hossain and Tasnim 2020). Child-friendly cities research often reflects the aims of global policy including the UNICEF Child Friendly Cities Initiative (UNICEF 2018) and 8 80 Cities project by Bernard van Leer Foundation (2017). Reports from these projects include goals that state 'Every child and young person has opportunities to enjoy [. . .] safe places to meet their friends and play' (UNICEF 2015, 12), and that cities must 'manage and maintain green spaces children and families play in' (Bernard van Leer Foundation 2017, 51). The premise often articulated in these project goals is the importance of cities having site-specific urban zones that are designed for children's play and activity, containing equipment, features and structures that create bounded spaces deemed age-appropriate for children and families to socialise and play in relative safety. Dedicated site-specific zones are important for children to access and use, however they are not the only spaces children need access to, to enable them to develop their civic connection and identity. Children often cross the city with adult others, and in these times they encounter shopping malls, buses, carparks, walkways, offices, museums and more. This chapter argues that children encounter many more spaces than those of the park or playground. Commonly, the urban civic space is densely built with close-set buildings interlaced with traffic routes. The design of urban spaces and cities include walkways and pedestrian areas that effectively direct urban navigation via a finite range of configurations. Pathways and alleys between buildings, pedestrian zones such as malls, shopping precincts, markets, green spaces and parks and underpasses are the ways people move through the city to get from one area to another. These spaces have affective impact on children; their materialities and spatialities, as well as their registers of affect, impact on encounters in physical and sensorial ways. It is through their movement in and with wide urban spatialities and materialities that a child's civics and citizenship emerges. And the affective agency of spatialities and materialities in co-curating movements presents a vitalist posthuman urban civics borne of imprints and marks, connections and belonging.

A posthuman theorisation of urban civics sees that urban rights and responsibilities take form within highly detailed and densely relational urban milieus comprising ecologies of things, bodies, registers, affects, histories and movements. The usually backgrounded, non-human aspects such as urban planning, design, infrastructure and building, as well as urban critters such as insects, birds and small mammals are resituated and activated, meaning that posthuman governances are shaped through the touch, encounter, movement, space, and location of different bodies and agencies, and the different affective registers these interactions and interrelations provoke.

Taking up the conceptual work of chapter 2, in this chapter we explore the concept of posthuman civics, which emerges from encounters between bodies and agencies in vibrant urban ecologies. Rosi Braidotti's (2019) writings into posthuman knowledge, Felix Guattari's (2014) work into subjects and relationalities and Erin Manning's (2013) scholarship into relational movement provide important theoretical guidance.

CIVIC CONTACT ZONES

Extending on from our discussions into posthuman civics in chapter 2, Braidotti (2019) offers the posthuman as an orienting term for the emergence of social and political discourses of the 'mutations that are engendered by advanced technological developments [. . .] it is a working hypothesis about the kinds of subjects we are becoming' (2). Posthumanism conceptually explores and describes the ways technologies blur bodily lines and demarcations between *a life* (human, and also, others), living and objects and environments and speech, ideas and beliefs. Posthumanism intellectually considers and translates the conditions and effects of evolving interrelationality. Further, in speculating about the co-constitution of future bodies, Braidotti draws attention to the role of advanced technological developments in directing subjectivity. She is interested in the semiotics of things and interfaces that virtually and physically connect us: music, cameras, scooters, lighting, airplanes; all of which generate subjects composed of multiple interfaces with their own respective significations. Braidotti suggests, therefore, that the posthuman body should be thought of as 'materially embedded and embodied, differential, affective and relational' (11) and co-constituted by the other bodies and surfaces it encounters. In the case of posthuman civics this means not thinking of humans as separately encountering urban materialities but that city and citizen are mutually co-constructing and urban civics emerges through the affects of these interrelationalities. The buildings, creatures, ecologies, materials and atmospheres in the urban milieu are not inert and only brought to life once a human steps in; there is an interplay between independently lively and active bodies and agentic material surfaces in richly atmospheric and sensorial spaces. As an example, the interior spaces of a shopping mall include cavernous walkways, diffused natural light from glass atriums, polished glass walls of shop fronts, bright, unified lighting. The shopping mall is situated in an inner-city block so the exterior of the mall is edged by back alleys and side streets. These spaces have old surfaces that are not cleaned every day, there are strong smells from kitchens and industrial refuse bins, small roads and narrow paths that connect to major roads and thoroughfares, insects and small animals and residual matter such as oil, paint and excretia. These two spaces enact different material and sensorial affects, and have directing agencies on the bodies moving in, with and through them. Braidotti proposes that material and atmospheric elements have associative meanings and semiotics so it is never simply an encounter between a child and a shopping mall or back alley. The components of the event: the corporeal, material, sensorial and semiotic aspects are an urban milieu that also includes the politics of land, place, belonging, exclusion, participation, rights and access. Collectively these are a posthuman civics.

Collectivity is a mode to think about the purpose of the activity of the milieu. Collectivity is also a way to think about community in posthuman ways; as a 'complex multiplicity' (Braidotti 2019, 18) of action 'through alliances, [and] transversal connections' (19) that are social and also sustaining. The co-animation of multiple bodies within the urban milieu is collective because they contest the tendencies of human-centric readings of space that hierarchise people against everything else. To think about children physically moving through a city, it is not just a case of focusing on their actions against a static field. A posthuman collectivity sees connection through their physical actions of touching surfaces and leaving imprints, and in relation with many other bodies in lively urban ecologies. A socially sustaining collectivity is produced in the encounter, which Braidotti proposes as the locational orientation of the meeting of onto-epistemological difference. Braidotti (2019) is interested in 'the multiple perspectives generated by embodied and embedded middle grounds', (52) a wonderful term that describes the zone where energies collide and exchange, where particles move back and forth. Where matters and bodies must negotiate each other and where productions emerge. The touch, scrape, residue is the collective sociality generated by the encounter of different surfaces, and this lively event brings about transversal urban civics. Transversality describes the many 'connections among material and symbolic, concrete and discursive lines of relation or forces' (Braidotti 2013, 95) happening across human and more-than-human encounters.

We bring Guattari's (2014) three ecologies into this discussion at this point because Guattari was also interested in the interrelationships between subjects and external more-than-human onto-epistemological forces. Guattari wrote *The Three Ecologies* in 1989 in response to rising integrated world capitalism, the explosion of mass media and his concern for its reductive and homogenising impacts on culture and subjectivity. Guattari identified the three ecologies as environment, social relations and human subjectivity. Environment, social relations and human subjectivity are the ethico-political groupings through which we can conceptualise the world and how living is affectively co-constituted. Collectively the three ecologies comprise

ecosophy, which Guattari proposed as a critical counter to a creeping
technocratic, standardised life. Guattari saw the three ecologies not as self-
contained, sparse systems but as wild and full, 'capable of bifurcating into
stratified and deathly repetitions', (36) perpetuating complexity and difference and keeping life interesting and complex. Guattari targeted mass-media
as the primary culprit in working against complexity because it creates
images of life that are 'generally reduced to their meanest expression' (17);
mass produced images that create a desire for subjects to become like those
seen in advertising, social media, TV and film, shifting the world towards a
monocultural standardised identity ideal. The impact of this, for Guattari, is
a compromised 'relationship between subjectivity and its exteriority' (17); a
reduced connection to the many different things that generate difference and
individuation. Guattari proposed that ecosophy provides 'an ethico-political
articulation' (18) of how social heterogeneity might thrive or be maintained,
and that these heterogeneous articulations reside in the vibrant convergence
zones across the three ecologies and are processually activated. Guattari's
emphasis on the value of processual action in these zones infers the importance of transversality across practices and materialities in the co-constituting
of diverse subjects. Pindar and Sutton (in Guattari 2014) suggest that Guattari
'compares our interior life or "interiority" to a crossroads where several
components of subjectification meet to make up who we think we are' (9).
Guattari (2019) talked about the negative impacts of solidification – using
the term 'ossified' to suggest that difference and fluidity were in danger of
becoming cemented into a singular, homogenous subject thanks to the growing ubiquity of technology. Guattari termed his suspicion of technologic
progressions a 'nagging paradox' (20) because the hopes that technology
will provide the means to address our ecological crises and 'reinstate socially
useful activities' are overshadowed by its monocultural, homogentisic nature,
and this prevents mass media being put to work for social transformation.
The lure is that technology can create a different life, however this lure is
always thwarted by the reality that mass media is mesmerising and reductive.
Guattari's nagging paradox sees that technologies can connect isolated people
and build a sense of community identity (think place-based, local community
online groups for example), while being algorithmically controlled in ways
that prevent true independence from the programme or platform. As such, it is
important that life is ecosophical, shaped by divergent and shifting ecologies
that perpetuate difference.

Guattari's (2019) nagging paradox and ecosophy inform the development
of posthuman civics and citizenship because it advocates for transversal
practice through different mediated encounters. Guattari's suspicion of mass
media and its shortcomings can be critiqued however, by expanding a narrow
definition of the 'technologic' beyond the specifics of certain forms of digital

media, and diversifying the material expectations of 'the interface'. This expanded interface, which might also include geologic forms, cement walls, grass, wood, pets and so on, disrupts Guattari's nagging paradox because this expanded interface is ascribed with the multiple meanings, associations, semiotics and versions of life of its different materialities. Subjectification is differently, heterogeneously formed through and by interaction with interfaces that have different agentic and material properties: digital, but also organic and biologic technologies, in diverse environments, forming multiple relationalities. A posthuman civics emerges in the contact zones where these diverse components collide, through a 'logic of intensities, of auto-referential existential assemblages engaging in irreversible durations' (Guattari 2014, 29) happening differently, for each posthuman subject in the event.

SCALING THE CITY

In Scaling the City, the children's creative movement in dance and gestural mapping processually traversed different material interfaces across the three ecologies of environment, social relations and human subjectivity. As we explained in chapter three, the project worked with groups of children aged between four and ten years in Brisbane, Australia, and Auckland, Aotearoa New Zealand. The two groups, named the Urban Activators (NZ) and Downtown Mappas (AUS), met in urban locations and created artistic works using creative movement and chalk marking in response to the space (Figures 6.1 and 6.2).

The overall proposal of the project was that the two creative modes would help children think about their connection to community, the city and their civic roles and rights as citizens. The project focused on dance and mapping to reflect some of the common ways children move through a city. Children don't drive car, so unless they are driven by an adult they are often on foot, or riding a bicycle or scooter or walking between public transport and their destination. These modes of transport place children in close proximity to city spaces, and the project was interested in maintaining those proximities while enabling children to experiment with forms of moving other than those they use everyday. Creative dance in a group setting created a changed perspective and a changed encounter with the spaces, and with other people in the space. The dance movements would prompt different considerations, interactions, relations and responses to the space. Urban planning, design and architecture prioritises the lives and needs of adults (Cockburn 2013) so children, and youth particularly, often claim a space or declare their presence in unsanctioned, undesirable ways such as through marking territory through graffiti, street art and tagging. Mapping with children's pavement chalks, which wash

Figure 6.1   Downtown Mappas, Brisbane, Australia. Photograph by Linda Knight.

Figure 6.2   Urban Activators, Auckland, New Zealand. Photograph by Linda Knight.

off easily, enabled the project to critically explore young people's 'deface-ment' practices as well as figuratively/literally 'marking' children's presence in the city and the routes they take through it. The chalk marks created visual tracings and residues of past moments when children had been there. The marks were both a defacement and a proof of occupation; giving children a presence they don't normally have in the city. Making the chalked mapping marks was also a creative process because it required children to think about how they would map themselves into the scene.

As noted earlier, at the beginning of each meeting it was explained to the children that we were thinking about citizenship and civics.[2] We held discus-sions focused on who could be a citizen? Could other living things such as animals and plants be citizens? Could non-living things such as the weather, rocks, play equipment, buildings, be a citizen? The children asked questions and speculated on these posthuman ideas of citizenship and subjectivity. We held the meetings in different settings in the two cities: an outdoor play area in a natural park with a nearby river; a below-street-level, semi-covered walk-way that ran alongside a glass-walled building and busy road; a pedestrian-accessible flat roof; and a walled garden in a university complex.

These initial discussions enabled the children to look around their immedi-ate environment to think about the civic agency of the more-than-human bod-ies and things there and to prompt the kinds of mappings and movements they wanted to make. The children and researchers completed warm-up exercises to enable the children to experiment with using their bodies to make differ-ent creative movements[3] and whole-body, gestural, drawn mapping marks using pavement chalks. The groups then spent a short time walking around the space to explore and familiarise themselves before spending between one and two hours co-curating mapping marks and co-choreographing body movements. The children worked in variously sized groups, continuously and spontaneously generating responses to the topic of citizenship and civics which they translated into movements and mapping marks. They sometimes collaborated with the adults, although not always. Their creative responses were in direct interaction with the conversations about citizenship and civics and with the material and affective aspects of the spaces including tempera-tures, sunlight and shade,[4] surface materials, angles of surfaces, large and small spaces, pathways and coverings, and also birds, animals, other people, insects, plants, refuse, parked vehicles and bicycles. The movements and mapping marks were photo and video recorded by the researchers. The chil-dren did not make any recordings.

Guattari (2014) proposes that 'Social ecosophy will consist in developing specific practices that will modify and reinvent the ways in which we live . . . in an urban context' and that 'It will be a question of literally reconstructing the modalities [. . . for] implementing effective practices of experimentation'

(22). Guattari advocates for creatively exploring how to expand the ways for/ of making contact-with, because these inquiries activate differently sensing apparatus points and increase individuated experience, and that the multiplicity of these contact points help to counter homogeneity. Scaling the City enacted a social ecosophy because, through practice, it generated interactions that brought the three lively ecologies into contact. Through movement in and with urban space the environment was experienced, felt, responded to; not as a backdrop but in close proximity and in detail. 'Environment' became less of a scape and more an active, activating nonhuman 'Other' with civic agency and rights. The interactions with the environment nurtured social relations that were not homogeneously reductive and media-based, they were emergent and grew through the meeting of many different bodies and materialities. Human subjectivity was thus shaped, dependent upon and directed through the semiotics of the social interactions between these diverse technological interfaces, building a civics individually and collectively.

Braidotti (2013) and Guattari (2014) hold different opinions on the impact of technology on subjectivity. However their ideas about how technologies mutate life converge somewhat, in that 'the acceleration of techno-scientific mutations' (Guattari 2014, 18) 'have a strong biopolitical effect upon the embodied subject they intersect with' (Braidotti 2013, 90). Guattari and Braidotti propose that technologies intersect the ecological, the social and the material; and this means that children, who are participants in the contemporary world, are already posthuman, technologic subjects because their daily lives and subjectivities are produced through technologically mediated experiences.

The Urban Activators were a pre-existing dance group, based in Auckland New Zealand, of boys aged between eight and ten years. The group experimented with a mix of contemporary dance, gymnastics and parkour in works they choreographed with their female dance teacher, and they sometimes also worked with visiting male dancers. The Urban Activators would select a site in the city or surrounding suburbs and choreograph a dance piece in response to the site. The prior experience the boys had with dance enabled them to focus significantly in this project on interfaces and technologies, pushing the experimental possibilities for ways of working with the spaces and surfaces available. This is seen in Fig. 6.2 where the boys have found a narrow space and creatively placed their bodies in relation with it. The group also pushed the technologic interface of the pavement chalk and experimented with many different ways to 'hold' the chalk so that they could make marks and dance movements simultaneously. A popular technique was to prehensively[5] grab the chalk by the toes and make marks during dance movements (Fig. 6.3).

The Downtown Mappas were a group of children aged between – four and ten years, brought together for the purposes of the project, and it was not

Figure 6.3   Urban Activators, Auckland, New Zealand. Photograph by Linda Knight.

known what their prior experiences with movement were. The children in the Downtown Mappas predominantly held the chalk in their hands, although they experimented with positioning their bodies differently as they generated marks (fig. 6.1). The children were creative in their negotiations with the weather and found ways to participate in movement activities while avoiding direct sun and heat.

Scaling the City facilitated an examination of how wild ecologies such as the environment, social relations and human subjectivity converge in middle grounds. Surface distinctions such as the demarcated boundaries that assert one body from another were softened in an expanded field that includes biologic, material and elemental technologies and interfaces. The semiotics of these interfaces, which are already thick and wild with heterogeneous meaning merge in a middle ground encounter, become wilder and denser, germinating relationships between the child subject and exteriority. The middle ground between the children and the surfaces as they touch, bounce, roll, tread and as chalk drags across and leaves its trace, there enacts a transversal urban citizenship across forms, beings, bodies and agents. As dust hits skin, as chalk gets dragged across grass blades, or through a wet puddle lined with silty moss, interrelationalities are formed between these technologies in this middle ground, this zone of encounter, this processual zone. Concrete, grass, chalk, skin, water, fabric, dust, rubbish and so on are each a technology that is replete with particular signs and semiotics which it transfers through its own interface. These technologies and signs coalesce in embodied and embedded middle grounds to generate emergent posthuman subjectivities, and the transversal encounters are materially and subjectively co-constructing a posthuman civics of more-than-human care and reciprocity.

The children moved within a space, moved with a space and were moved by a space. Likewise the non-human and inhuman others were also moved; by and with the children and the chalks they wielded. These movements and encounters are a co-constitution of bodies (a chalk-concrete-hand body or a foot-sock-shoe-wall-air body) that generate new futures through their impact on and from the encounter. The Anthropocene is widely understood as a term that describes how the inhuman and non-human world is being increasingly co-constituted by humans into new future forms; likewise, the inhuman and non-human co-constitute the human into new futures in these interactions.

The co-constituting interactions between the dancers, pavements, walls, plants, chalks, dust motes, birds and so on co-construct them each as citizens *and* as the city, and a posthuman civics emerges through the affective power of these interrelational encounters. The Urban Activators and the Downtown Mappas had different relational experiences brought about through creative and corporeal activity that was simultaneously individual and collective, and always in relation with the exterior. The Urban Activators experienced places that were different kinds of thoroughfare: a university quadrangle, a subterranean walkway alongside a glass-fronted office and a rooftop space that connected lecture halls and a cafe building. The Downtown Mappas experienced public parks that were filled with plants, trees and grass as well as playground structures. The materiality of these spaces impacted on the types of movements that each group could make, for example the Downtown Mappas could swing, slide, lay across pathways, stay still and crouch, while the Urban Activators could climb, jump against walls, slide against glass. The creative movement led to 'a problematization that is transversal to them' (Guattari 2014, 21); transversal, as in it related to their own ideas of themselves as a citizen, their bodies as civic entity, their presence and rights in spaces, their interactions with spaces and materials and the affective powers of those spaces and materials. What makes these events examples of a posthuman civics and not simply a movement event, is because a posthuman civic subject emerges from the ecosophic middle grounds where encounters generate care for and about the materiality and technology of spaces, for in/non/human others in the space, consideration of how these others move through the space and why the space is important, why it is a space that calls its subjects to attention. In a posthuman civics the interaction with other bodies, technologies and materialities in space is a gesture of responsibility and civility.

THE CREATIVE GESTURES OF CIVIC ACTION

Scaling the City employed dance and gestural mapping because these practices facilitate imaginative and corporeal encounters and because creative practice is effective in provoking different kinds of thoughts, actions and feelings about the altered subject, the technologic subject, new socialities and what kind of humans are we becoming. Pindar and Sutton (in Guattari 2014) interpret that it is artists in *The Three Ecologies* 'who provide us with the most profound insights into the human condition' (9) because they continuously return to experimentation and speculation. Creative practice is especially pertinent to projects because it can introduce children to concepts of posthumanism, and new meanings around civics and citizenship through performative, semiotic, experimental and creative modes which traverse the material, physical and conceptual. Artists 'start over and over again from scratch, uncertain with each new attempt precisely where their next experiment will take them' (Pindar and Sutton 2014, 9). The Urban Activators cycled through movements, experimenting with placing their bodies in different arrangements and trialling movement sequences in ways that brought other things actively into the choreography. The young dancers were being led as much by the bodies in the urban milieu as by their own and others' bodies, and they considered the details of these movements through an expressive and creative gesture. The Downtown Mappas were attuned to the non-human others in the park, observing their movements and listening to their calls, repeating these in their own body movements and chalk markings, and moving alongside the critters in a form of physical relation.

The repetitive and speculative artistic practices in Scaling the City created the conditions for affective middle grounds comprising different matters and technologies, and different citizens collectively generating posthuman civics. Michelle Duffy (2016) suggests that affect attunes us to the humming 'relations in-between the human and nonhuman elements of a space', (385) referring to a Spinozan reading of a body affecting and being affected by other bodies. Erin Manning's (2013) work can be employed to expand on this Spinozan articulation. In her text *A Body Is Always More Than One*, Manning references Whiteheadian, Deleuzian and Simmondonian concepts to propose that affect is not always a distinct exchange because the individual is not regarded as singular or separated from its surroundings, it is always part of an energy field that is composed of more than just itself. Bodies, and the affective resolutions that take place are always in a 'processual field of relation and the limit at which that field expresses itself', (Manning 2013, 17) meaning bodies occupy fields that are also full of multiple movements taking place, and affects reside in the concentrated, intensive 'about-to' zones at the very edge of these fields of multiple movements already expressed. Perhaps, then, more than a case of affect moving in one direction and from/to the other, affect always needs an 'in-relation' with, for affect to happen 'through'. For Manning (2013), affect 'returns as the force of becoming that incessantly creates collectivities in the making' (30) by tuning bodies and movements into the potentiality of difference. Manning's ideas of relationality and affect matter because in Scaling the City bodies which included the children, chalks and surfaces came into contact to form new ideas about civic identity and belonging. Like Guattari and Braidotti, Manning eschews a separated affected/affecting for affective co-composition, proposing that a body is 'an ecology of processes [. . .] always in co-constellation with the environmentality of which it is a part' (19), and that affective life generates in this lively zone of the encounter and the encounters to come. The propositions from Braidotti, Guattari and Manning on encountering suggest posthuman civics and citizenship only really develops through practices and that an affective posthuman civics is created through the co-mingling of bodies, energies, movements, potentialities, affects and means that children become citizens in and with their surroundings within ecosophic middle grounds and through processual 'activity that is intensively relational' (Manning 2013, 25). Each time a surface is touched, each time a body is in movement with the touch and other things, it builds a transindividual relation between citizens, and this becomes a posthuman civics.

Each co-mingled practice in Scaling the City brings about what Manning (2013) describes as 'a movement of thought', and a processual thinking that 'composes-with movement' (14) as movement occurs. In Scaling the City, the creative movement and chalk mapping intensified the co-mingling of things in relational zones, via processual modes that distilled 'from the weave of total movement a quality that composes a bodying in motion' (Manning 2013, 14), in other words, the creative movement and the mapping were each a mode for curating a gestural sequence carefully extracted from all movements occurring.

As an example, one of the Urban Activators sessions took place in a walled garden on a university campus. The garden wall was old and made from small red bricks, and the wall provided entries and exits to the garden, these were through arched doorways that had heavy wood doors attached. Inside the garden were pathways that sectioned off grassy lawns that were well trimmed and weed-free. In the centre of some of these lawns were old trees of different native and introduced species. There were garden beds dotted about the edges. The pathways were surfaced with chopped concrete and tarmac, making them easy to walk on but with a rough, stony surface. The paths had old iron bollards placed in them and were painted white and the iron was exposed in areas of high wear and tear. The weather on that day was dull and it had rained earlier so everything was still wet and there were puddles dotted about.

The boys had brought scooters to experiment with different ways of moving in the space, and to experiment with how they might use the pavement chalks to create mappings of and with the space. We began with walking around the space to familiarise ourselves with it, then the boys began some initial planning of the movements and mappings they wanted to make. They were all very keen to integrate their scooters into their work, and so the boys took to their scooters at this point to brainstorm movements and choreographic sequences. They also took sticks of the chalk and began experimenting with ways to simultaneously ride their scooter, make dance movements and also make chalk markings. Some movements they trialled included squatting on the scooter while holding the chalk to the floor and then dragging the chalk alongside as they scootered along the paths, or trying to scooter on the dirt and the grass as they made chalk markings. They tested how effectively the chalk marked surfaces such as tree bark, painted and unpainted metal, brick, concrete, grass, puddle and glass, and began to curate ideas around the results of those tests. The children found a path on a slope, the path had bollards set in to it, and it also had dips filled with puddles so they devised a movement sequence whereby they moved in a line, starting at the top of the slope and pushing off so they could squat on their scooter and make a long chalk line, briefly dip the chalk into a puddle then resume the same mark making gesture as they headed down the slope. They then chalked lines around a bollard, circled around the bollard then stood up on their scooter to scoot back up the hill without chalking. The boys repeated this sequence in a looping line, building up long trails of pale chalk that became much more intense after the chalk was dipped in a puddle and covering the bollard in small dashed marks.

While this was happening, adults were walking through the garden to go into buildings or to exit the other side of the garden. There were moments when groups of children on scooters encountered adults walking in groups or alone – heading in the same or opposite direction. The encounters sparked everyone to abruptly move in unexpected ways to try and negotiate the others they met.

Processually, in mapping, the precursive gesture towards producing a scraped chalk mark issues from a coalition of thought, affect and movement, and these forces travel into the gesture which carries the coalition through and into a curated trace, placed on a surface. The movements for making the chalked marks are movements for that mark-making. The process of marking a surface brings attention to that surface, and initiates a relation with urban space. Processually, dance, thought, breath and the precursive preparations of energies and tensing of biologic materials distinguish from all movements happening, and these distinctions become the beginning of a movement performed against all other movements. And at the same time, in mapping and in dance, these gestural sequences fall into the all-other movements of others to be processually co-mingled and co-composed into further movements. The chalked marks and movements were peaking moments in the milieu. These peaking moments, produced individually, collectively and interactively in relation with and between all the in/non/human participants of the Urban Activators and the Downtown Mappas, formed civic, ecological co-compositions from 'a thinking in act, a movement of thought' (Manning 2013, 15). The co-composed, repetitive and speculative processual movements in Scaling the City enact an affective civics through creative practices that perpetually explore immanent possibility, 'understood as the preacceleration of experience as it acts on the becoming-body' (Manning 2013, 5), bringing about a perpetually emerging citizenship-in-relation with becoming-civics composed in the milieu.

The movements that were composed of bodies, scooters, walkways, a garden and more occurred and some were recorded via video and photography; however, the chalk tracings continued to reside after movements moved on. We wanted these chalk tracings not to lock down the movements into a static landscape but to act as actual and virtual markings of the children's presence. The dashed, dragged marks, once made, have their own physicality and their own contributing presence in the milieu; each mark composed of chalk particles clinging together in their formations and with the material surfaces they find themselves on. They also are an imprinted account of an uncommon gathering of non/in/human citizens in the urban milieu, visualising a 'co-composition through a common tracing that allows the uncommon to emerge' (Manning 2013, 193). Manning's interest in Fernand Deligny's mapping project with autistic children focuses on how marks in mappings are made with and during the meeting of things in the milieu, and she notes that these marks cannot occur without that meeting. Also, the things exist beyond the marks, so the marks need to be created in an excess to record that excess by visualising partiality. In Scaling the City, and the example of the children scootering in the walled garden, the marks record just the partiality of the excesses of the movements in the event. The children's technique of dancing and chalk marking surfaces was a call to acknowledge the urban civics of uncommon in/non/human citizens. The citizens: chalk, scooters, pavements, bollards, people, puddles, temperatures, atmospheres and more build a posthuman civics through movements and encounters in middle grounds, and the chalk marks are a residue of a partial recording of all the in/non/human citizens in their lively civic activity, and are a tracing of an event of the 'collective individuation' (Manning 2013, 35) of bodies moving in-relation. The tracings are a temporary accounting because they disappear as they become dispersed through the disturbances of being walked on, brushed or rained on. Nevertheless they creatively declare a point in time and are a reminder that civics and citizenship rely upon co-configurations and co-constitutions, placing emphasis on how 'affectivity and relationality is an alternative to individualist autonomy' (Braidotti 2019, 12).

CHILDREN BECOMING ACTIVE URBANCITIZENS

Guattari (2014), Manning (2013) and Braidotti (2019) conceptualise the milieu and its contents differently; however, their respective conceptualisations have connection points. In *The Three Ecologies*, Guattari (2014) considers how to disrupt the ubiquity of a mass-mediated image of life through reconnection with lively and wildly producing ecologies to 'reinvent the ways in which we live' (22) in the urban context. In *Always More Than One,* Manning (2013) thinks in detail about how difference happens, suggesting that 'It happens across strata, both actual and virtual [. . .] both concrete and abstract' (2) in a multi-dimensional relationscape. And in *Posthuman Knowledge*, Braidotti (2019) calls for a recasting of 'ethical and political subjectivity for posthuman times' (34) not based on status, or the right to vote, but on a transversal politics that emerges out of intertwined and symbiotic relations. A posthuman civics is not limited to human rights and responsibilities, a posthuman civics emerges in the intensive zones of encounter, imagined differently by Guattari, Manning and Braidotti through their propositions into interrelationality and intersubjectivity and their attention to the agency and vitality of all things. Their propositions collectively articulate that posthuman civics develops in and through reciprocal exchanges between transversal bodies in movement.

Scaling the City exemplifies how posthuman civics and citizenship develops in interrelational and intersubjective exchanges between things and bodies, and used creative, playful movement and mapping practices to increase children's urban agency within a posthuman conceptual framing of children's civics and citizenship. The project did not attempt to assist children's urban agency through co-design, architecture or designing playful cities. While projects like these are incredibly important and productive, they were not the focus here. Instead, Scaling the City was oriented by posthuman concepts and centralised active movement and gestural mapping to explore how children interact with spaces such as playgrounds, skate parks, swimming pools and so on. The mapping combined large-scale drawing techniques, gestural drawing techniques and performance drawing techniques with abstract mark making. The creative movement was a fusion of parkour, gymnastics and contemporary dance, and collectively these practices helped children build civic relations with a city's materialities. The drawing techniques, which involved wielding chalks, water and paintbrushes offered a way to disrupt more common cartographic practices because the large-scale, gestural drawings generated what Davisi Boontharm (2019) describes as 'non-measurable dimensions of place' (65). Boontharm sees that using drawing practices in mapping creates these different kinds of dimensional readings because drawing itself is a particular kind of practice and will produce something different from the exegeses generated from other cartographic approaches. As a practice, the act of drawing, for scholar artists in the Drawing Research Network, produces a visualisation of 'the difference between what is seen and what is conceived, and [. . .] what is conceived and what appears' (Downs et al. 2009, xix). Introducing the children to large-scale, expressive, gestural, movement drawing techniques effectively introduced them to processes of mapping that could not rely upon schematic coding, or topographical representation. Our mapping relied on making records of points of encounter, marking where they felt it was important to inscribe a civic space, and the criteria for marking was not based on an objectivist or extractivist reading of the land, it was a way of mapping occurrences of transindividual sociality. The drawing practices could initiate these forms of mapping because, as Pamela Lee (1999) states, in drawing 'the gesture is equally informed by the thing upon which it acts' (43) meaning that drawing is collaborative and transversal; emerging from the interactions between materials, ideas, movements, topics, environments, objects. The mappings made in Scaling the City were not cartographies of, but were mappings with, produced at the lively, brief meeting points of citizens in the urban milieu.

The movement techniques evolved from a mixture of parkour-inspired practices along with contemporary movement and dance that the Urban Activators had already been exploring in their prior work and were interested to continue to use in this project. The combining of these movement techniques created a hybrid practice that quite purposefully and meaningfully brought the children into close bodily contact with places and spaces. This means the children were not dancing against an urban backdrop; they were being directed by and were responsive to the materialities and bodies in spaces in ways that are familiar to those who practice parkour. Although critical readings of parkour highlight the need to consider urban access and issues of subjectivity and intersectionality (Mould 2016) there is acknowledgement that urban spaces are inscribed differently and that parkour offers 'an emancipatory potential from the confinement of existing urban power structures, however covert, tacit, and "soft" this emancipation may be' (Mould 2016, 315). As dancers, the boys in the Urban Activators were motivated to explore these emancipatory potentials and to explore elements of parkour in combination with dance moves and gymnastics to build their civic connection with, and in those spaces. The hybrid movement practices that they developed in Scaling the City enabled them to encounter urban space and initiate their citizenship by 'rediscovering the urban environment around their own beliefs, expressions, and desires' (Mould 2016, 313).

The Scaling the City project speculated on emergent concepts of urban civics that are not limited to humanist readings of citizenship and political agency. The children experimented with creative mapping and movement practices and created a series of curated responses that allowed them to think more expansively about civics and citizenship, and the diverse bodies who contribute to the urban community. The curations also offered a critical starting point for the children to think about posthuman concepts of urban civics and a posthuman politics that is respectful of non-human and inhuman participation and civic agency. Additionally, the expressive curations repositioned the child as a citizen and brought different conceptions of citizenship into focus as they negotiated these urban zones.

Although Scaling the City was facilitated by adults, and adults were always present at the activities, the children were centrally positioned because, as researchers, we support that 'researching "with" children acknowledges that they are active participants in their communities' (Duffy 2016, 386), and that children need to be able to experiment but within safe conditions. The children were taken to different locations by adults; the children did not choose these. The urban sites chosen were mainly not sites approved for play or physical activity, they were spaces that are determined to have specific use: walkways, paths, underpasses and so on. There are often negative and restrictive public reactions to youth moving in their own ways in urban spaces, such as young people gathering in public spaces to take drugs or to have sex , or children going 'wild' and causing damage to private and public property and so on (Arends and Hordijk 2016). These negative scenarios germinate and act to undermine normative ideas about the kinds of physical occupation and behaviours that young people 'should' perform in a space. These negative scenarios act as cautionary tales against disrupting social rules and expectations and help to maintain common perceptions of what the spaces have been 'officially' designated for (Mould 2016; Arends and Hordijk 2016). The public mistrust of young people in 'non-designated' spaces indicate that urban spaces are privy to sociological norms and that disruptions to these norms: essentially in the form of young people being present expose the governances of urban participation and belonging. Subverting these governances by enabling young people to chalk and creatively move in non-designated spaces is a social and spatial political act that addresses civics and citizenship, and how young people's urban citizenship, civic membership and contributions are controlled. Choosing non-designated locations by the adults enabled children to make connections to new spaces they would not normally be able to access because of these regulatory expectations. Adult selection of locations offered wider access to city spaces and supported the children to have freedom to select what aspects of the space they wanted to use. Working across generations has helped to subvert the negative associations that can attach to young people occupying space on their own terms (Arends and Hordijk 2016) and doing unexpected things there. The Urban Activators and the Downtown Mappas weren't 'behaving' as expected for young people. Although adults were there, the children were chalking, leaving marks, dancing, loitering, jumping on surfaces, climbing. making noise, acting in groups. The children interrupted the walking paths of the adults, they left records of their occupation. The adults did not officiate.

Although the adult researchers sometimes participated in the movement and mapping, the children had the freedom to organise themselves and to devise their responses. The Scaling the City project involved adults and children being in a space together and working intergenerationally to make creative movements and responses to emergent ideas of civics and citizenship. The Downtown Mappas were children who did not know each other previously, while the Urban Activators knew each other previously so the choreographies and mappings were created with friends or strangers, in unfamiliar spaces and not often involving adults. Nevertheless, the children directed the progress of the sessions; they could change their ideas at any point and work together or in smaller groups, or pairs. It was important that the children had this freedom so that they could use mapping and movement to explore concepts of identity and agency, belonging, participation and citizenship. At the end of the sessions we asked the children to write evaluative comments on post-it notes. These short comments, which included 'its good to be ina flock', 'work together as a teme', 'I enjoyed leading', 'you need too try too keep with your flok' and 'There are lots of animals at The Gap and lots of beings' indicate that the process of moving and mapping helped the children to think about and explore citizenship and belonging in experimental and expansive ways.

Creative practice was central to this project and vital methodologically in helping the children to corporeally articulate their desire to take up space, be a citizen and develop their civic connection and responsibilities. The dance-based, cartographic, drawing-based methods were creative and applied within a participatory art methodologic framework. Although the Scaling the City project had a focus on exploring posthuman civics and citizenship, the project had a research-creation approach, whereby ideas and concepts of posthuman civics and citizenship continued to develop throughout. Children were taken to spaces that helped them understand ideas about posthumanism, spaces that helped them to connect to the urban milieu such as the different scales and registers there, the materiality of surfaces, temperatures, light and shadow and plant and animal life. These spaces helped them to develop their ideas and responses through their curations with the movement and mapping. The richness of each project meeting meant that the project continually developed, and exemplifies the research-creation approach.

CONCLUSION

This chapter has argued that children need expressive modes, brought about through the arts, to experiment and speculate on complex ideas. In Scaling the City, two groups of children were able to make artistic works to help them learn about and consider posthuman ideas of belonging, identity and community, which they experimented imaginatively and actively, to prepare for urban possibilities in a time of great change and at a formative stage in their lives. Creative movement and gestural mapping were centrally important to the project and the children's experimentations. Their use of artistic research practices to explore urban belonging 'make possible new ways to consider the everyday, the arena in which researchers have usually framed children as being both socialized and contained' (Duffy 2016, 387). The children were able to experiment with the ways that artistic practices can be put intellectually to work to think about big ideas, theoretically and also in and through practice. The acts and practices within creative movement and in gestural mapping brought the children into contact with the urban milieu, not only in terms of its different materialities but also the conceptual ideas and propositions that compose and frame their surroundings as a 'posthuman urban milieu'. The practices within acts of moving, practices of mapping, required different physical shiftings, different positionings, choices, flexes and slowed life down enough for them to consider, ponder, speculate, propose and to extend their thinking to interact as a civic citizen with and in space more widely. The practices initiated creative responses that address how children can participate in political civic action. The imprints and traces they left offered a comment on the norms and expectations of children's urban geographies and the ways that children's urban movement is majoritively determined by 'adult-centered spatial and social codes of conduct' (Mould 2016, 318). The chalked residues that remained after the activities were a visual continuation of their having been there; the dashed marks and dusty lines recorded that young people have rights to urban space, reminding others that children occupy cities and are already citizens with rights to all parts of the space.

Creative practices helped facilitate how children think about belonging and the feelings of being in the space with all others in the milieu: interacting with friends, material surfaces, spaces, creatures, materialities, as well as with concepts, propositions and speculations, and how these meet in intensive zones of encounter. The children had interactions with non-human and inhuman urban others through their creative and performative curations, with materials, animals and matters that have long historical presence and connection with the urban space. As the children scaled the city in creative and unpredictable ways, they created civic spaces that tended to 'the political in creative and unforeseen ways' (Manning 2013, 37). Just by arriving, by dancing and moving, by mapping and marking 'there', a gathering took place in that moment, of citizens of the city, and they were briefly together moving in civic – and political – relation. These participatory art methods creatively experimented with concepts of civics and citizenship in ways that were conceptual but also physical, leaving imprinted residues across bodies and surfaces in the milieu, including the children. Those residual imprints are affective and have changed what was before, changing the directions of ideas, thoughts and bodies. No posthuman body is excluded here, however, despite this there is no possibility of being able to suggest a definitive statement on how human bodies are included: how children become citizens, or how they understand civics. Everything about Scaling the City was designed to explore speculations into posthuman civics and citizenship and examine the ways that civics and citizenship develops for diverse bodies and identities. Guattari, Braidotti and Manning indicate that exciting things happen in contact zones that are full of movement, so it is perhaps from there that a posthuman civics and citizenship emerges – for all that are present.

Chapter 7

Climate Change and the End of Childhood

The Bible, among many other popular cultural texts, features the statement that children will inherit the earth (see Psalm 25:13 but this point is also inferred in Matthew 5:4). While the Bible can be thought of as one of the most singularly influential Western cultural texts, popular cultural references to this statement also feature in music, film, novels, poetry: many and varied cultural texts. The more specific point made in Matthew 5:4 is that the *meek* will inherit the earth, which is not quite that children will inherit the earth, but does align with the sentiment that the less powerful among society will end up being the most successful. Today, running against this early assurance that innocent children will 'inherit the earth' are media images of children being born and dying in refugee camps, infants wrapped in shock blankets as they are rescued from sinking ships, and images of drowned child bodies washed up on beaches. Not only is there little innocence in the age of the climate crisis, there is no apparent safety for many children. This risk and lack of safety comes from being born into political danger, economic uncertainty and universal environmental disaster. In this chapter we examine the fact that, in inheriting the earth, children are asked to negotiate the complex and perhaps unsolvable issues of climate change that threaten life on earth. Data from the Interfaith Childhoods project shows how children respond to climate change by imagining and posthuman futures in which they might find safety and refuge and form empathetic kinship with others.

We introduce posthuman publics as a concept that can be used to map both the start and end of the idea of childhood in the Anthropocene. The climate crisis brings with it the impossibility of childhood innocence and safety in the 'natural world' as originally imagined by scholars such as Jean-Jacques Rousseau. This is because, as well as being born into unsafe and changing environments, children are born into tumultuous political climates that can threaten borders, safety and life. Such political battles are more often than not fought over fossil fuels and possibilities for mining; practices that lead to climate change also create political instability. Ontologically and politically, the contemporary global climate is insecure, and children inherit this complex insecurity. This renders notions of 'nature' as the cradle of childhood innocence mute. In this chapter, we use data from the Interfaith Childhoods project as proof that childhood 'innocence' has been annulled by the Anthropocene and that child publics have always-already been posthuman. The contemporary climate that children are born into brings with it a responsibility of undoing the devastating actions of those before them, and the futures imagined by children in this context reflect deep awareness of this responsibility. As a way of negotiating this ontological and political insecurity, a series of workshops invited children to explore concepts of home and safety. The children made art about 'what really matters', 'what makes a home' or 'what makes me feel safe', which was then used to decorate 'refuges', or small canvas tents. These tents became assemblages of safety, and formed little children's publics, which, as noted, are always-already amalgams of nature-animal-human-otherworldly communities. Part of this work entailed children thinking about some of their own migrant journeys and periods of homelessness, or reflecting on these experiences in others. The tents made and decorated by children became architectures of empathy; refuges holding all the precious things that give children's life meaning and security, but also small urban publics in which children without a migrant background could form empathetic connections with their peers who had fled war, division, persecution, extreme climate events or poverty. Assembled together, the refuges formed tent cities, reminding the children and the viewer of the absence of a childhood filled with possibilities in the Anthropocene, perhaps more similar to the realities of refugee camps than parents might think. The children's architectures of empathy, or tent cities, model a kind of posthuman citizenship that has been formed in direct response to the realities of climate change, a citizenship entangled with the more-than-human environment and empathetic kinship with other children and other planet-dwellers. This chapter shows the relationality of children's sense of citizenship as they collectively reconfigure their environments through processes of habitation, sensing, moving, enacting, thinking, making and talking about connections with place. These processes are open, shifting the conditions of value and othering and the delineation of matter as 'human' and 'non-human'. But their tent-city citizenship is also characterised by a profound awareness of the end of Romantic and traditional notions of childhood innocence. In their formulation of their posthuman 'tent-city' publics, children find ways to face the realities of the Anthropocene.

This chapter begins with a brief outline of the refuge workshops of the Interfaith Childhoods project, before examining the recurrent themes that emerged in relation to – and often as definitions of – 'safety', 'home' and 'refuge'. We found that children not only took refuge in practical things like a house, warmth or food, but also in less tangible things such as heritage, cultural trends and objects, and a keen sense of self. Above all, children found safety in a sense of connection, with their families, their friends, their communities and even with themselves, which highlights how children's sense of refuge is deeply relational, drawing on wide assemblages of people, places, animals and things; connection is a response to posthuman encounters. Working with children from migrant and refugee backgrounds also showed us how children with little control over their external sense of safety would often turn inwards, finding refuge in their self and their self-love. We then turn to the kinds of relational, empathetic and care-based citizenship that was formed in and facilitated by the posthuman publics of the tent cities. The workshops allowed this citizenship to be based on empathy between children who had experienced displacement and violence and those who had not. In response to the always-already posthuman nature of childhood publics, we turn to the role of nature in the formation of this citizenship, and form critiques of 'nature' as the cradle of Rousseau's childhood innocence that the Anthropocene has brought to an end. We conclude with an examination of the kinds of non-innocent publics the children have formed in response to the danger of the Anthropocene, and how this again draws on posthuman conceptualisations of the children's relationship with the environment, animals, themselves, their peers and their homes.

We thread ethnographic observations through the analysis, but these observations are not only of the children but also of ourselves as we negotiated the realities of fieldwork. This data – about long tube rides, tents that just wouldn't work and collapsing papier-mâché – form the rich and thick data of posthuman and new materialist ethnographic research (Hickey-Moody et al. 2021), draws in the mess, failures and lively materiality of fieldwork as a central part of analysis. This mess is key to the feministic ethnographic perspective from which this project operates; as we argue elsewhere, 'ethnography as a field needs to understand the embodied and psychic labours of being open to change, being responsive, being overcommitted, giving one's domestic world over to work' (Hickey-Moody 2019b, np). We weave these embodied and psychic labours throughout the chapter, entangling them with our ethnographic data.

REFUGE

The Interfaith Childhoods workshops on refuge began by talking about home and safety, structured around the questions of 'what really matters?' and 'what makes a home?' A broad conversation developed into a discussion of the most important things the children would take with them if they had to suddenly leave their home, which then inevitably evolved into an exploration of some children's experiences of seeking refuge. This is a confronting subject for many of the research participants, namely, for those who live in poverty, have been displaced, or have been homeless while seeking political asylum. The workshops prompted children to reflect on their ontological insecurity. Those children who come from secure family backgrounds, some of whom have spent their whole lives in the same family home, were able to think empathetically about the experience of children with less secure homes. As such, the initial discussion was very generative, with some children sharing stories of treacherous journeys by boat and the death of family members, and other children learning about the precariousness of life for many of their peers. These conversations were instrumental in shaping how some children later decorated their refuges and collaboratively built their architectures of empathy, which emerged as structures that scaffolded their understanding of the precarious lives of their peers. The lists of objects the children would take with them became things the children made into mobiles and decorations for their refuges. These places of refuge were several small canvas and bamboo tents that we brought to the final workshop and assembled with assistance from the children. Assembled together, these tents created small 'tent cities' covered in artwork of safety, homeliness, belonging and empathy.

'WHAT MAKES A HOUSE A HOME?'

The refuge workshops began in London in 2018. For the first three workshops, we custom-built the tents for each workshop with six bamboo poles and gauze fabric. The first iteration of the workshop (Figures 7.1, 7.2 and 7.3) was held at P21 Gallery in central London, the second at Harbinger School in Isle of Dogs, and the third at Cherry Orchard School in Charlton.

While many of the children involved in the Interfaith Childhoods project were asylum seekers and refugees, the majority of children from these backgrounds were in Australia or Manchester, and very few were in London. While many children in the Cherry Orchard School live with financial insecurity (see Hickey-Moody in press), the school is a multi-cultural, not predominantly refugee, community. The children at Harbinger School have a similar, slightly more ethnically diverse and financially secure demographic profile. These initial workshops therefore provided an opportunity for the children to think about, and empathise with, refugee experiences, and for the migrant children in the class to share their backgrounds with those whose families had been living in London for many generations.

Children have a keen sense of needing to escape the present moment, and while relationships with family can provide solace and happiness, the vast

Figure 7.1 **Refuge Made at P21 Gallery in London.** Photograph by Anna Hickey-Moody.

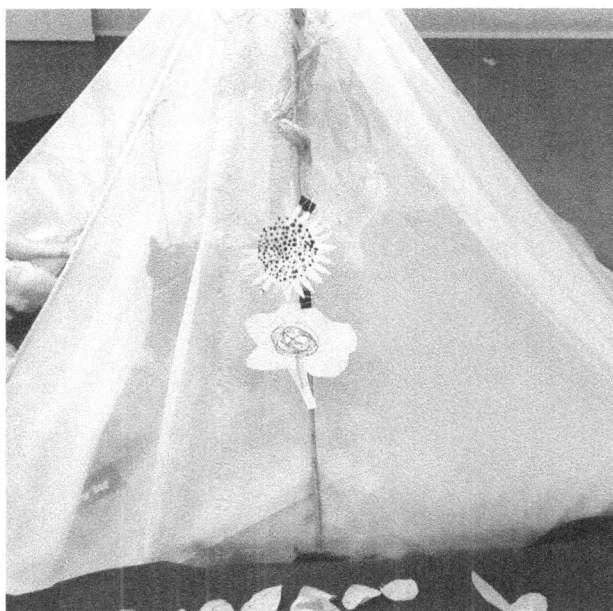

Figure 7.2 **Art Decorating a Refuge Made at P21 Gallery in London.** Photograph by Anna Hickey-Moody.

Figure 7.3   Refuge Made at P21 Gallery in London. Photograph by Anna Hickey-Moody.

majority of things in which children in these two workshops took refuge helped them get away from the stress and worry of everyday life. At P21, these objects included a veggies patch, books, goldfish and the sun. But, already in the first iterations of the workshops we found references to a permeable, relational significance of nature and the natural world. Figures 7.4 and 7.5 are examples of the art attached to the refuges created at Cherry Orchard. Each image attached to the gauze presented a child's story of home and what makes their home special. These drawings and collages include family, friendships, pets (goldfish, a bird and a flying cat) and a picture of the world surrounded by people holding hands. Another piece of art featured writing that almost resembled poetry:

LIFE your
Heart.
Animals.
Breathing.
Air.

This art also featured the artist's two goldfish, who he had said 'really matters' because they are his pets; it's unclear whether his 'poem' is referring to himself or to his fish. This distinction is almost beside the point: the poem

Figure 7.4 Art Decorating a Refuge Made at Cherry Orchard Primary School, London.
Photograph by Anna Hickey-Moody.

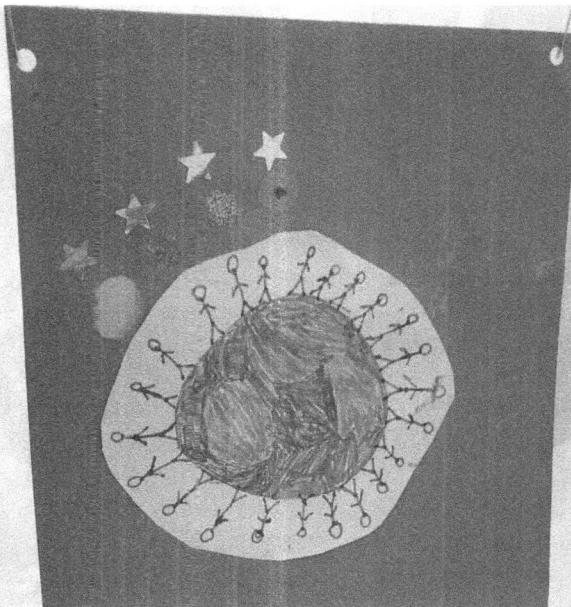

Figure 7.5 Art Decorating a Refuge Made at Cherry Orchard Primary School, London.
Photograph by Anna Hickey-Moody.

speaks of a permeable, fluid relationship between heart, breath, air, animals. The child artist takes refuge in this reciprocal and almost cyclical relationship between human and animal. Another image on the same tent drew a 'life cycle' of a person transitioning from a baby, to adulthood and to old age. This cycle was a circular diagram that hovered above an ocean, which was full of fish and hearts and stars. It also shows the words 'kids are the future', a collage of a range of different ideas of animals, family, life and temporality.

The Cherry Orchard children were alive to the possibilities of the imagination, especially during our 2018 fieldwork, which occurred while PunchDrunk's enrichment programme 'The Lost Lending Library' was at the school. PunchDrunk is an internationally renowned performing arts company based in London that stages work across the globe. The company is known for creating experiences that engage the imagination and inspire audiences. 'The Lost Lending Library' is an education enrichment programme that has been developed as a form of literacy support and has been shown in Australia, North America and the United Kingdom. The company built a hidden library within the school and staged a site-specific performance that accompanied the work: a librarian, having supposedly discovered her library has unexpectedly landed in the school (like *Dr Who*'s TARDIS), reads to the children and invites them to browse her magical library. The 'library' itself is a work of art, filled with tiny antique model houses, old books, paper butterflies, dioramas and photographs collected in order to tell stories about other times and other places. 'The Lost Lending Library' suggests that other worlds are possible, and indeed are already present in the form of books.

The children who were working with us to create their refuge told me the 'secret' of the existence and the locations of 'The Lost Lending Library' (which is not supposed to be shared with adults) and were clearly excited to share their adventure stories. But their work on their refuges was much less of an adventure, and at a time that was characterised by imagining new places for the children, the refuge workshops were focused on turning inwards and thinking about emotional sustenance and security. This was also found in Australian fieldwork sites discussed below, where children with less control over their external safety – often because of migration or seeking asylum, as well as acts of racial vilification. Exploring these themes resulted in children turning inwards to find safety, to their sense of self and their love of themselves.

The third London location for the workshop's discussion of home and refuge was Harbinger Primary School in the Isle of Dogs. Religion, family, food and cultural heritage play very important roles in the lives of this community, and this was evident in their representations of 'what really matters' and 'what makes a home'. The refuges were covered in images of mosques, hearts and a paperchain of family and friends, linked together and draped over the top of the tent. Hand prints and small figures, expressing identity, also decorate the refuge, as seen in Figures 7.6 and 7.7. Many children drew safety as their favourite things, the things that mattered to them such as *Fortnite*, their families, their favourite colour and flags of their nationalities. 'Nature' featured more than once on these tents, in the form of forests, flowers, stars and animals. The self also appeared regularly, and again reflecting how many children turn inwards to find safety and refuge.

The workshops at the southeast London schools and in P21 Gallery similarly provided structures for children to create and characterise their own sense of safety and refuges. These early iterations of the project allowed children to express their ideas of home and safety around the themes of 'what really matters'.

The end of the Harbinger project marked the end of our work on refuge and empathy in London, until some of the work was shown at the Goldsmiths gallery a year later (see chapter 4). The image below shows a child playing in one of the refuges assembled for the exhibition. This particular structure is decorated with the work of children from across the English schools, and includes self-portraits of the children, images of the ocean ('swimming is one of the things I love'), and a star labelled with 'happiness'. This tent formed part of the exhibition discussed in chapter 4, where children, many of whom hadn't taken part in the workshops, occupied and played with and through the tents, inhabiting and transforming the refuges into schools and spaceships.

After weeks of transporting long bamboo poles and suitcases filled with fabric and art making materials on the sweaty, crowded London underground, we decided that building the tents from scratch at each workshop was not sustainable. It took time and energy, both of which are already in great demand when undertaking such a labour-intensive form of research. More than this, the plethora of irate suit-wearing tube travellers who glared at the long and awkward bamboo poles on overheated trains were more than we could continue to bear. An online search of craft shops led to the discovery of pre-made children's tents that did not need to be tied together and came with plastic attachments to hold the pole structure together. We bought twelve. Upon commencing our fieldwork for the year in Manchester, I began catching Ubers with the boxed pre-made tents, which was a lot less exhausting and more time efficient, although the tents sadly looked much less unique.

SAFETY IN RELATIONALITY

As the workshops progressed, we began to identify how the children's ideas and feelings of refuge were expressed through the more-than-human. The refuge workshops work in Manchester occurred in two schools, Claremont

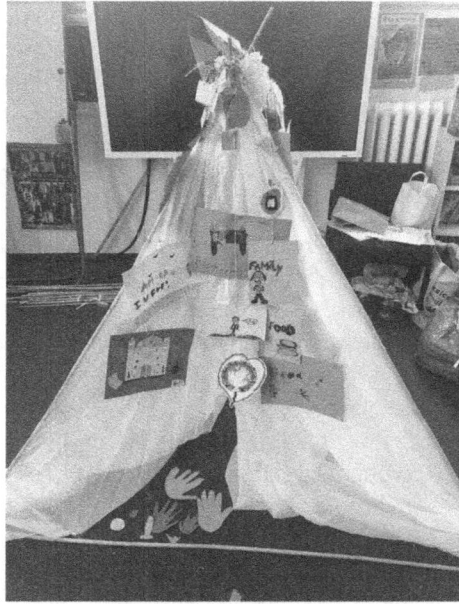

Figure 7.6   Refuge Made at Harbinger Primary School, London. Photograph by Anna Hickey-Moody.

Primary School and Alma Park Primary School, and in the Whitworth art gallery. We begin with a discussion of the work at Claremont, presented in Figures 7.8 and 7.9.

Set outside on an English summer day, the Claremont children's refuges foreground heritage, family and diaspora in similar ways to the London field sites. The tent in Figure 7.8 features the flag of Pakistan, a love heart, flowers and objects of attachment. The tent in Figure 7.9 features the French and Pakistani flags sitting side by side, underneath the words 'family' and 'reliable', and a detailed collage of family members, activities, hobbies and goals.

The images that adorned the children's refuges showed a marked concern with ideas of home and safety along quite creative and not necessarily practical lines. The children were concerned with practical safety entwined with emotional or spiritual safety, but also with things we would not necessarily have associated with 'home'. For example, at Claremont, Simon included a pirate ship as 'a type of transport', a heart because 'you need a heart to live', the sun 'because without the sun it would be just raining' and a rainbow, because 'when you see rainbows it makes you feel special'. There is also a tent, drawn with a figure sheltered inside it: 'Sometimes you don't have a place to stay and a tent is one of your options'" Simon explained. Simon's art and the narratives surrounding his practice signal a concern with regard to

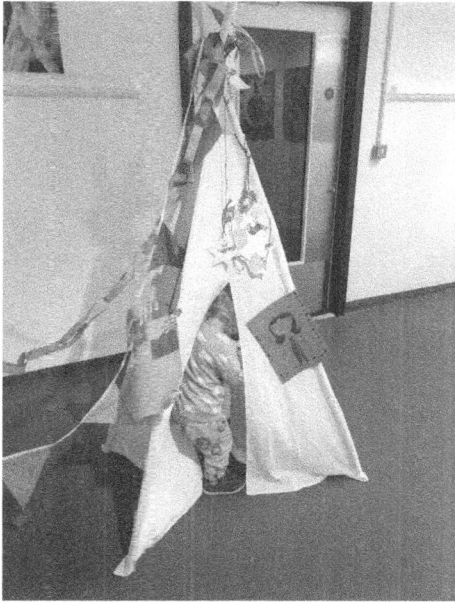

Figure 7.7 Refuge as Playspace, at Goldsmiths' James Hatcham Church Exhibition.
Photograph by Anna Hickey-Moody.

Figure 7.8 Refuge Made at Claremont Primary School, Manchester. Photograph by
Kate Lonie.

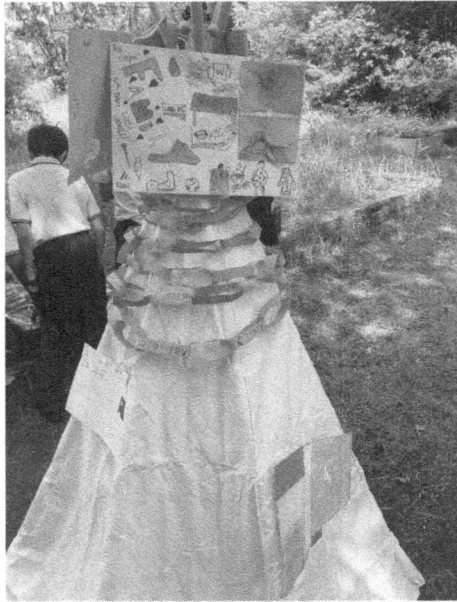

Figure 7.9 Refuge Made at Claremont Primary School, Manchester. Photograph by Beverly Irving.

housing, to shelter, to safety in caring, sharing and housing people. Simon's art is a curious combination of fanciful and practical – a pirate ship is used not as a symbol of adventure and mischief but as *a form of transport*; a tent is a place of safety and utility when you have nowhere else, but it is entangled with its function as a place of play (you can hear the other children playing in and out of the tent as Simon speaks).

Again we saw the importance of objects that help children escape the present or express themselves creatively. In Figure 7.10, 'Things I associate with refuge' are books and family for one child, family, sports and swimming for another child, family and *Nintendo* games for another. Family and some kind of escape from the daily grind of life through novels, games and sports emerge as clear themes.

The other Manchester school that participated in the refuge workshops was Alma Park, and the children explored similar themes of safety, belonging, shelter, family, community and the environment. Soccer was a theme of enduring significance, partially because fieldwork was taking place at the same time as the 2018 FIFA World Cup, and as such the children were alive with the ever-changing soccer score and the skills of and battles between the players. Their artworks were populated with abbreviated soccer player's names, their position numbers and pictures of the sport. Clearly this game

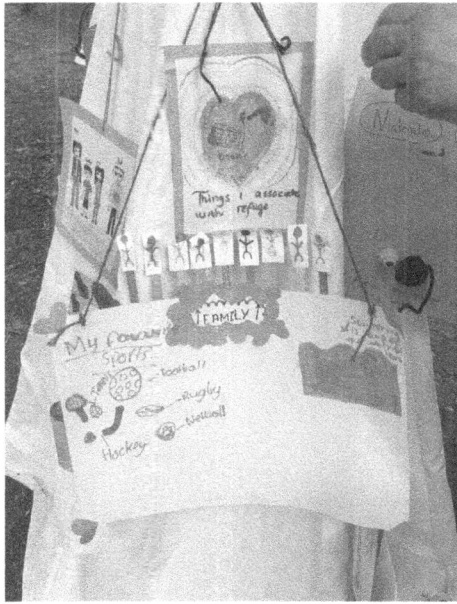

Figure 7.10 Refuge Made at Claremont Primary School, Manchester. Photograph by Beverly Irving.

presents a community in which the children take refuge and feel part of, indeed, to which they belong.

But the workshops at Alma Park also continued the sense of relationality that pervaded the children's sense of home and safety. This was often expressed as a relationality with other humans – family, community, friends and peers – which we explore more below. There was also a definite sense of safety expressed through one's position in the *natural* world. Before the refuge projects began at Alma Park, links between 'safety' and 'nature' emerged spontaneously from a walk that occurred during a workshop in 2017. We left the classroom to walk around the school, finding 'special places' – places of safety, play, food, gathering, friendship, worship and learning. In particular, we were drawn to the large wooded area that exists on Alma Park's school grounds (Figure 7.11). This 'natural' space stood in contrast to the urban surrounds of inner-city Manchester, and featured a number of play and sculpture materials such as ropes, nets, tires and rock formations. These materials were continuously being re-appropriated through children's outdoor play, and we applied similar architectonic constructions and reconstructions to the 'special places' we imagined through our walk. We would later use these sites to form a series of installations exploring the children's relationship with nature (see for more detail Hickey-Moody et al. 2021). After the initial walk, we returned

Figure 7.11   Path Leading to the Wood Next to School Playground, Alma Park Primary, Manchester. Photograph by Anna Hickey-Moody.

to the classroom to discuss the kinds of spaces we would form and make. The first was the establishment of a 'home space':

Anna: So, we're going to make a home. This is the bit, there's a little clearing of trees, how would you describe the home space.
Felix: It's small and wet.
Anna: (Laughs) So small, wet. And, so what are some things that make home a home?
Felix: It needs to be cosy.
Anna: It needs to be cosy, Okay. What else makes home a home?
Anna: It protects from rain, it's cosy. What else makes home a home?
Anna: Healthy. And who do you share your home with? Yeah?
Felix: Mum and Dad, brother and sister, and Mum and Dad, so family. (Manchester 2017)

Through this walking and mapping of the forested spaces of their school, the children's conceptualisation of refuge and home was distinctly posthuman; the children drew together the ideas of home and safety with their other-worldly communities (which we explore in greater detail below).

Similarly, while the tent cities were built around initial discussions of refuge, and this inevitably evoked notions of safety and home, they also evoked a kind of care based on collectivity that reaches beyond humanity. The children expressed an inherently relational understanding of values around safety and refuge: questions of 'what really matters' drew out responses such as the need to 'make sure everyone's got a home', and this concern often grew to incorporate the non-human. To express her sense of refuge and safety, Sophie created, rather than drew, a model of herself and her mum 'hugging on a cloud' and used it to adorn her tent refuge. The model is three-dimensional: featuring a cloud made from blue crepe paper, and Sophie and her mum are represented by two figures made from pipe cleaners that are intertwined with one another. Sophie expresses a sense of safety that is inextricable from the sky: she feels safe on a cloud because 'nobody can hurt us' there and her mum is made from blue and white pipe cleaners, like the cloud, because 'she likes the sky'. Another child at Alma Park created a refuge picture as a mix of natural and man-made things in a park: sky, sun, grass, an apple tree and a red gate 'to keep you safe'. Despite the red safety gate, the park is apparently 'for everybody' and the addition of an apple tree provides food 'if somebody is hungry'. This echoes a recurring concern of the children of 'everybody' being fed and housed, cared for, a sense of collective responsibility of care that is inextricable from their environment, from the non-human (these ideas are discussed in greater detail in chapter 4).

The school workshops in Manchester culminated in a public workshop in the Withworth art gallery, which had a family focus and at which the refuge tents were decorated by children and parents working together. What was striking at these workshops was again the broad spectrum of things in which children find comfort, and how once again these are not necessarily practical. For example, one participant stated strong attachments to feminism and *Dr Who*, their parent valued coffee machines, others liked mice and *Tetris* and other digital games (Figure 7.12). We can see just from this initial analysis that the concerns of the demographic who attend the art gallery are different from those expressed by the school groups in less affluent communities (discussed in depth in chapter 4). But what is more engaging is the fact that impractical things like Dr Who, coffee, and feminism, made this child feel safe, and made her feel like she had a home.

The workshop at the Whitworth prompted a set of very different kinds of conversations about the essentials of life, in which rich cultural and political influences on the children's life emerged as central to their sense of safety. Whilst this may point to the relative safety of these particular participant communities – very few of the participants at the Whitworth, for example, had fled violence or had sought asylum – the artwork nonetheless showed the rich inner worlds of children that are formed in part by drawing on these political and cultural factors when constructing notions of safety. Safety was not just physical for these children, but is a political and cultural matter.

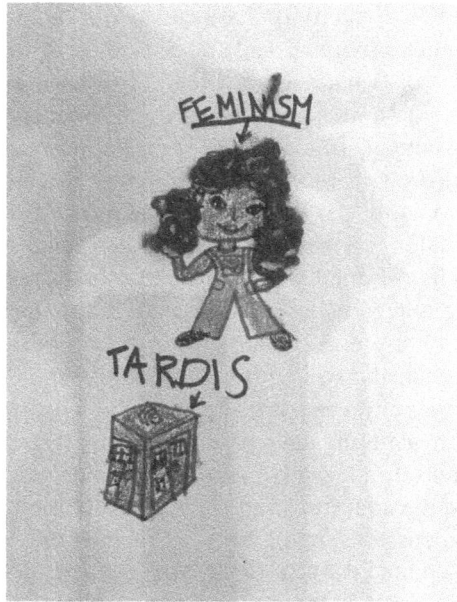

Figure 7.12 'What Really Matters' on Tents at the Whitworth Gallery, Manchester. Photograph by Anna Hickey-Moody.

Ideas of 'cultural safety' are frequently discussed in relation to healthcare and child protection (e.g., Curtis et al. 2019; Koptie 2009; Nelson and Wilson 2018) with a particular focus on threats to cultural safety faced by Indigenous populations living under colonial health and care systems. In 1999, Robyn Williams defined *cultural safety* as 'an environment that is spiritually, socially and emotionally safe, as well as physically safe for people; where there is no assault, challenge or denial of their identity, of who they are and what they need' (213). Under this definition and outside of healthcare settings, cultural safety comes to encompass feelings of belonging and inclusion, things that emerged repeatedly as important to our participants, both adults and children. We might also look to an idea of safety in a cultural sense as part of the cultural and political contexts that make children feel truly safe – for one child it was feminism and Dr Who, but for another, particularly those from migrant or refugee backgrounds, safety likely means freedom *in* their culture and freedom from racism, religious persecution or marginalisation. We discuss this further below, but it is important to highlight here that even in child populations that have little refugee or migration backgrounds, the safety in cultural and political expressions of self remain key to children's ideas of refuge.

Once again, the artworks at the Whitworth (Figure 7.13) also featured the more-than-human as much, if not more than, the human aspects of children's

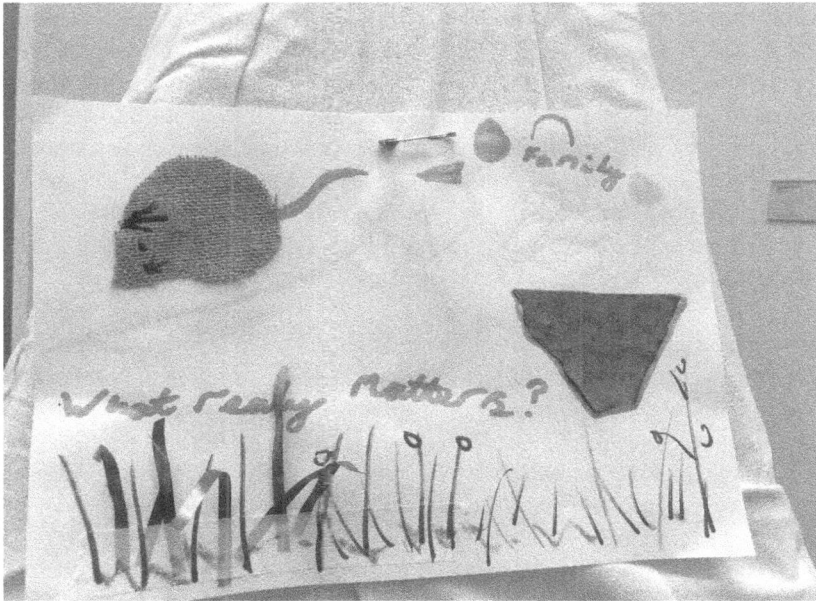

Figure 7.13 'What Really Matters' on Tents at the Whitworth Gallery, Manchester. Photograph by Anna Hickey-Moody.

lives, demonstrating once again the specific calls to action around the non-human or 'natural' world that directly inform how children position themselves in relation to the climate crisis. Children's notion of safety is evidently grounded in a networked sense of care and kinship across boundaries of the self and of humanity. What makes these children feel safe and secure is not only the practical requirements of shelter, food and safety – things which are nonetheless deeply threatened by the climate crisis – but also a sense of safety for *others*, for other women ('feminism') or other animals ('family', represented by a mouse in a field) (Figure 7.13). Safety and refuge draw on more than self-interested concern for members of a home – they include concern and care for the posthuman public of which the children are citizens.

REFUGE IN PRECARITY: A TURN INWARDS

One Australian site at which we facilitated the refuge workshops was the Marion Mosque in Adelaide. These workshops were very different from those at another Adelaide workshop, which took place at community church groups in Littlehampton and Norwood and some of which are discussed below. The idea of refuge took on a different meaning at the mosque because all the participants were from migrant or refugee families, many of whom had sought asylum from political and/or religious persecution. This community had come to appreciate safety after leaving an unsafe home, and also as a result of being persecuted when outside their home in Australia. While we turn to the refuge workshops with children momentarily, the following discussion first draws on the stories of mothers of children we worked with at the Marion Mosque that were shared in a parent focus group discussion. In this group discussion, some of the parents explained how unsafe they often felt in Australia, after moving to Australia to seek refuge. Amira began the conversation:

Amira: After I came to Australia . . . I came just two months prior to September 11. So I was wearing a full head scarf. Going out to the streets after September 11 was a scary experience. It was like 'I came just two months prior' and you can see the shift in people's attitude and how they received Muslims. Before, [when] you go out, everyone is smiling at you, greeting you. After, it was frowns, verbal abuse. So it wasn't very nice. That stage I was, like questioning everything. Not just the religion, questioning me coming to Australia. Questioning the people who done the September 11 and. . . . So yeah, I went through so many thoughts and feelings and I think that period really affected me in a great way on how I perceive people around me. How I perceive religion. So yeah. . . . The feeling of belonging. That's a weird one, because sometimes I do feel like I belong here, but other times I don't. . . It's never like a yes or a no. It's just you are always in between. And you tell the minute I go to visit my family in Jordan, the feeling's just different.
Anna: How do you feel in Jordan? Do you feel more attached?
Amira: Not attached, but you feel home. Like you don't feel the burden that you have here. That you have to always justify what you are wearing. You don't have to justify the religion you believe or the god you believe in. (Marion Mosque Focus Group 2018)

Noticeable in Amira's description of place is a feeling of exile experienced in the streets of one's own country of residence. The impact that a public response to her religion has on her feeling of belonging is also quite clear. The conversation about cultural safety from racism in Adelaide continued in this focus group, with another mother explaining:

Maryam: Yeah, racism I think is alive and running in Adelaide. I remember once I took my first born, my son to a play group and he was around three years old. So it was three years after September 11 and I went there all confident, it's going to be fine and when I get to a new place I have to just really keep talking to myself to encourage myself to go out. All right. So I went there, they are all Aussies, white and no one greeted us. No one said a word and no one even made an effort to smile and I just took my son and went home and never went back again. It was awful. It's awful also – I once went to a shop, also with my son when he was 15 years old and he wanted to really buy these cool shoes and we waited for assistant, we waited for assistant and no one even like came. Then I went to guy there and was like 'excuse me, we need some help. Can you show us – like I need this size from this shoes'. He's like 'we don't have it'. He didn't even look. He didn't even like say 'what size are you?' Nothing. So I said to my son 'even if they have the size, I'm not going to buy it from this shop'. So yeah, you deal with racism on a daily basis. (Marion Mosque Focus Group 2018)

There are extensive stories from this group about their experiences of racism in the workplace, in public space (at bus stops) and at university. Given this ongoing kind of emotional assault, a safe home is especially important to these communities. But the focus groups also revealed how community members find refuge in religion, family, culture and literature.

It is inevitable that children's artworks will reflect aspects of their parents' experiences, as they live with and alongside these experiences. There are few safe public places for these members of the community and, as such, their children's explorations of refuge brought extra weight. But despite daily threats to their safety, what stood out more than anything was the emphasis on self-love that the parents at Marion Mosque had developed in their children. Foucault (1990) frames care for the self as a form of freedom (Fornet-Betancourt et al. 1987), and we might look to the children in these populations as practicing their freedom from external threats of racism and persecution through a care of the self. Foucault (1990) explains this cultivation of the self as an:

[I]nsistence on the attention that should be brought to bear on oneself . . . it is the importance attributed to self-respect, not just so far as one's status is concerned, but as concerns one's rational nature . . . it was not a strengthening of public authority that accounted for the development of that rigorous ethics, but rather a weakening of the political and social framework within which the lives of individuals used to unfold. (41)

In response to experiences of racism and lack of external valuation offered in Australian popular culture, these young Muslim girls have developed a focus on 'self-love' and mutual appreciation. As suggested by Foucault (1990), a response to a 'weakening of social and political framework' can lead to an 'insistence on the attention that should be brought to bear on oneself' (41).

Indeed, this attention brought to bear on the self is visible in the self-portraits created in earlier workshops at the mosque, such as Figure 7.14, as well as in the self-love and mutual appreciation themed decorations for refuges that the children created later on.

Figure 7.14   Self-Portrait Made at Marion Mosque, Adelaide, Australia. Photograph by Anna Hickey-Moody

Figure 7.14 radiates happiness and celebrates the character and colour of the artist. For us, looking at this image evokes an infectious sense of well-being and possibility. This ethics of care, in which the self is valued, cared for, and loved, carried into the workshops in which the children decorated their refuges. There too, the children foregrounded the significance of self-love.

Figure 7.15 is one such decoration, showing two girls supporting each other through positive reinforcement, the artists called the picture 'self-love'. We see a similar vignette in Figure 7.16, in which friendship is interpreted as self-love. The relationship between the self-acting on the self and the self-acting on others are seemingly interchangeable in these decorations, and one would usually think of self-love as simply the self-acting on the self. However, the artwork shows the children being friends, their 'self-love' titles as an enactment of care for another. This is hugely significant in the context of the aggressive behaviour described by their parents and witnessed by children, as is the overall theme of positive reinforcement. Broadly speaking, the children's refuges at the Marion Mosque show self-love and friendship as safe retreats from racist Australian publics.

The children at Marion Mosque had clearly been taught to accept and support themselves and each other, and their sense of safety lay in inward processes of self-care, friendship and positive affirmations. This contrasted

Figure 7.15   Refuge Decoration, Marion Mosque 2019. Photograph: Anna Hickey-Moody.

Figure 7.16   Refuge decoration, Marion Mosque 2019. Photograph: Anna Hickey-Moody.

to the work of children on other sites, who were often very outward-focused: they took refuge in books, games, animals, places. Looking at the art of the children who attended the Marion Mosque, it could be argued that this was because things outside of these children's control were less likely to bring them refuge. Their parent's stories clearly illustrate the kinds of prejudice that are part of everyday life, and as a way of coping with such extreme racism, the children have learnt to turn inwards to find self-assurance and safety, and to care for each other in conscious ways. Another group involved in the refuge project had similarities to those as the Marian Mosque in that they came from cultures that are too often marginalised in Australian popular culture and everyday life. In discussing their stories, we now turn to the outer southeast Melbourne fieldwork site.

A DIVERSITY OF EXPERIENCES – REFUGE FOR REFUGEES

The outer South East Melbourne fieldwork site was a weekend art class run for children from 'disadvantaged' backgrounds; mainly newly arrived communities, many of whom have refugee status. Halilovich (2013) offers instructive insights into both refugee experience and the social construction of the refugee, explaining:

Refugees and asylum seekers, 'by definition', are highly vulnerable people whose lives and freedoms are threatened, while their 'well-founded fear' relates to threats of death, torture, starvation, rape, robbery and other forms of cruel, inhuman or degrading treatment. However, many non-refugees, including those who write about refugees, often fail to recognise that 'being a refugee' does not equate to some distinct individual or collective identity; rather, it defines a temporary – and more than often not a prolonged – state in which ordinary people find themselves, when going through extraordinary ordeals as a result of social and political upheaval in their homelands. (129)

More than this, as Halilovich also explains, researchers too quickly focus on trauma when working with refugee groups. Rather than looking for trauma and reinscribing past wounds, researchers need to 'look for a diversity of experiences'"(Halilovich 2013, 130). Our workshops' orientation to a diversity of experiences when working with communities from a refugee background reveals how their ideas of refuge often explore many different places and things *beyond* trauma. For example, Figures 7.17 and 7.18 show some of the things the participants in the Melbourne fieldwork site love: singing and rap, art and nature, gaming, looking at hot air balloons, martial arts and

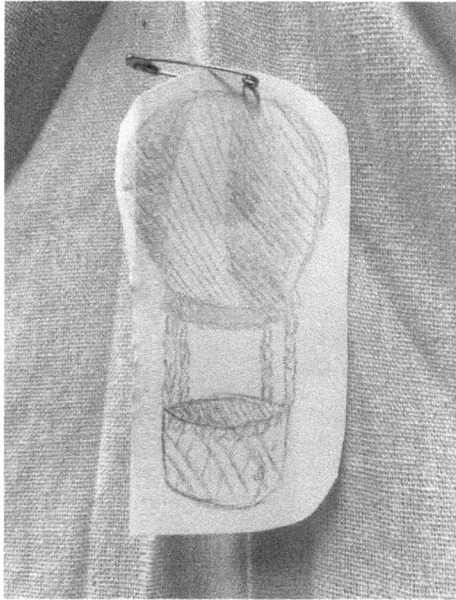

Figure 7.17 **'What Really Matters' Refuge Decorations Created in Outer South East Melbourne.** Photograph by Anna Hickey-Moody.

Figure 7.18 **'What Really Matters' Refuge Decorations Created in Outer South East Melbourne.** Photograph by Anna Hickey-Moody.

the outdoors. The refuge workshop at this site actively sought to position the sense of safety identified by children with refugee and migrant backgrounds as part of a rich assemblage of factors, of which their trauma or fear of fleeing persecution, experiencing racism or feeling like they don't belong, is but one element. Alongside their tumultuous histories of flight or persecution is a feeling of safety in hot air balloons or rap music; a diversity of experiences on which we must draw when examining children's sense of home, safety and belonging.

Hot air balloons are visible on the Melbourne skyline most mornings, and this artwork celebrates the hopeful site of the hot air balloon and the fun of making raps with siblings. Once again at the Melbourne site, the tent cities emerged as an amalgam of shared values and the children's sense of self. The architectures of empathy that the children constructed with their tents and their depictions of 'what really matters' and 'what made them feel safe' model a kind of citizenship without adults, one built on connection and kinship with others, both human and non-human.

TENT CITIZENSHIP: EMPATHY

After the fieldwork in London, the first refuge workshop we facilitated in Australia was with a church group in the Adelaide hills, around the state capital of South Australia. These hills are quiet, and the part in which we worked, Littlehampton, is very forested, which contrasted to the urban school playgrounds and classrooms of England, and even the calm space of the Whitworth. The outdoor spaces in England we had been able to use, even the large Whitworth Gardens, had been much more urban and less wooded. Amid the trees in Littlehampton stands an old church and small side building, which was originally built as a Sunday school. This building has a large balcony, which served as a perfect location to build the refuge tents, decorate them and assemble a tent city.

Themes of family were recurrent in Littlehampton, along with popular video games (although here *Fortnite*, rather than *Tetris*, featured). Some of the children made artwork about the video game worlds to which they belong, turning their favourite characters into mobiles and three-dimensional toys. A boy in Littlehampton made a mobile of *Fortnite* characters, and children recreated images from the game in Sydney, London and Melbourne. The work echoes of the *Dr Who* and *Tetris* decorations made earlier. Books (including *The Witches* by Roald Dhal) were other popular decorations on the tents, as well as rainbows and underwater worlds. The fact that the environment (rainbows, fish, water) was something that children associated with home and 'what really matters' surprised us. Once again the 'natural' world featured heavily in children's sense of safety and refuge, again drawing on an ethics of care that incorporates the more-than-human we discovered in Manchester and discussed in chapter 4.

Once the children had finished decorating their tents they put them all together to make a physical community of tents. The children collected sticks to make a 'fire' in the middle of their tent city, and actively played in their city for the best part of a day.

The small tent city that children created can be read as a practice of modelling citizenship: children created homes that were catalogues of their values on the scale of a miniature city, but occupied this city as a form of urban practice, gathering around the fire, moving through the 'streets', playing in and out of the homes they had built. Drawing again on the formulations of posthuman urban scapes discussed in chapter 4, the small tent cities created at Littlehampton emerge as a structure through which children could empathise with the 'others often not like us' (Neimanis 2016, 3) that emerge when one looks at one's entanglement with the world through a posthuman lens. The tent cities can therefore be thought of as miniature posthuman urban publics, characterised by a dispersed sense of agency and a civics characterised by care, but also by an inherent empathy with an 'other'.

While there were no students at Littlehampton with refugee backgrounds, at Alma Park in Manchester there were a mix of children from both secure and insecure migration histories. Looking to a site like Alma Park, we might consider the multiplicity of perspectives on home, belonging and safety that emerge out of an assemblage of children with both diasporas and local backgrounds. The refuge projects in these instances allowed a structure through which children could not only express and negotiate their migrant journeys, but other children could empathise with refugee experiences and ways of thinking about what makes a home and what matters at home. Children who had no migrant background, no experience of fleeing violence, persecution or effects of the climate crises, took up a position in a posthuman, tent-city public sphere alongside, and in empathy with, children who did have these backgrounds. Empathy moves across borders of the self and is often central to understandings of movement in wider, geopolitical processes; Pedwell (2016) looks at 'empathy's dynamic relationships to transnational processes of location, translation, imagination and attunement' (27), specifically engaging how empathy works in transnational relations of power. Taking up a position within these tent-publics means engaging with these relations across boundaries that exist between children's ideas of home and safety, which can vary widely. Crucially, these processes are affective, rather than purely cognitive. Pedwell's empathy is one premised not on 'knowledge, accuracy, and prediction', but one posed as 'a mode of affective translation involving attunement, negotiation, and invention' (2016, 5). The crafting, inhabiting and embodiment of the empathy-tent-cities allow a form of this affective empathy to establish connections between the children and with their fellow planet dwellers, allowing deep affective attunements to one another's diverse experiences of home, refuge and belonging. As we explore below, the tent cities also allowed affective responses to the climate crisis to emerge as *responses* to questions of safety and security, often in terms that showed a distinct end of childhood innocence and the need to configure posthuman publics as a response to the threat of the Anthropocene.

The project of creating these urban architectures of relationality and *empathy* helps to build resilience, by teaching children that safety as a mobile practice, one that is to be continually formed and reformed through relations with other humans and non-humans. As such, while the refuge project created a space in which children explored their family relationships, they also embraced this opportunity to appreciate their love for the more-than-human world. Children's artwork on and around the tent city draws out the children's relationship to rain, weather and themselves and their surroundings, but this sense of relationally is drawn outwards to incorporate collectives of people, animals, plants, environments, buildings and machines. Animals, computers, virtual worlds constructed by fiction, video games or the imagination responding to physical environments also constituted the populations of these posthuman, empathetic, tent-city publics. It is to these components of these 'unnatural publics' that we now turn.

UNNATURAL PUBLICS

While comparative analyses of data from the larger project have been published elsewhere (Hickey-Moody 2018, 2019), there are many events that featured in the research where children explored climate change. In this section we examine children's posthuman public spheres as they are formed in relation to the 'natural' world that is no longer a safe cradle in which the Roussauean ideal of childhood innocence can flower. The realities of the Anthropocene, seen in our project through the lens of mass forced migration and a deep awareness of the impending threat of climate change, have forced the construction of publics in which childhood innocence is gone. While the posthuman publics we discuss here largely comprise animals and nature, drawing on the work of Halbertsam (2020), Gere (2019) and others, we want to suggest that 'nature' needs to be seen as being more than 'the environment'. 'Nature' can be anarchy and sexuality; the non-human world can mean the uncontrollable, the untamed, the queer, the defiant (Halberstam 2020). In the age of climate crisis, 'nature' is not a safe cradle in which the pure child can rest or play; rather 'nature' disrupts all assumptions we have about how things are, or could be. In the Anthropocene, nature is a force that is bigger than all humans, more powerful than humans. Gere (2019) cites Zizek in stating that 'if there is one good thing about capitalism, it is that, precisely, mother earth now no longer exists' (14). We contend that 'nature' and indeed 'mother earth', needs to be seen as 'unexplained' (Halberstam 2020, 23); the outdoors and its (dis)contents as 'existing without explanation, without a niche, outside of an orderly and inevitable scheme of life' (Halberstam 2020, 22).

In their construction of posthuman publics, children often imagine having some rule over this disorder, they imagine being both among it and magically controlling it. Presiding over insects, cats, rocks and forests is a practice that explores libido, community, the unknown, the possible and many other things. The following artworks position the landscape as very significant, or focus on non-human actants as *central* agents. While in chapter 4 we discussed 'nature' and its entanglement with the urban landscapes through which the children moved, created and formed public, here we look to nature as a force that has caught up the children and their imaginaries of their place in the world, threatening their sense of safety – or of control – by becoming deeply entangled with themselves. This emerges as a direct effect of the Anthropocene. In a world characterised by flood, famine and climate refugees, children no longer feel they can control or find safety in the romantic 'cradle' of nature.

The children persistently and consistently showed a deep-seated awareness of the entanglement of nature with the self, which directly informed the publics they formed in response to the disruption of the climate crises. Figure 7.19 is an identity picture drawn by a boy in Manchester. When asked to explain the image, the child said that it was a 'picture of him *in* the rocks, by the water' (emphasis added). Clearly there are both a tree and a sandy beach in close proximity to the figure of the artist, and it looks like someone is swimming in a small pool at the foreshore. The rock formations are the most noticeable feature of this image: enveloping the boy like a cloud around him, he seems embedded in, rather than standing upon, the rocks. This primary significance of the rocks is followed by that of the sea, the sand, and the tree. The 'self-portrait' part of the image, namely, the artist's representation of himself, is central but small, and fits in with the colours of the natural landscape surrounding him. The child has camouflaged his human self to fit his environment, like a bird, fish or insect might. The human figure recedes in this image, taking up not a central position of stewardship or control, but an embedded position within a network of *other* equal, perhaps more important, actors: sea, rocks, sky, sand.

Continuing on this theme of reverence for the more-than-human, Figures 7.20 and 7.21 are children' examples of 'what really matters'. They

Figure 7.19   Boy on Rocks, Image of 'What Really Matters' Alma Park Primary School, Manchester. Photography by Anna Hickey-Moody.

Figure 7.20   Image of 'What Really Matters' at Alma Park Primary School, Manchester. Photography by Anna Hickey-Moody.

Figure 7.21   Image of 'What Really Matters' at Alma Park Primary School, Manchester. Photography by Anna Hickey-Moody.

are two cats, drawn with varying levels of skill, presented here as the children's choice of what matters most in their worlds.

The red 'ginger' cat on the right-hand side was introduced to us as the family pet, and while we know little about the cat on the left, the fact that it has been chosen to represent 'what really matters' in the child's life, over human beings and other places, animals and objects, is significant. These choices foreground the significance of non-verbal communication in children's lives and their animal attachments, but also the role that the non-human plays in what we might assume are exclusively human activities and connections such as family and homelife.

At the same time, children would often imagine a world over which they can preside when imagining a situation in which they can actively stop climate change. These imaginings also critically represent political events causing climate change, and the children's struggle to position themselves within these events. Figure 7.22 is a collaboratively drawn canvas that was devised and created by three nine-year-old boys in North Melbourne.

Figure 7.22 demonstrates the close relationship between climate change and the political and ontological insecurity in childrens' experiences of the present. The large green square at the left-hand bottom of the picture is a recycling centre, which is connected across to city buildings by the green strip

Figure 7.22   'M.S.A Future', North Melbourne. Photograph by Anna Hickey-Moody.

reading 'M.S.A recycling centre', M, S and A being the initials of the artists. Up above in the upper right-hand corner, dead bodies fall out of helicopters. The bodies are clearly lifeless and almost ghostlike scattered across the cemetery. The child who drew the dead bodies falling out of planes is a refugee from Papua New Guinea who had witnessed war and death prior to being relocated to Australia to live with his uncle. He suffers from post-traumatic stress, and both the experience of war and the perilous journey to Australia remain very much part of his imagination. At one stage of development, this collaborative canvass featured images of all three artists. However, upon seeing his friends draw a picture of him, the boy from Papua New Guinea cried and screamed uncontrollably, insisting that his friends' drawing of him was removed. Attempting to ease his anxiety, his friends covered him up by drawing a minaret over the top of him coming up behind the 'MSA future' apartments. Interestingly, in this image, the cemetery, hospital and apartment buildings are similar sizes, demonstrating the children's perception that illness and death are just as prevalent as life itself. Saving the planet and surviving war is clearly the agenda for life presented by this collaborative artwork, which most certainly presents a sobering perspective on the experiences of children in contemporary society.

Indeed, the theme of children saving the planet through stopping climate change runs through the artwork from all the project sites (see for example chapter 4). Below is an example in the form of a discussion between a research assistant and participant in Melbourne:

Anna: So that's the scientists taking over the country, uh over the world?
Franko: Nice. (laughs) oh my god. That is brilliant
Anna: I know. And this one. . . . This is the past where there's crime, this is current society where there's a lot of buildings, and this is the future when Earth takes over the world. (South East Melbourne, 2018)

Here, the *earth* takes over the world, reclaiming ground that has been lost to human development and exploitation. The removal of humans is offered as an inventive way of healing the earth, demonstrating children's understanding of, and engagement with, a public sphere that is composed of non-human objects as much, if not more than, the human. This emphasis on the posthuman publics to which children belong, and over which they preside, shows the broad extent to which children's identities are relational, and are formed in the space between themselves and other objects.

Figure 7.23 shows a future world in which children are again trying to combat climate change through invention. The mosque flies on a carbon-neutral cloud and passengers parachute out of a flying car with pink wings. Roads

Figure 7.23 **'Bubble City', North Melbourne.** Photograph by Anna Hickey-Moody.

are green and made of grass, and there is a large river running alongside the grassy road, making bubbles that are floating up to the sky.

The fact that any conception of the future must bring with it radically new ways of living demonstrates the significance of climate change and the impact of the Anthropocene on children of today. Indeed, if childhood was originally imagined as a period free from responsibility, a 'natural' time of development, we would suggest that contemporary children are burdened with more responsibility than they have been for a long time, and that the new 'nature' undoes the romantic premise of 'nature' at every turn.

THE END OF 'INNOCENCE'

In a world characterised by the degradation of both the environment and childhood, the link between childhood and 'nature' that has been a way of signalling or characterising 'innocence' through Rousseau's conception of childhood falls away. Rousseau's figurative 'Nature's Child' places children in nature as a cradle, as a source of safety and refuge. It is this notion, Taylor (2017) argues, that perpetuates the common Western understanding that children have an innate affinity with nature: 'From [Rousseau's] legacy, the assumption is that, if nurtured, children's "biophilia" (or innate love of nature) will predispose them to become environmental stewards' (5). We must move past the 'entrenched and romantic notions of nature as a separate and pure domain, to which innocent children might be returned and through which they can be saved' (Taylor 2017, 61), because these notions do not stand up to the realities of children's relationship with the planet in the age of the Anthropocene.

Can we, then, conceive of the child in relation to the Anthropocene? Certainly not in the ways originally associated with the term 'childhood'. A worry-free childhood cannot happen in asylum seeker 'tent cities', where children live with remaining family members without schooling, medical care or proper food. Similarly, being born and dying in refugee camps is not an 'innocent' childhood filled with hope and dreams. We might argue childhood has been killed by the Anthropocene, and by the global politics that is responsible for the creation of the Anthropocene.

To understand how childhood might function in the Anthropocene, we enmesh the historic Rousseauian notion of childhood innocence and 'biophilia' with a posthuman relationship to the Anthropocene. As we have seen repeatedly, children do not see themselves as *in* 'nature', as a separate, 'wild' entity', but *of* nature, as part of thoroughly entangled life-worlds. Taylor (2017) argues that such a relational, posthuman perspective of childhood offers alternatives to stewardship pedagogies, in which the child is figured

– and indeed tries to figure herself – as looking after and indeed looking *over* 'the world'. The children of the Interfaith Childhoods project formulate post-human future worlds in which they are inextricably entwined and over which they have no mastery, but nonetheless are worlds that they can plan to 'save'. They form these imaginary posthuman publics to account for the realities of the Anthropocene. Most notably, these publics are devoid of the traditional 'innocence' of childhood. The Anthropocene-ready cities that the children imagine out of tents and 'what really matters' are responses to the loss of innocence that the climate crisis brings. As children either experience, or empathise with, the insecurity and lack of refuge that is synonymous with the Anthropocene, they create publics in which these realities can be managed or at least 'lived with'. Their artworks 'in different but intersecting ways, draw attention to how better futures are imagined, engaged, and brought into being and to the non-linear relations between presents and futures' (Coleman 2020, 12–13). These imagined publics are posthuman, and they are posthuman specifically in response to the post-humanising force of the Anthropocene.

CONCLUSION

In this chapter we have examined the values and practices of care that make up children's home lives and worlds, and the worldviews that these beliefs and practices express. We have shown that making collaboratively is an effective form of peer-to-peer education and a vehicle for critical reflection. We also examined the ways that children adapt and respond to the global uncertainties of our contemporary situation. While we have catalogued many ways that children imagine solving extant problems in the future, we have also demonstrated the ingenious ways they re-make hope, to build a better and more sustainable future and hope for change on a structural level. While the research sites discussed in this chapter are geographically and culturally very different (middle-class Adelaide and working-class Manchester), there are noticeable parallels in the themes the children chose. Digital and analogue games, animals, nature, love and self-love and carbon natural inventions clearly unite children from both sides of the world. Whether they have been born into uncertainty and large change, or into fairly established homes, children see themselves as part of a larger, more-than-human landscape and as having the power to create new ways of living that repair some of the environmental damage that characterises the Anthropocene.

Chapter 8

Participatory Community-Building with Transnational Others

In this chapter we describe how participatory approaches to community building activate children's performative civics. What we advocate for, however, in this chapter is not only the importance of participatory practices for children; we are interested in the ways that participatory projects are important for community building with more-than-human others. These more-than-human others are different, transnational bodies and things that come into and out of the space and form fluid, posthuman collectives. This participatory form of posthuman community building, we argue, should be understood as the way that children are part of larger milieus engaging and shaping civic life. In chapter 2 we explained that classicist readings of the public sphere as being a place for men, were selective and skewed because these men were part of larger assemblages of food, lovers, trade, money, livestock and possessions. We identify that the different texts that Habermas described as being disseminated in the public sphere and that begin to shape public discourse, have not featured children, even though children create and perform public texts. In this book we offer detailed descriptions of how children participate and shape the public sphere through their civic participation and their understanding of what it is to be a citizen. Participatory methods have been processually vital in bringing our examples into being, and, we propose, are a primary approach for activating posthuman community-building projects.

We will describe the posthuman participatory approach used in a specific creative work in the Scaling the City project. This creative work, called 'Godwit Neighbours' explored how children and godwit birds briefly form a civic community during a feed stop the birds make to the Tuata Peninsula in Auckland, Aotearoa New Zealand. Engaging in collaborative experimentations between the bodies and surfaces of environments, humans, materials and the atmospheric and affective weather conditions, knowledge, habits and traditions in the particular context of working with a temporary community made from local schoolchildren, estuarine ecologies and transient bird flocks offered ways for thinking about different forms and modes of community building.

Theatre and performance studies scholar Sruti Bala (2018) asks 'In what ways does participatory art participate in civic, public life?' (2) We would extend on this question to ask how might participatory art *shape* civic and public life? The question might seem very close to Bala's; however, there is a subtle difference: participatory art can do more than just be a mode of responding to life. The active immersion in space, creating with other bodies and things also bring about new civics and publics. Participatory approaches can facilitate transversal collectivity between posthuman citizens within the urban milieu. Laura Ianelli and Carolina Marelli (2019) also support this view. Their research with performers and publics during a government election led them to observe how 'artistic performances of citizenship [. . . that] democratize the field of public art [. . .] we see artists as doing citizenship, through [. . .] practices of political participation' (634). Ianelli and Marelli's project demonstrated how participatory practices and approaches facilitate physical modes for 'artists [to perform] their knowledge and democratic values' and to 'activate the citizens' interest in alternative representations of urban spaces' (639). Similarly, Susan Wake and Sally Birdsall's (2016) project into children's interactions with school gardens didn't simply teach children about gardens; the participatory approach brought about new transversal civic relations and actions between child and plant bodies through 'participatory learning approaches, codesign practices, [. . .] that promotes enduring guardianship' (109) between bodies and things which co-exist in spaces. In chapter 6 we discuss how a posthuman civics takes place in lively zones of encounter; these examples support the need for participatory approaches because generating transversal encounters triggers 'intersections between individual and collective forms of embodiment' (Bala 2018, 16–17); vibrant meetings between bodies, materials, energies and ideas, and also desires and needs. These all shape civic and public life. As Bala (2018) observes, creative participatory approaches enact a 'redistributing authorship and creative functions' (5) of diverse citizens, resulting in richer explorations of civics and publics by all concerned. We define participation here as being the active community-building practice that takes place between more-than-human bodies, things and aspects. We regard different things as having material vibrancy and agency and that this animacy proposes participation, expressed through different affective scales and registers. This transversal participation occurs in lively zones that are playful, and, as we articulate in chapter 6, these lively middle grounds (Braidotti 2019) are important to pay attention to in research using posthuman ideas of community and activity.

This chapter methodologically examines middle grounds by exploring participatory practice approaches and extending these beyond the human-centric. A posthuman participatory practice is effective for fostering cross-species neighbourly knowledge because it experimentally but purposefully examines how bodies and materialities make contributions and generate responses with and to others in the urban milieu.

PARTICIPATORY ART WITH MORE-THAN-HUMAN OTHERS

Posthuman participatory approaches work with 'non-humans through methodologies that invite non-humans to participate actively [. . .] or that find ways of identifying and amplifying the role of non-human agency in the construction of research practices' (Noorani and Brigstocke 2018, 10). In Godwit Neighbours the godwits and their temporary but annual surroundings, the estuary and its ecologies shaped and directed the construction of research practices. We discuss the project in more detail below, but briefly, the agency of the more-than-human included: selecting a school near the birds to work with; the physical movements of the godwits directed the creative movement choices of the children's bodies; and the estuarine ecologies kept the godwits at a safe distance from the humans and forced us to use binoculars and web-based resources to interact with them. The humans in this collective were not able to 'use' their human-ness to force changes to these conditions; the humans were kept in place by the other components in the event. We don't suggest in this situation that the estuary is making decisions to keep humans and birds separate. In their summary report to the Connected Communities programme,[1] a ten-year project into the changing nature of communities led by the Arts and Humanities Research Council, UK, Noorani and Brigstocke (2018) state 'more-than-human research does not seek to reveal the minds of non-humans, as if non-humans could suddenly speak' (34). The diverse paradigmatic and philosophic approaches to researching with non-human others conceptualise relational interactions differently, not trying to make things seem more 'human' but to speculatively explore the world in ways that dislodge the human from a centralised axis point.

We explore how, historically, citizenship is attributed to the individual, to the individual human citizen and, in Europe and North America certainly, primarily to the White, male, human citizen. The propositions and research project examples throughout this book actively contest this human-centric vision of the White, male citizen. We expand the concepts and politics of citizenship outwards, declaring that citizens come in all shapes, sizes, bodies and materialities. Posthuman citizens are more-than-human, are differently alive and are variously agentic. Collectively, these diverse posthuman citizens enact a more-than-human politics and community building in intense zones of encounter, within urban milieus bursting with movement. Thinking of participation beyond the human prompts a deeper, critical consideration of transversal relations, and our example projects described throughout the book declare how art particularly, can catalogue the details of this expanded collectivity, including 'those moments in which the withdrawal or refusal of participation might function as a critical form of participation' (Bala 2018, 3). In Godwit Neighbours the relational organisation, and different participations/refusals/withdrawals of the estuary, godwits, children, school, weather and more were critically understood and creatively expressed. For the children, participatory arts conceptually provided 'the power to depict their own lives' (Butcher 2016, 295), helping them to understand they are members of a civic community and that they cohabit and negotiate space with other bodies and things. Specifically, in Godwit Neighbours, the use of gestural drawing and creative movement introduced children to body-based participatory art through corporeal practice that promotes conceptual awareness of physicality and how 'what a particular body can do is always cultural, social and political. Body work is theoretical work, building insight in the moment of movement' (Hast 2021, 56); purposefully and carefully moving the body to bring awareness that 'this' body is part of a bigger community. Participatory art, like other art practices, is constantly moving – or, put another way, it is never a static replication of a procedure. What takes place in the production of participatory art is always different because it must have participants, and these are always bodies and things that are moving and changing (Bala 2018; Jaskolski 2016). Participatory art therefore has a constantly changing nature to enable it to move with the contexts and circumstances of its production, and this makes participatory art approaches methodologically rich for projects concerned with theorising bodies and participations, and a demonstration of this is held within the gesture.

Bala (2018) identifies how performance studies have theorised the gesture as being 'at the intersection between the *image* and the *act*' (17, original emphasis) and proposes the gesture is central in participatory art because it is non-representational, an 'indicative, decomposed, interrupted move that extends beyond itself' (18) and occurs beyond the boundary of the body pushing towards the limits of movement expressed and events occurred. The explorative gesture, which is 'situated in between image, speech and action, no longer image but not yet act, not strictly within the coordinates of language but also not wholly external to it' (Bala 2018, 15) is the expressed coalescence of things felt, thought, seen, interacted with, coming together and concentrated in a motion that leads into the act to come. In the posthuman context, gesture is useful because its dynamism is the performed expression of 'a transition, often involving a bodily movement [. . .] a socially recognizable form of conduct' (Bala 2018, 17) which reaches out to the wider event. For Bala (2018) the gesture is 'simultaneously an expression of an emotional condition or an inner attitude, as well as a social habitude [. . . it is] performance into the sphere of public, civic life' (16). Gesture is not limited to humans; all bodies and things make gestures. Participatory approaches can nurture and curate the gestures of things and bodies towards each other across the urban milieu 'in a relationship of simultaneity, one gesturing (to) the other' (Bala 2018, 18).

Posthuman participatory approaches extend how 'participatory art is characterized by gestural qualities' (Bala 2018, 16) communicating civic possibilities by, between and across bodies, materialities and affects. Participatory approaches also assist children to engage and shape civic life, because, as Michelle Duffy (2016) articulates, such approaches 'emphasize the child as an active participant within his/her community' (381). Children's active participation in social art practice projects helps them to examine and understand 'power relations, agenda setting, ownership and outcomes' (Duffy 2016, 386) and this is because participatory approaches target the specific needs and conditions of participants 'in their place-based and cultural contexts' (Seppala et al. 2021, 2). Posthuman research also facilitates children acknowledging the needs and conditions of all the diverse participant bodies and things that are part of the research process. In Godwit Neighbours it was fascinating to see how the children engaged and shaped civic life with diverse others. As the children mapped and danced through the urban spaces they encountered, and reacted to different other bodies and things, the researchers observed an emerging citizenship taking place through bodily movements in relation with other bodies in space. The Godwit Neighbours project took children to different interior and exterior spaces at the school, and also to the estuary. Their creative responses with the surfaces generated points of encounter and formed a neighbourly, civic connection to the school space and estuary space as a citizen among other non-human and inhuman citizens. Noorani and Brigstocke (2018) assert the influence that Dewey's ideas around communication and consultation in public contexts, suggesting Dewey 'had a profound influence on contemporary understandings of participatory research and democracy' (13) because he essentialised the ways humans can build civic cohesion through social experiences in times of complexity or difficulty. Noorani and Brigstocke go on to say that Dewey's thinking of social, civic cohesion is influential to more-than-human participatory research because it is ecological and takes in wider contexts and environments. However they identify, as others have done (Cohen 1940; Snaza 2018; Fendrich 1975; Bingham 2016), that Dewey's scholarship remains firmly humanist and therefore 'does not go far enough in recognising the vital role of more-than-human actors in the constitution of democratic publics' (Noorani and Brigstocke 2018, 14). In chapter 2 we further discuss Dewey's relevance and look at Bennett's (2010) examination of Dewey as perhaps not completely humanist and that his ideas are useful in crafting a posthuman concept of publics. In Godwit Neighbours the children were not the only things moving or participating. Although their movements were easy to see, the other bodies participating were also directing the movements and events in the milieu. The godwits, for example, although not present in the close space of the school, or among the bodies of the children, were actively present in the space of the estuary, and their bodies and their modes of living which included an annual neighbourly visit ignited human bodies to move in civic relation as the public came to visit the estuary, and as children moved their bodies in godwit-fashion in order to understand their temporary neighbours more deeply.

Dewey's ideas around experiential learning might fall short in the posthuman context, because they focus on the human alone, however Indigenous worldviews about relationality are highly appropriate to think with in relation to posthuman research. Indigenous scholarship can disrupt and contest colonial, humanist theorisations. Indigenous scholarship into transversal relationalities (see Bignall 2020; Weir 2017; Moreton-Roberston 2017; Dudgeon and Bray 2019; Datta 2015) between place, country, creatures and elements of the landscape, for example, explain how metaphysical registers such as history, ancestry, art, stories and futures are a 'dynamic ontology that exists within Indigenous cultural ideology' (Martin 2013, 185) to guide understandings of the world and how it operates through interconnected networks of bodies, things and aspects. Noorani and Brigstocke (2018) propose that non-Indigenous scholars address issues of race and colonialism by making commitments to referencing Indigenous theories in more-than-human participatory projects that are focused on diverse bodies and things. Projects need to continue to work through 'decolonizing and indigenous ethics of care and responsibility' (16) because Indigenous onto-epistemologies are essential for ensuring participatory projects that address what Bala (2018) lists as 'larger issues of citizenship, democratic praxis, collective action and social justice' (15) from critical race standpoints/perspectives. Although posthuman research is interested in more-than-human bodies, these bodies still need to be conceptualised within scholarly frameworks that strive for 'the same kind of relations of care, collaboration and mutual respect that characterises human research at its best and most ethical' (Noorani and Brigstocke 2018, 10). As such, it is important to centralise Indigenous worldviews when using participatory approaches with children. How this occurs is varied, and Bala (2018) suggests 'It can be a manner of doing, a manner of perceiving, and a manner of perceiving doing' (6) which means there are openings for Indigenous scholarship, ontologies and worldviews throughout a whole project. We are aware that there can be tensions between Indigenous ontologies and posthuman theorisations; these are well documented and have addressed the specifics of standpoint theories (Moreton-Robinson 2013; Braidotti and Bignall 2018), Western science (DiNovelli-Lang 2013; Zembylas 2018; Todd 2016; Eglash et al. 2020), cosmological theories (Vetlesen 2019; Bignall 2020) and others. A posthuman approach to participatory research does not automatically side-step the impacts of colonisation and earthly damage due to extractivist practices; however. participatory approaches can offer different modes for working with and through these big topics, and it is here we return to the gesture.

In chapter 6 we discussed Braidotti's (2019) middle ground as a potent site for transversal, onto-epistemological encounters. The middle ground is a meeting point for different bodily, material and sensorial gestures to reach towards each other to make an encounter. The space offers a sparking energy for new imaginaries to grow, and to become open to different perspectives, different histories, experiences, politics and futures. For children particularly, being able to enter a space of transversal encounter through participatory art projects enables children to 'be differently' in a local environment. In Godwit Neighbours children learnt about their environment through different ontological theories and through the gestures brought about by speculative movement and mapping, forming new relationships with other posthuman citizens in their neighbourhood. The participatory approach enabled many different bodies, things and aspects to contribute to the project. We shall now discuss the Godwit Neighbours project in more detail.

THE GODWIT NEIGHBOURS PROJECT

Godwit Neighbours is a particular creative work within the Scaling the City research project, introduced earlier in this book. The researchers and artists who designed and facilitated Scaling the City also led Godwit Neighbours.[2] The participatory art practice approach was chosen specifically to foster neighbourly relations between urban collectives that included children, an estuary and a migratory bird.

The godwit is named in Latin as *Umosa lapponica,* but is also known by the many names given to it by the humans it encounters in the stopping points it makes during its cyclic journeys between the north and south poles. Its common name in English is bar-tailed godwit, but it is also named kuaka by the Maori (Welch and Fitzgerald 2009), keundwisbulidoyo by Koreans (Glosbe 2021) and teguteguaq by the Alaskan Yupik (Alaska Native Knowledge Network nd). We will use the English common name here. The godwit is famous in ornithological circles for its extreme migratory pattern which involves the birds after their breeding season making a massive, non-stop 12,000-kilometre, 8–9-day continuous flight from the top of the globe to the bottom, before making the return journey via numerous refuelling stops around the Yellow Sea (Welch and Fitzgerald 2009). Godwits, unsurprisingly, possess incredible navigation skills that are aided by the habitual pathways they develop. The godwits learn to stop in very specific places, hence their many names. We met the godwits after they had flown thousands of kilometres down to New Zealand.

Godwit navigation means that the birds habitually visit the same spot each year. New Zealand has many estuaries they like to inhabit; we met them on the Te Atatū peninsula in the outskirts of Auckland, a waterside city perched on volcanic forms and with extensive estuaries and shorelines. Sizeable numbers of godwits visit the Te Atatū peninsula from September to December to refuel before beginning their return journey north to the Arctic; and so the godwit bird, which is significant to local Maori community (New Zealand Birds Online nd.), migrates to the same spots of the coastline, that is, the same estuaries. And the birds arrive emaciated because they have travelled non-stop from the Arctic. The enormous nine-day trek leaves them expended of fat and muscle and almost completely spent. The New Zealand estuaries offer the nutritional wealth of their ecologies providing the godwits with mud, water, slugs and other food creatures to help the birds to bulk up before their long flight. The low tides of the estuaries enable the birds to remain distant to predators and the receding waters expose a wealth of foods and nutrients in the silt. And this is where the godwits remain until some inner signal tells them it is time to leave, which they do, almost together. Their arrivals and exits make it seem that one day they are there, and then, suddenly, they are not.

Godwit Neighbours was a creative response to the annual event taking place at the time that godwits were present in the Te Atatū peninsula estuary. The participatory project brought us together with children from a primary school located near the estuary and near a transient community of godwits, adding to our work into urban citizenships in our Scaling the City project. Some of the young dancers already involved in Scaling the City came to work with us and the children at the primary school, and together we constructed a movement and mapping project with the birds, school spaces, the estuary, with technologies and with different stories and details about godwits and migratory birds. We initially held a number of movement and mapping workshops in the school hall and the schoolchildren attended these in year groups. The children who wanted to continue being involved formed part of a multi-age group and we worked with them for the remainder of the project.

With the smaller group, we went on to create movement and mapping works in the school hall as well as around the outdoor spaces. In these workshops we used laptops to access online resources about godwit birds and migratory bird habits. The children and researchers then worked together in different types of activity to generally become more familiar with the lives of godwit birds (Figure 8.1). In one activity the children used laptops to study the migratory pathways godwits took from the north of the planet to the south and back again. The children and adults discussed the video and web-based resources and how these might be used as a basis for making large performative works across the school hall. The discussions focused on how gestural mapping and the placing of parcel string could be interwoven with dance moves to generate a collaborative participatory work about godwit migrations.

The children worked in groups with the researchers, negotiating how to use the pavement chalks and the string to convey migration routes and at the same time to guide their dance movements about migrating as a flock of birds.

The participation of different bodies, things and agencies in the project played out in various ways. For example, even though the school was close to a godwit site, children had distanced physical connection with the birds due to the participation of the estuary. We took the children who were interested to visit the estuary shoreline after the school day. The children couldn't get physically close to the birds because the birds were off in the estuary and that we were unable to leave the shore so we used binoculars and telescopic glasses to observe the birds feeding (Figures 8.2 and 8.3). The

Figure 8.1   Children Mapping Godwit Migratory Pathways. Photograph by Linda Knight.

Figure 8.2   Visiting the Te Atatū Peninsula Estuary. Photograph by Claire Battersby.

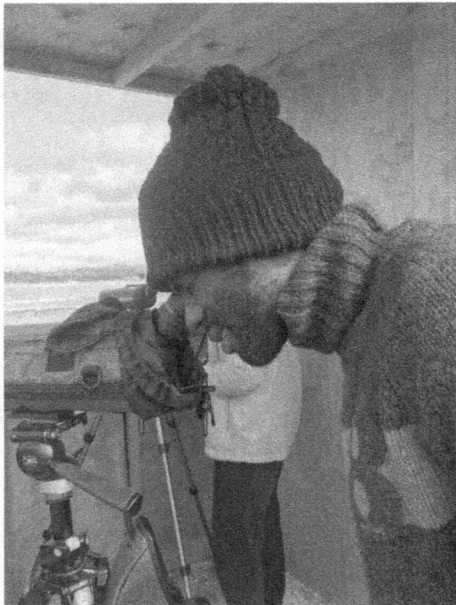

Figure 8.3   Using Specialised Equipment to View the Godwits in the Estuary. Photograph by Claire Battersby.

children entered the fringes of the estuary and created spontaneous creative movement responses with the estuarine surfaces and ecology, and made long-distance connections to the godwits who were gathered far off in the distance. Sticks and stones were used to make marks in the soft, wet mud that stayed only momentarily, bodies jumped down onto the spongy surface and feet made splashes in the shallow puddles. The clouds and sky seemed also to be included as their reflection became both distorted and animated as child, stick and stone bodies disturbed the glassy water. The technologic enhancements offered by the telescopic lenses created posthuman eyes and a way for being in neighbourly relation with an avian community that is simultaneously familiar and unknown. The creative movements and gestural mapping from these observations in the fringes of the estuary brought about a participatory community building with transnational others, stretched out over the wide expanses of the estuary.

As in Scaling the City, Godwit Neighbours was a creative movement and gestural mapping project into civics and citizenship, so the children were using their bodies in their explorations. The participations of other things helped as the children accessed their fellow citizens through video footage, photographs or binoculars. The contributions of these other things became incredibly important to the quality of the project: because they couldn't physically interact with the birds, the children initially defaulted to a poor quality movement to 'mimic' the birds through generic, flapping 'bird' motions. This meant they did not move their bodies differently, they simply ran around moving their arms in up and down movements. The participation of other bodies and things which included other dancers, the video footage, photographs and binoculars shifted how the children moved their bodies as they began to understand the feeding movement of the godwit as the bird sticks its beak into the sand, into the mud, drizzles out a grub and throws back its head to send the food down its gullet. The movement of godwit bodies helped the children to understand the godwit through their own bodies, and the godwit became more than an archetypal bird that simply 'flaps its wings', it has 'a life', a community and its habits of movement are nuanced to the different activities it performs. This enhanced, technologic knowledge generated new participatory actions as children explored concepts of migration more deeply, and examined how birds must work collaboratively as a flock as they make the arduous journey back and forth from the north of the globe to the south (Figures 8.4, 8.5 and 8.6). The children began to choreograph movements around collectivity, survival, community and endurance, and they conveyed this through creative, participatory works that wove around the school grounds, imagining the space as the vast areas of water the godwits must cover to reach the estuary, and then returning over these seas and stopping off in other estuaries to feed in their journey north.

Figure 8.4 Children and Researchers Creating Participatory Work Based on Godwit Migration. Photograph by Linda Knight.

Figure 8.5 Children and Researchers Creating Participatory Work Based on Godwit Migration. Photograph by Linda Knight.

Figure 8.6   Children and Researchers Creating Participatory Work Based on Godwit Migration. Photograph by Linda Knight.

The movement and the mapping, as modes of expression or modes or exploration, gave the children different ways of making a civic relationship with their fellow planet dwellers, helping them to think about civics and citizenship in relation to their relationship with these migratory bird citizens. Creative movement and inefficiently mapping were expressive, explorative modes for forming civic relationships with other bird bodies, estuary ecologies, cultural knowledges and relationalities, and how their abilities to form neighbourly and civic relationships is affected by factors such as environment, bird knowledges and estuarine conditions. The school had requested that the children present something on the project at the weekly assembly so we concluded our week at the school by showing a short film from sections of our video and photographic data of the workshops along with information about godwits to the school and parents. These presentations effectively extended the participants outwards to engage with attending family members, and in this way the community also expanded as the audience learned about their transient neighbours through the creative movements of children and the digital media pieces.

Godwit Neighbours has some similarities with *Listening to Climate Change*, by George Revill (2017), a project using more-than-human participatory methods and a coastal nature reserve.[3] Focusing on sounds, the project brought sound artists, scientists, the coastline and creatures in the reserve, and local residents together to critically experience, produce and think about sounds that collectively reflected on climate change. The more-than-human participatory methods enabled the project to use 'different kinds of listening to explore the ways in which the coast is changing' and to create 'rich public debate concerning the place of non-humans' (Noorani and Brigstocke 2018, 25). The Listening to Climate Change project site features maps that locate soundscapes and oral histories of place and is an immensely rich account of the many components that comprise a coastal, more-than-human community.

Where Revill oriented his project around the impacts and affects of climate change, Godwit Neighbours is oriented around migratory birds as posthuman citizens, and the shifting civics that occur as these citizens arrive periodically each year. Our posthuman participatory arts approach invited open explorations from children, estuary, school, birds, weather and knowledges into the ways that humanist concepts of the citizen and civic rights do not acknowledge the cosmopolitics of more-than-human, transnational urban communities – namely, migratory birds. The open explorations by all involved played out in the following ways: the school offered its location as something useful to the project, being close to the estuary and birds, to the local Maori community who had cultural connection to kuaka; the estuary offered its ecology of low tides and silt as a safe space for godwits and the food and shelter needs of the godwits; the children offered their bodies and thoughts for expressive and conceptual contributions and interactions; the birds visited and offered their migratory feats and habits; the weather contributed each day and contributed to what could be undertaken; the knowledges offered contextual framings that took the project in particular directions. This list is not exhaustive and much more was going on, however collectively these different participations investigated how different, transnational bodies and things come into and out of space and form fluid, posthuman publics and civics.

COMMUNITY-BUILDING WITH TRANSNATIONAL OTHERS

The annual arrival of avian citizens generates a continuously evolving urban civic milieu. These migrations and relocations recognise that posthuman citizens are transnational, perhaps moving minimally from one place to another or moving frequently or continuously and across global locations. Rather than think of the godwits as necessary materials to enable the children and adults to do research, a more-than-human approach to participatory research sees how all things and bodies actively contribute, generating 'embodied empathy and and attunement, as different feeling, seeing and thinking bodies undo and redo each other, reciprocally but not symmetrically' (Noorani and Brigstocke 2018, 28) within the milieu. The participatory approach of Godwit Neighbours initiated a disruption to the patterns of encounter taking place between the components; this brought diverse bodies and things into contact and sparked affective impacts. For example, the spectacle of the godwits' annual arrival affords them a presence in the community, whether as a novelty or as the signifier of a culturally important event. Some of the schoolchildren might not have known much about the godwits beyond its novelty before the project, and certainly some of the children voiced that they hadn't given much thought to the reasons for the birds' annual arrival. Bringing different bodies, things and agencies together in a posthuman participatory project helped create ideas around the other citizens, the godwits. And not just the birds, but the birds in relation to the other things that were offering themselves, like the grubs in the sand and the protection of the estuary, and the biological reasons why the godwits select the space because of its ecologies and its nutritional richness; and the estuary being in this land known as Aotearoa, New Zealand.

We were made aware of how a participatory project enriched the understanding of civics and citizenship for the human bodies because we all spoke English; we could observe the changed ways the human children moved their bodies singly and in relation to each other, and we heard the children speak about their ideas and understandings. Additionally, we had ethical permission from the children, families and teachers to work with the schoolchildren. Taking a posthuman participatory approach does raise important issues of ethics and consent. Simply put, we wonder: Did the birds, did the location also consent to be involved? Did these other participants convey their experiences of the project, and did we understand these? Noorani and Brigstocke (2018) highlight there are conceptual and ethical conundrums around doing research which claims to be 'posthuman'. These include addressing the ways humanist participatory methods such as interviews and focus groups centre on the human, the ethics of consent and participation by those not able to voice that, giving due citation to the long histories of Indigenous scholarship, ontologies and cosmologies that have influenced the posthuman 'turn', and also, how 'innovative research practices might enable more than human actors to participate more fully?' (Noorani and Brigstocke 2018, 11) These considerations should not initiate disdain or suspicion for attempting to engage with the posthuman, or more-than-human participatory methodologies. Such disregard comes from a colonial, scientific orientation to research which officiates certain onto-epistemologies in order to benefit colonial interests, and where humanist research is based on consent, demonstrably given by the participant. The humanist reading of consent, which emerges from a Descartian idea of the cognisant, singular being (Descartes and Cress 1998), is connected to ideas of benefit and how research benefits individuals and societies, even if other bodies and things also receive some form of benefit from the research. Although challenging, the notion of consent needs critically examining for research that includes more-than-human bodies. We realise we are on shaky ethical ground here, because this view has been used to advantage research that uses animal-testing, and also military/defence research, such as bomb testing and both these forms of research have very poor regard for more-than-human bodies when compared to our approaches. We are aware, too, however, that more-than-human concepts of 'consent' have also been used to advantage conservation researchers and lobbyists as well as traditional custodians in the protection of cultural lands. In each set of examples the proponents argue that, although not able to 'voice' their consent, the more-than-human participants can be ethically treated and are actively regarded as essential contributors to the research, a view discussed at length by Haraway (2008). We are not saying here that we personally support animal-based or land-based testing, rather, we disagree with it, but what we raise is that consent and participation are already conceived differently, accepted and used in research, scholarship, society and law.

Although Godwit Neighbours did not regard the landscapes as passive and neither did we objectify bodies, we acknowledge that we didn't get the godwit's consent or perspective, or the consent and perspective of the land and the different materials included. We were mindful of this as we conducted the project, and were careful to think ethically about the different modes of participation by the many things, bodies and agencies present and involved. The posthuman ethical framework we attempted to conduct ourselves and the project by was also demonstrated by Naomi Millner during her project on community forestry in the Maya Biosphere Reserve in Guatemala (in Noorani and Brigstocke 2018). Millner took a more-than-human approach to consent while collecting the oral histories of local foresters. During the project the 'interruptions from the site itself (the sounds of the forest; a sudden downpour; the silence of a two-thousand-year-old stone structure) were . . . the imbricated living networks that the interviewee participated in and was shaped by' (in Noorani and Brigstocke 2018, 30). Although not receiving a signed consent form, Millner was ethically open to the more-than-human participation of things and understood that these 'participations' contributed to the study, and were actively part of what occurred in the fieldwork (Bastian 2017) not as environmental or objectified specimens but as active research participant participations.

Posthuman approaches to participation and consent acknowledges that the world extends way beyond the human. To focus so closely, to carefully attune to and to purposefully interact with the other 'things' in the picture effectively decentralise the human. In Godwit Neighbours the shifted focus, the attuning and the interaction by the schoolchildren shifted their centrality as they began to move from acting-on, to participating-with. The children began to conceptually stand to one side as these other participating things came into view. And the children's shifting to the side wasn't prompted by other living things; that is, it wasn't just for the godwits. The things, machines, technologies, agencies and the atmospheric components of the urban spaces where we took the children were no longer vague backgrounds but became understood more through their individual specificities in relation to their materiality, how they were in the space and the affective qualities of these different bodies in space. And the decentralising came about through the children actually being allowed to move around in certain spaces in which they had never been, accessing spaces that were previously unknown or perhaps they thought were forbidden to them. Decentralising came about through the intense exchanges in spaces where things came together. The more-than-human participations directed how bodies could move in relation to surfaces, weather conditions, air quality and heat. The atmospheric conditions and different dimensionalities and angles and positions of material surfaces generated a posthuman consenting and participation between different bodies in 'discursively entangled relations' (Hovde et al. 2021, 77). Finally, the project activities, and the knowledges the children gained about godwits and their status as transient, temporary neighbours would not have been possible without the participation of local spaces, without the (albeit distant) presence of the godwits in the estuary, the estuary ecologies, the technologies that extended vision and provided access to knowledge and research, the tools such as chalk and string and the different interior and exterior surfaces in the school. Human activity does not and cannot act in a vacuum; it needs to be understood as becoming possible only through the interactive participation of other bodies, matters, elements, energies and things.

Beyond the incidences of more-than-human consent, Godwit Neighbours facilitated diverse participatory relations between humans and non-humans. These relations were not intensively identical, nor were they the same in terms of their affective condition. The 'more-than-human' descriptor of the participants in Godwit Neighbours did not automatically mean that all these other things could only or did only generate a single kind of flat relationality with each other and with the human participants. And relationality was not limited to the godwits, children, grubs, estuary silt, parkland and inlet. In classifactory terms relational participation occurred between things differently categorised. The unrefined and unmanufactured world included those listed above as well as trees and plants, and waters (sea, rivers, rain, tap water). Different relationalities could be formed through memories and prior experiences of being on holidays, going for walks, swimming, cooling down, being shaded, climbing, playing, touching, swinging and so on. The manufactured world category included things such as pavement chalks, play equipment, school buildings, music equipment, computers, string, and so on (Go-Pro and gimbal, Bluetooth speaker). Different relationalities could be formed through school routines, home play, prior learning or researching events, scents or memories. And the sensorial world category included weathers (sunlight and lots of wind), temperatures, sounds, smells (estuary mud, school hall linoleum) and colours. Black featured strongly in the project due to the colour of the volcanic stone, as did the pale blue of the Auckland sky, and also the colours of the estuary: the pale yellow of estuary sand; the deep brown of the estuary silt; the steely blue of the coastal waters; the incredible ultramarine blue of the linoleum floor of the school hall; the greenness of the grass, the colours of concrete; sandy and dashed with all the colours of the little pebbles within it. Different relationalities arise through these sensorial encounters along with the affective prompts they generate. Bodies, things and agencies across the categories can participate in different ways in community-building projects, activating performative civics with more-than-human others.

CONCLUSION

In Godwit Neighbours, the curations, practices and choreographies of dance works, and the researching, material manipulation and choreographies of gestural mapping were a collection of actions that pulled in different, transversal participatory collusions that became intensely concentrated through the two practices and that generated collective investigations into belonging, community, reciprocal connection and individual rights of access. The children, despite their age spread, and working physically with their different bodies, and their different body capacities and scales, used expansive zones of perception across their brains and bodies to enter into a posthuman, more-than-human theoretical space and to explore really big and unusual ideas about transnational, more-than-human communities. The creative and participatory practices helped the children to work through these incredibly complex theories. The dance and mapping were artistic tools that supported creative participatory work with more-than-human others and provided the children with modes of expression to help them to think through and explore the concepts embedded in posthuman theories in interesting and appropriate ways for them. The children's classroom-based learning, in partnership with corporeal practices helped them to discover about the science of godwit / kuaka migrations, and bird migration generally, and the Godwit Neighbours project supported their practical and critical investigations into diverse communities, and in their comprehension and engagement with the topic. The dance and mapping offered corporeal modes for the children to learn with and through, and to enact a participatory community building through. For example, the children learned about the science of migratory birds in the classroom, and through movement and mapping in a posthuman participatory arts project they learned how godwits enact a swooping motion when they are feeding.

The gestural mapping and movement helped the children start understanding the godwit as a fellow citizen, rather than it being just a 'bird'. The participatory approach helped nurture a more genuine engagement with the godwit because through creatively imagined touchpoints the godwit became more present and agentic to the children. What we mean here is that the relational encounters with different others helped the children conceive of the importance of the estuarine ecologies, the time of year and that the godwits need to fill up on grubs, build up their fat stores and increase their body size from scrawny, underfed and spent to being really fat and hardly able to fly.

Global transience and migration means that the pathways to becoming a citizen are no longer straightforward. Children directly or indirectly experience discontinuous connection to place, and this impacts the development of their sense of civic connection and legal status. Participatory approaches can initiate forms of transversal social collectivity that constitute a posthuman civics inclusive of diverse biologic, morphologic, technologic material beings as well as the ephemeral, sensorial and atmospheric citizens present. Through posthuman participatory projects, notions of posthuman civics and citizenship can germinate that celebrate transversal reciprocity with other bodies and beings. Usually, civics and citizenship is about communities with other people and not much else. We advocate for projects about building civics with the otherwise building communities that are solely human.

Chapter 9

New Geographies of Praxis

Research that engages children's art as a method for research, or examines the impacts and benefits of children's art, has an interdisciplinary history that spans the fields of psychology, child development and education. Across these very different practical and theoretical spaces, we can say that consensus is reached on the fact that, in many ways, art supports and enriches children's lives. Within these interdisciplinary communities of childhood research, practitioners have employed a range of different methods to investigate children's emotional states and mental well-being and have also drawn on collaborative arts practices with parents and children to examine the interrelationships between families. Others have used drawing to elicit oral or written narratives in collaboration with children (see Driessnack 2005). Using visual methods can assist children to retain and communicate memories of events, and enable them to understand and remember complex ideas. This includes using drawing to speculate on different kinds of child identities (Knight and Rayner 2015). In addition to extending traditions of arts-based research and participatory research, we see our work as a means of choreographing an ethics of posthuman engagement, attunement and civic practice in the age of the Anthropocene. This is an ethical project in which the child's lifeworlds extend beyond the individual to encompass and create place, communities and more-than-human publics. Across all the case studies and examples drawn upon in this book, the children co-creators and co-researchers in our projects all presented a view of the world in which humans and their environments are deeply connected. The human and non-human – the biological, technological, material and discursive – elements that make up children's worlds, were repeatedly shown to be enmeshed, entangled or networked. Page (2020) explores this interconnectivity by suggesting:

[I]nseparability is not Othering, separating Self from Other, or individuating bodies, that is, getting inside someone else's skin. This is about making connections and commitments where we take responsibility and accountability for these relationalities of which we are part – the practising of withness. This responsibility is where we respond to, not impose or assume, and where we listen, acknowledge, recognise, take care and are responsive to the other, who is not separate from the self. (153)

The ethics of engagement canvassed by Page resonates with our approach to research practices as ethical modes of 'being with' as Page would say, or 'being different together' (Hickey-Moody and Willcox 2019). Collaborative art-making is a form of place-making, subjectivation and more-than-human-relationality. This book brings together diverse approaches, locations, people and non-human actants through a shared ethics of engagement that is attuned to more-than-human emergent geographies of praxis. To put this another way, the process of humans and non-humans collaborating to create future images of a better world simultaneously imagines new ways of being together in these new futures. This concluding chapter explores these contours of human and non-human engagement and outlines the contributions of the book to theorizing children's posthuman civics and publics in the Anthropocene. We have shown the possibilities and implications of theorising the posthuman child as a political subject and citizen who, through their collaborative and entangled acts of art-making, form posthuman civics and publics during, and in response to, the great social and environmental upheaval of the climate crisis. Through the lens of the public sphere we have shown how children's publics are always and already posthuman, and that children position themselves within a relational network of political and civic participation that is specifically imbued with an ethics of care and empathy. Despite the end of Romantic notions of childhood in the face of climate catastrophe, we have shown how children continue to imagine futures defined by care and empathy in order to survive rising tides and temperatures and wars of displacement and resource scarcity. In this future we also argue for the rethinking of urban environments and reconsidering how they are designed for different civic and public use; children not only navigate these assemblages of human and the more-than-human as they constitute civic participation in the Anthropocene, but their imagined future cities demand deeper entanglement with their non-human fellow urban citizens. A posthuman civics for the Anthropocene must therefore be based on an ethics of care for the more-than-human of urban environments, acknowledging the cosmopolitical force of the more-than-human urban dwellers in children's formation of posthuman citizenship. Finally, we conceptualise posthuman publics and civics in relation to family, education, play, animality and flora, arguing that multimodal forms of expression through art and gestural mapping allow children to articulate the complexities of their posthuman futures. The process of posthuman collaborative art making is a way to call expanded publics to attention through children's art and occupation of urban and cultural space.

THE POSTHUMAN CHILD AS A POLITICAL SUBJECT AND CITIZEN

The 'innocent child', entwined with healthy 'mother nature', was famously imagined by William Blake (1975) in his 1789 sonnet *Songs of Innocence*. Such a child seems so far from the realities of contemporary ethnographic work with children. For those not familiar with the poem, its first stanza reads as follows:

Piping down the valleys wild,
Piping songs of pleasant glee,
On a cloud I saw a child,
And he laughing said to me:

'Pipe a song about a Lamb!'
So I piped with merry chear.
'Piper, pipe that song again;'
So I piped: he wept to hear.

'Drop thy pipe, thy happy pipe,
'Sing thy songs of happy chear:'
So I sung the same again,
While he wept with joy to hear.

'Piper, sit thee down and write
'In a book that all may read.'
So he vanish'd from my sight,
And I pluck'd a hollow reed,

And I made a rural pen,
And I stain'd the water clear,
And I wrote my happy songs
Every child may joy to hear. (Blake 1975[1787], 26)

The poem echoes the ancient Greek myth of Pan, god of nature, piping children to follow him into the wilderness. Pan became a figurehead for the European Romantic era of the 1800s. Written in 1789, Blake's *Songs of Innocence* can be seen as foreshadowing and inspiring the rise of this Romanticism. Taylor (2013) argues that this Romantic vision of childhood needs hijacking to 'politicize, reorient and reconfigure [childhood] as a lively and unforeclosed set of relations with a different set of political and ethical affordances' (xiv). The imagined 'natural' pedagogical relationship between adult and child, and the childish delight we see depicted in Blake's suggestion that the child is learning 'happy cheer' from adults, now seems an almost garish scene that taunts the much more complicated nature of our work with children. The clear water of rural settings that inspires imagined happy songs has been replaced in the Anthropocene by concrete surfaces and acid rain, and children's lives eked out in slums built on mountains of landfill or slowly survived in refugee camps. Children living in the Anthropocene are, according to Malone (2018) 'working or living near factories; [. . .] exposed to pollutants in the soil, air and water; [. . .] losing homes to rising sea levels and suffering from the impact of natural disasters' (2). The question of what contemporary childhood is, or what childhood can be, remains a proposition that is being asked of contemporary society (or perhaps we should say is being made) by the Anthropocene. To put this another way, the Anthropocene is posing the question of 'what is childhood'? What is left of ideals of childhood and what has childhood become? And not only that, but, as Malone (2018) points out, 'we are not all in the Anthropocene together – the poor and the dispossessed, the children and non-human animals are far more in it than others' (249) The impact that the Anthropocene has had on childhood needs to be explored in much greater detail by children and researchers. A singular answer to these propositions is not possible; rather, multiple answers will be embedded in and emerge through shifting landscapes of possibilities and limits that characterise young lives. Limits set around possibilities for childhood impact not only the lives of children and youth but also the work of those who think about children and young people. As we have suggested in chapters 2 and 7, children's agency and the very nature of what being a child is have changed substantially across the past four decades. Children are responsively embedded in contexts (the family, the mother's opinions, the school) and less aware of themselves as an actor than adults are. The crucial task for researchers working with children in the Anthropocene is therefore to strive to recognise the agency of actions, understand the 'entangled nature of children's lives with the non-human world that embraces them, holds them, works through them' (Malone 2018, 253) and explicitly engage with the embedded nature of this agency.

Our research shows that children and young people's processes of subjectivation and citizen acts are inextricably enmeshed with the materiality of their surroundings. New materialism offers a specific line of approach to these political registers, calling for attention to be paid to the materialisation of political acts as well as the motility of these acts: the being together, making, breaking, changing actions that leave residues in the people and places to which they are connected (Murris 2016). The process of making art is politics in the making: the minutiae of intra-actions in daily life are composite parts of larger bodies that are recognisable as having a political identity, or being a political action. As we suggest in the introduction, our choice to examine political and civic issues at a micro-political level allows a focus on the techtonics of making and remaking identities, bodies or entities. The processes through which subjects become are inextricable from the subject themselves and their actions. The embeddedness of children in their cultural and material worlds therefore emerges as a new geography of praxis for childhood research in the Anthropocene, and needs to be undertaken with sensitivity to the responsibilities into which children are born. Saving a planet that is burning alive is no small feat in anybody's terms.

RETHINKING URBAN ENVIRONMENTS

Place-based findings of our research that characterise the possibilities for posthumanist childhood research to rethink and reshape urban environments run throughout our work in this book and form the focus of chapters 5, 6 and 8. These accounts extend the work of scholars such as Page (2020), Ellsworth (2005), Barrett (2012) and Fors et al. (2013) in considering how entanglements between environments and people are ethical and political encounters. Participating, being in and moving *with place* are requisite components of forming posthuman publics and civics. As demonstrated in chapters 5, 6 and 7, place isn't a static background against and in which humans act; it is co-constitutive of participatory citizenship. Our projects demonstrate this through the intersection of art and landscape that characterises children's work. Chapters 5, 6 and 8 in particular draw out children's always-already posthuman connections with their cities, their environments and other non-human beings. The possible future cities children create in chapter 5 feature water-roads entangled with buildings, dragons, flying hospitals and animals caring for humans emerge as examples of posthuman forms of civics and publics that could be formed in a future defined by climate change. Using participatory practice to connect with non-human, transient community members in chapter 8 extended children's conceptions of community and how these might thrive during environmental change. Chapter 5 engages the political and cultural functions of bringing children's art into public space of galleries and universities, examining the physical and cultural location of art-making and art-display as a process of forming publics. Children also took art into civic spaces in chapter 6 to generate public commentary on the expectations around children's presence and access in urban space. As both spaces of pedagogy and ecologies of learning, the schools, community arts centres, religious community buildings, art galleries and universities in which the children's art was made and displayed, became directly imbricated in the kinds of posthuman publics and civics that could be formed. In these spaces the children's future cities emerged as direct calls to attention for publics, but also as a direct *call to action* to the world of adults regarding ways of being and, indeed, as Page suggests, 'being-with' in the face of climate catastrophe. Chapter 5 saw the imagined futures on the canvas be moved into public spaces in which children seldom have voice or agency, and in chapter 6 these imagined futures were realised through chalked marks and dashes on pavements and walls. In art galleries, museums and universities, and in urban pedestrian spaces, children's imaginings of an urban future called upon the world of adults to create futures in which the human and more-than-human are deeply entwined.

RELATIONAL ETHICS OF CARE

Importantly, the call to action that children made through their art specifically envisioned a future characterised by connectivity and care, or what, after Haraway (2016), we might call 'kinship'. The inherent relationality of children's lifeworlds emerged in their demands for a future defined by care. Our concern with the techtonics and affects of relationality threads throughout our inquiry. Reframing practices of relationality as children's posthuman ethics is one of the most significant contributions we look to make with this book. Research is an ethics of care, a practice of caring for others through enquiring about *how* they want to be and become known. Children establish terms of relation with the more-than-human world that define how they become, and the terms upon which they want to be known. Page (2020) explains her related focus on relationality:

> *The ethics of new material practice research is to research with care, to take care socio-materially, and not separate from the practices and processes of researching, making and learning. Mind, body, spirit with matter we can make and take responsibility and consciously engage in disrupting the practices and discourses that dominate and oppress, to work the spaces between.* (164)

We see children make these disruptions every day as they work the spaces in between the human and non human, adult and child, animal and human. Children's embodied imaginations disrupt categorising discourses and re-purpose space and place in line with the processes they instigate. The amazing possibilities of the spaces in between how things are said to be and how they are experienced are opportunities both for critique and for positive change in children's worlds. On some levels, dominant discourses framing children's worlds sell them a misleading picture of what their futures might hold. For example, adults can but hope that schooling systems are preparing their children for the future world. Who really knows what world will remain in twenty years' time, if the predictions of climate change science are accurate? We cannot know that jobs of today will continue to shape employment opportunities in the future, or even that our planet will remain inhabitable to humans. Despite this, and despite children's awareness of this complex reality, school systems rely on assumptions about the enduring nature of our contemporary planet's economy and geography. We are not teaching for climate disaster prevention, even if children know they need to prepare for climate disasters. Children, however, (as we have shown in chapters 5 and 7), work the spaces in between dominant discourses about the continuation of capitalism and existing labour markets and the science of climate change, in order to explore climate change. Children try to invent ways to stop climate change, imagining ways of living *with* it in ways that don't exacerbate it and shifting how we relate to the more-than-human world. As we saw in chapter 5, prompted with questions of 'values' and 'what really matters', children begin crafting future cities that are characterised by an ethics of care, an ethics entangled with non-human life and matter of the city. This was also demonstrated in chapter 8, where children expanded their understanding of citizenship to include migratory birds. The elements of these cities called a wide public to attention, often in the form of a call to action to be more caring and more environmentally friendly, but these calls were also often framed around the ways children and cities could respond to the climate crisis. The imagined futures and survival strategies for the present that emerged in discussion in chapter 7 showed how childhood is being re-defined (if not completely undone) by the Anthropocene, and that children respond to the discursive and material manifestations of climate change in their art and the way they relate to their peers. The tales of empathy, migration, refuge and safety that emerged in the Interfaith Childhoods workshops, the Godwit Neighbours project and Scaling the City speak directly to the already occurring realities of the climate crisis, and show how children operate within their own, and adults', responses to these realities.

The projects show how children make, maintain and re-make relational ethics of care through their interactions with others. But what of the relational ethics of care of the research team and the research environment? One of the most significant things we can recommend in terms of the relational ethics of care embedded in research practices with children is to leave space for children's broad and creative re-interpretations, indeed, re-inventions, of the adult world. Listening to children and engaging with their hopes and beliefs as expressed by their wild imaginations and inventive art, as shown in chapters 2, 3, 5, 6 and 7, offer adult researchers opportunities to learn from and with children. We show that participatory approaches, which flatten the usual power relations between adults and children, are highly effective in opening up spaces for experimental thinking and making. This is especially important for projects that address speculative ideas and that are art- and practice-based. Hearing voices and opinions that are expressed through indirect discourse and imaginative making is an essential practice here. Child-centred and child-responsive research practices and imaginations are key here.

REFUGE IN RELATIONALITY

In chapter 7 we examine what children take refuge in, and what matters the most to them in times characterised by impermanence. We also explored the possibility for art to bring different communities together, and the geographic- and class-based limits of this possibility of togetherness. Refuge is a complicated concept and practice in contemporary culture. As our data shows, contemporary children often take refuge in digital virtual worlds. The safe places that children built are populated by mobiles that testify the significance of Tetris, Minecraft, Fortnite and other digital games in their emotional worlds. Games offer a form of escape, but also a form of security. Games have rules that children can't change. They are a system that, once one is within, can't be questioned and must be abided by (perhaps this is part of the broad and significant appeal of games for children?). In times when our environmental surroundings and futures remain so terribly uncertain, complete yet contextually specific certainty is offered by the virtual worlds of games, their rules, their scoring systems, their requirement that the player suspends their disbelief (e.g., through a young man who appears on screen as tall muscular and a big breasted woman who wears a purple suit of armour). Clearly this offers appeal and respite from the ever-changing and tumultuous contemporary world.

As we discuss, children also call the more-than-human world to attention and make themselves part of more-than-human collectives through their art-making. Children's artworks centred on the significance of relationships with family, the relation of self to self and relation of self to the more-than-human. In exploring this practice of relationality, Braidotti (2019) suggests that in accounting for the human in posthuman times we need to:

> *carefully ground the statement 'we humans'. For 'we' are not one and the same*
> *. . . the human needs to be assessed as materially embedded and embodied,*

differential, affective and relational. . . . For the subject to be materially embedded means to take distance from abstract universalism. To be embodied and embrained entails decentering transcendental consciousness. To view the subject as differential implies to extract difference from the oppositional or binary logic that reduces difference to being different from, as in being less than. Difference is an imminent, positive and dynamic category. The emphasis on affectivity and relationality is an alternative to individualist autonomy. (11–12)

Affectively and relationally, in different ways, children's relationships with their parents and families offer them refuge in times of uncertainty. So too do imagined possibilities arising from a variety of different future scenarios that children create through imagining future worlds. Here we see the focus of *the-human-being-in-relation-to* that is part of a posthuman perspective. As explored in chapter 1, concerns have been raised about the capacity of new materialism to explore the lived politics of society. Considering the-human-being-in-relation-to is central to examining not just issues of political concern but also a means of better understanding the micro-politics of how political situations unfold. In chapters 2 and 3 we have offered some tools with which to understand the human-being-in-relation-to the human and the more-than-human world.

The Scaling the City project built skills in the participants through independent curatorial and collaborative working. These processes built participant's capacity to make decisions along curatorial lines, and undertake quality-based analyses of ideas and aesthetics. They also learnt about migratory birds so they gained a scientific knowledge of something in their field. But most importantly, the children built connections with the space that they were in. Through both research projects, we were able to capture how the children's environment took up a more affective presence in their lives and a greater materiality. In the art they made in classrooms, the galleries in which their art hung and the bodily mapping of urban spaces and migratory patterns, various spatialities were articulated on planes of awareness and planes of affect.

These expanded spatialities, as well as the capacious modes of expression, civics and publics they engaged, eventually lead to a more engaged form of citizenry, one that was inherently entangled with the more-than-human parts of their world. The birds, the grubs on which they fed, the mud, concrete, asphalt, leaves, sunlight, humidity, wind, salt, sun, chalk and water took up space and constituted a practice of posthuman civics where the human was no longer central. Both projects allowed for the recognition of civics and public spheres in which the human is not the centre but, rather, a node of an assemblage. In the Scaling the City project, both on the asphalt of Brisbane and Auckland and in the mud alongside the peninsula estuary, posthuman relationships became foregrounded.

As we have noted, both projects engender practices of posthuman civics and publics and, in terms of considering the politics of their materiality, we would say that our methods are forms of posthuman pedagogy that employ the more-than-human to impact on the human, and change their processes of subjectivation.

POSTHUMAN PEDAGOGIES

In this section we reflect on the processes of collaboration we have presented in this book as a modality (Colman 2019) of posthuman pedagogy in which children are changed by their experiences of engaging with the more-than-human. Posthuman theories are key to understanding intra-active relationality, and the research projects we canvass in this book do more than instrumentalise theories; they are key to understanding and forming the findings of the projects. A similar, co-constitutive, relationship between theory and method is explained by Coleman (2020, 17) in her suggestion that 'to develop an account of things it is necessary to see theory and method as entangled; that is, the conceptual and methodological aspects of "things" are entwined and co-constitutive'. This quotation expresses our approach, as our methods were both expressions of our onotoepistemological positions and responsive, fluid engagements with contexts.

Part of the material-discursive entanglement that constitutes our research process is the practice of observing the ways art practice teaches the children who make it, and teaches those who observe the art when it is exhibited or performed to think about other possible futures. In thinking about the posthuman pedagogical affects of our research process we work with a model offered by Deleuze and Guattari (1994) for thinking about posthuman pedagogy, as a way of coming to terms with how non-human things (in this instance, art practice, materials, urban environments, birds, parks) can impact on the human. Among other things, Deleuze and Guattari show us that art is *more* than a mode of producing subjectivity and a way of modulating community. This argument relies on a specific definition of 'art'. Deleuze and Guattari argue that works of art consist of compounded collections of percepts and affects. A *percept* is a physical fragment of the world imagined in and through the artwork. An *affect* is the sense, or *feeling*, that is enmeshed with the materiality of the artwork. Combined together in art, percepts and affects constitute what Deleuze and Guattari term a 'bloc of sensations' (176), and these blocs are pedagogical: they are the language with which art speaks. To employ Deleuze and Guattari's (1994) words:

[A]rt is the language of sensations. Art does not have opinions. Art undoes the triple organisation of perceptions, affections and opinions in order to substitute

a monument composed of percepts, affects and blocs of sensations that take the
place of language. . . . A monument does not commemorate or celebrate some-
thing that happened but confides to the ear of the future the persistent sensations
that embody the event: the constantly renewed suffering of men and women,
their re-created protestations, their constantly resumed struggle. (176–177)

For example, the children's canvases depicting future cities also give their viewers a sense of what it might feel like to inhabit the future city, what one might
see in that city and even what the city as a collective subject might see. Likewise,
the children's creative movements and dashed chalk markings presented what
life was like for a child in a city to those adults who watched the performances.
To put this another way, knowledge is communicated through and by art and
creative participatory processes in ways that exceed language, and is often communicated by things that are not human. Artworks are monuments, entities that
propel the political agendas of those for whom they speak. In doing so, they
create a new sensory landscape (and, in our example, a new possible future),
for their beholder. These simultaneous acts of propelling a political agenda and
creating a sensory landscape occur *through* an artwork's affective potential.
This is the way a work of art can make its observer feel; the connection(s) a
work prompts its observer to make. The materiality of the artwork, the blocs of
sensation of which it is composed, embody affects that are specific to the work.
No two artworks make a viewer feel the same way. As such, each bloc of sensation has its own affective force or quality. If a bloc of sensations made by a
canvas or a way of moving has an affective capacity, then it follows that art has
the aptitude to re-work a body's limits. It changes people's capacities to act: it
teaches them. The materiality of art can re-adjust what a person is or is not able
to understand, produce and connect to. This is not to say that a work of art necessarily *will* change viewers in prescribed ways, rather, that artworks *can* create
new associations and habits of clustering emotion around new images. Art can
think for us, and with us, it can machine thoughts and feelings.

Extending this argument that art makes new feelings, Deleuze and Guattari
(1994) suggest that percepts and affects exist within a work of art because
they have been created as part of a work of art, upon terms established by,
and situated within the work, terms that are specific to the *way* the work of art
has been constructed. For example, the world of Tetris or Fortnight as a controlled escape from the chaos of everyday life is conveyed through the refuge
decorations precisely because the images of games were developed to reflect
things in which the children took refuge. In other contexts, digital games
could have entirely different meanings. An affect is a new milieu of sense, or
series of personal associations, that are created in relation to percepts: 'affects
are precisely these nonhuman becomings of man [sic]' (Deleuze and Guattari
1994, 169). Such minor transformations are non-human because, although an

affect is an embodied change, a readjustment of personal 'limit' or capacity, affect is not produced in relation to another person (i.e., a writer, a dancer, a painter) but rather, in relation to the material product, the work, that the child artist has created. A work of art develops a miniature universe that performs a pedagogic function through crafting and imbuing previously non-existent elements of difference upon its spectator.

The term *percept* is a way of describing aspects of the physicality of the artwork in its completed form. In describing the way a percept works, and what percepts are, Deleuze and Guattari (1994) suggest:

> *[A] percept is material crafted into a sensation . . . it is difficult to say where in fact the material ends and sensation begins; preparation of the canvas, the track of the brush's hair, and many other things besides are obviously part of the sensation.* (166)

Children's art often comprises multiple, childish affects. However, more than this, and extending the human into the more-than-human, the affects produced by percepts in children's art are not speaking with children's voices, and do not tell stories from children's lived experience. This is because affects that are produced by percepts can only be developed 'internally' to a work of art, upon terms that are specific to the work in question. New lived sensibilities, or personal vocabularies, are often the *products* of artistic affects. Affects occur within the context of a minor universe constructed by a work of art. In a work of art, blocs of sensation are offered up to the world by a work of art in a slightly revolutionary moment. In describing this potential for the creation of newness and transformation, or characterising the posthuman, pedagogical dimensions of art, Deleuze and Guattari (1994) argue that:

> *'blocs' of percepts and affects are innovative by nature; they are not about preserving previous events or works of art, but are the creation of a new solidarity. . . . Even if the material only lasts for a few seconds it will give sensation the power to exist and be preserved in itself in the eternity that exists for that short duration.* (166)

Translating this sentiment into subjective or 'human' terms, even if a child's body moving in space is only re-making space in new ways for a short space of time, those who witness this process of remaking will retain the new sense of place and will, from that point onwards, see the space in question anew. The implications of what Deleuze and Guattari (1994) suggest then are that the person who experiences the force produced by an affect made through art can retain this force, and can also be changed as a result of their experience. However, the way in which an affect is experienced, and the way(s) in which an affect works, will always be specific to the body in question. Whether or not a work of art is perceived as having affect at all, is always specific to the viewing body in question.

Importantly for us, in this line of thought, the non-human object here is the vector of change. The artwork (or rock/bird/snail/smell/body/material composition) is effecting change, not a person. Deleuze and Guattari (1994) contend that:

> *[a work of art] is no less independent of the viewer or hearer, who only experience it after, if they have the strength for it.* (164)

As such, the power of percepts and affects must be seen as situated: as context-specific and highly subjective. The forces produced by works of art exist in relation to those who experience them, those who 'have the strength for it' (Deleuze and Guattari 1994, 164). The production of art is contingent upon its opening up to chaos; a line of deterritorialisation that creates a territorial refrain and connects it to other spaces. The labour of the artist remains implicit in Deleuze and Guattari's analysis.

Operating in relation to the cultural context of an artwork, aesthetic figures created within an artwork offer us a way of thinking through the cultural politics of art. Deleuze and Guattari (1994) describe aesthetic figures by suggesting that:

> *Aesthetic figures, and the style that creates them, have nothing to do with rhetoric. They are sensations, percepts and affects, landscapes and faces, visions and becomings. But is not the philosophical concept defined by becoming, and almost on the same terms? Still aesthetic figures are not the same as conceptual personae. It may be that they pass into one another, in either direction . . . insofar as there are sensations of concepts and concepts of sensations.* (177)

By inviting us to think outside the boundaries of 'majoritarian' thought, aesthetic figures push sensory becomings into the realm of the conceptual by creating experiences in which one is challenged to partake in 'the action by which the common event itself eludes what it is' (Deleuze and Guattari 1994, 177). Beings of sensation are created within artworks and these beings 'think for' (Deleuze and Guattari 1994, 63–68) the observer, in the respect that they translate materiality into a particular sensation. The examples canvassed in this book show how we created a wide range of forms of posthuman pedagogy, and these can be seen as aesthetic figures that rethink futures, remake places and recreate animal-human relationships. The posthuman pedagogies we explore through examining making also produce multiple beings of sensation.

CONCLUSIONS AND BEGINNINGS

Concluding our exploration of the posthuman publics, civics and pedagogies of the Interfaith Childhoods and Scaling the City projects is a matter of inviting new beginnings. Our writings on these subjects are offered as a (hopefully) generative source of inspiration and an ethical, relational compass that will support researchers in facilitating making experiences with children and young people. Some questions you might like to take into your own praxis include:

- How does matter prompt responses from children and young people?
- In what ways do children and young people mediate and reply to landscapes and materials in their creative practices?
- What non-civic relational practices do you see children and young people developing?
- Who are the publics called to attention by the works children and young people create? What transversal lines are crossed in calling these publics to attention and what are the broader political implications of this?

You will most likely also develop orienting questions of your own. We would love to be brought into these conversations and collaborations through citational practice and knowledge exchange, so we can further develop these lines of inquiry in relation to your own extensions. We look forward to becoming in relation to your own posthuman praxis.

Notes

CHAPTER 2

1. Butsch began mapping this field in 2000 with *The Making of American Audiences: from stage to television, 1750–1990*, and his influence can clearly be seen in contemporary works such as Coleman and Ross (2010) *The Media and The Public: "them" and "us" in media discourse*.

CHAPTER 3

1. CRISPR stands for clusters of regularly interspaced short palindromic repeats. A short overview of the science around gene editing can be found at www.livescience .com/58790-crispr-explained.html

2. See www.raconteur.net/healthcare/healthcare-technology/timeline-of-scienti fic-discovery-gene-editing/

CHAPTER 6

1. Scaling the City was a collaborative project between Prof Carol Brown (VCA) and Clare Battersby (independent dance educator) with the Urban Activators dance group (NZ), and participant children in Brisbane, Aus. Ethics permission granted.

2. These are familiar terms to Australian and New Zealand schoolchildren as the topics are taught as part of the primary curriculum.

3. The children had varied prior dance experiences so the movements were often a combination of contemporary dance, parkour, gymnastics, and gross body movements.

4. The fieldwork was undertaken in the months of November and December, these are summer months in Australia and New Zealand and the weather can be very hot and sunny.

5. Prehensive means to be able to grasp, seize, or take hold of something. The children curled their toes around the chalks and were able to hold the chalks in this way to make marks.

CHAPTER 8

1. See https://connected-communities.org

2. The team comprised Professor Carol Brown (University of Melbourne), Claire Battersby (Independent dance educator), Dr Alfdaniels Mabingo (University of Auckland) and Associate Professor Linda Knight (RMIT University).

3. See www.soundingcoastalchange.org

Bibliography

Ahmed, Sara. 2008. "Open Forum Imaginary Prohibitions: Some Preliminary Remarks on the Founding Gestures of the New Materialism." *The European Journal of Women's Studies* 15 (1): 23–39. https://doi.org/10.1177/1350506807084854.

Akama, Yoko, Ann Light and Takahito Kamihira. 2020. "Expanding Participation to Design with More-Than-Human Concerns." In *Proceedings of the 16th Participatory Design Conference 2020—Participation(s) Otherwise—Volume 1*, 1–11. PDC '20. New York, NY: Association for Computing Machinery. https://doi.org/10.1145/3385010.3385016.

Alaimo, Stacy and Susan Hekman. 2008. *Material Feminisms*. Indiana University Press.

Alaska Native Knowledge Network. n.d. "Yupik Bird Book: Glossaries Search." Accessed May 26, 2021. http://ankn.uaf.edu/Resources/mod/glossary/showentry.php?courseid=15&eid=11186&displayformat=dictionary.

Alexander, Stephanie and Katherine Frohlich. 2019. "Levelling the Playing Fields: A Pilot Intervention." *European Journal of Public Health* 29 (Supplement 4). https://doi.org/10.1093/eurpub/ckz185.340.

Allen, Barry. 2011. "The Cultural Politics of Nonhuman Things." *Contemporary Pragmatism* 8 (1): 3–19.

Arends, I. S. M. and M Michaela Hordijk. 2016. "Physical and Virtual Public Spaces for Youth: The Importance of Claiming Spaces in Lima, Peru." *Geographies of Children and Young People* 3: 227–247.

Aslanian, Teresa K. 2018. "Recycling Piaget: Posthumanism and Making Children's Knowledge Matter." *Educational Philosophy and Theory* 50 (4): 417–27. https://doi.org/10.1080/00131857.2017.1377068.

Australia Council. 2020. *Creating Our Future: Results of the National Arts Participation Survey*.

Bala, Sruti. 2018. *The Gestures of Participatory Art*. Manchester University Press.

Barad, Karen. 2007. *Meeting the Universe Halfway: Quantum Physics and the Entanglement of Matter and Meaning*. Duke University Press.

Barker, Kezia. 2010. "Biosecure Citizenship: Politicising Symbiotic Associations and the Construction of Biological Threat." *Transactions of the Institute of British Geographers* 35 (3): 350–63.

Barrett, Jennifer. 2012. *Museums and the Public Sphere*. John Wiley & Sons.

Bastian, Michelle. 2017. "Towards a More-than-Human Participatory Research." In *Participatory Research in More-than-Human Worlds*, 19–37. Routledge Studies in Human Geography 67. London; New York: Routledge.

Bennett, Jane. 2010. *Vibrant Matter: A Political Ecology of Things*. Duke University Press.

Bennett, Tony, John Frow, Australia Council and Griffith University Institute for Cultural Policy Studies. 1991. *Art Galleries, Who Goes?: A Study of Visitors to Three Australian Art Galleries, with International Comparisons*. Prepared for the Australia Council by Tony Bennett and John Frow on Behalf of the Institute for Cultural Policy Studies, Division of Humanities, Griffith University. Australia Council.

Berlant, Lauren. 1997. *The Queen of America Goes to Washington City*. Duke University Press.

———. 2008. *The Female Complaint: The Unfinished Business of Sentimentality in American Culture*. Duke University Press.

———. 2011. *Cruel Optimism*. Duke University Press.

Berlant, Lauren and Michael Warner. 1998. "Sex in Public." *Critical Inquiry* 24 (2): 547–66.

Bernard van Leer Foundation. 2017. "Building Better Cities with Young Children and Families." https://www.880cities.org/portfolio_page/portfolio_pagebuilding-better -cities-with-young-children-and-families/.

Bignall, Simone. 2020. "Posthuman Publics". Jumbunna Indigenous Nations and Collaborative Futures. University of Technology Sydney. February.

Bingham, Charles. 2016. "Against Educational Humanism: Rethinking Spectatorship in Dewey and Freire." *Studies in Philosophy and Education* 35 (2): 181–93. https ://doi.org/10.1007/s11217-015-9490-3.

Blaise, Mindy. 2016. "Fabricated Childhoods: Uncanny Encounters with the More-than-Human." *Discourse: Studies in the Cultural Politics of Education* 37 (5): 617–26. https://doi.org/10.1080/01596306.2015.1075697.

Boontharm, Davisi. 2019. "Sketch and Script in Cultural Mapping." In *Artistic Approaches to Cultural Mapping: Activating Imaginaries and Means of Knowing*, Edited by William F. Garrett-Petts, Nancy Duxbury, and Alys Longley, 65–74. Routledge.

Braidotti, Rosi. 2013. *The Posthuman*. Polity Press.

———. 2019. *Posthuman Knowledge*. Polity Press.

———. 2020. "'We' Are In This Together, But We Are Not One and the Same." *Journal of Bioethical Inquiry* 17 (4): 465–69. https://doi.org/10.1007/s11673-020-10017-8.

Braidotti, Rosi and Simone Bignall. 2018. *Posthuman Ecologies: Complexity and Process after Deleuze*. Rowman & Littlefield.

Brown, Wendy. 2015. *Undoing the Demos: Neoliberalism's Stealth Revolution*. MIT Press.

———. 2020. *States of Injury: Power and Freedom in Late Modernity*. Princeton University Press.

Bruns, Axel, Jean Burgess, Tim Highfield, Lars Kirchhoff and Thomas Nicolai. 2011. "Mapping the Australian Networked Public Sphere." *Social Science Computer Review* 29 (3): 277–87.

Butcher, Melissa. 2016. "Reimagining Home: Visualizing the Multiple Meanings of Place." In *Space, Place, and Environment*. Vol. 3. Edited by Tracey Skelton, Karen Nairn, and Peter Kraftl. Geographies of Children and Young People. Singapore: Springer Singapore.

Butsch, Richard. 2000. *The Making of American Audiences: From Stage to Television, 1750–1990*. Cambridge University Press.

———. 2007. *Media and Public Spheres*. Palgrave Macmillan.

———. 2008. *The Citizen Audience: Crowds, Publics, and Individuals*. Routledge.

Campbell, Gwyn, Suzanne Miers and Joseph Calder Miller. 2011. *Child Slaves in the Modern World*. Ohio University Press.

Capous-Desyllas, Moshoula and Karen Morgaine. 2018. *Creating Social Change through Creativity*. Springer.

Chen, Mel Y. 2012. *Animacies. Biopolitics, Racial Mattering, and Queer Affect*. Duke University Press.

Clarke, Andrew, Cameron Parsell and Lutfun Nahar Lata. 2021. "Surveilling the Marginalised: How Manual, Embodied and Territorialised Surveillance Persists in the Age of 'Dataveillance.'" *The Sociological Review* 69 (2): 396–413. https://doi .org/10.1177/0038025120954785.

Cleaver, F. 2001. "Institutions Agency and the Limitations of Participatory Approaches to Development." In *Participation: The New Tyranny?*, Edited by B Cooke and U Kothari, 36–55. London; New York: Zed Books.

Cockburn, Tom. 2013. *Rethinking Children's Citizenship*. Palgrave Macmillan.

Cohen, Morris R. 1940. "Some Difficulties in Dewey's Anthropocentric Naturalism." *The Philosophical Review* 49 (2): 196–228.

Coleman, Rebecca. 2020a. *Glitterworlds: The Future Politics of a Ubiquitous Thing*. Goldsmiths Press.

Coleman, Stephen and Karen Ross. 2010. *The Media and the Public: "Them" and "Us" in Media Discourse*. Vol. 9. John Wiley & Sons.

Colman, Felicity. 2019. "Modality." *Philosophy Today* 63 (4): 983–98.

Cultural Ministers Council Statistics. 2006. *Social and Demographic Characteristics of Cultural Attendees*.

Curtis, Elana, Rhys Jones, David Tipene-Leach, Curtis Walker, Belinda Loring, Sarah-Jane Paine and Papaarangi Reid. 2019. "Why Cultural Safety Rather than Cultural Competency Is Required to Achieve Health Equity: A Literature Review and Recommended Definition." *International Journal for Equity in Health* 18 (1): 174. https://doi.org/10.1186/s12939-019-1082-3.

Cutter-Mackenzie-Knowles, Amy, Karen Malone and Elisabeth Barratt Hacking. 2019. "Childhoodnature—An Assemblage Adventure." In *Research Handbook on Childhoodnature: Assemblages of Childhood and Nature Research*, edited by Amy

Cutter-Mackenzie-Knowles, Karen Malone, and Elisabeth Barratt Hacking, 1–16. Springer International Handbooks of Education. Cham: Springer International Publishing. https://doi.org/10.1007/978-3-319-51949-4_2-1.

Dalley, Cameo. 2020. "The 'White Card' Is Grey: Survelliance, Endurance and the Cashless Debit Card." *The Australian Journal of Social Issues* 55 (1): 51–60. https://doi.org/10.1002/ajs4.100.

Dalrymple-Smith, Angus. 2019. *Commercial Transitions and Abolition in West Africa 1630–1860.* Vol. 9. Studies in Global Slavery, 2405–4585. Leiden, The Netherlands: Brill | Sense.

Datta, Ranjan. 2015. "A Relational Theoretical Framework and Meanings of Land, Nature, and Sustainability for Research with Indigenous Communities." *Local Environment* 20 (1): 102–13.

Deleuze, Gilles and Felix Guattari. 1977. *Anti-Oedipus: Capitalism and Schizophrenia.* University of Minnesota Press.

———. 1987. *A Thousand Plateaus.* University of Minnesota Press.

———. 1994. *What Is Philosophy?* Columbia University Press.

Descartes, Rene and Donald A. Cress. 1998. *Discourse on Method; and: Meditations on First Philosophy.* 6th ed. Indianapolis: Hackett Publications.

Dewey, John and Melvin L. Rogers. 2012. *The Public and Its Problems: An Essay in Political Inquiry.* Penn State Press.

DiNovelli-Lang, Danielle. 2013. "The Return of the Animal: Posthumanism, Indigeneity, and Anthropology." *Environment and Society* 4 (1): 137–56. https://doi.org/10.3167/ares.2013.040109.

Downs, Simon, Russell Marshall, Phil Sawdon, Andrew Selby and Jane Tormey. 2009. *Drawing Now: Between the Lines of Contemporary Art.* I.B. Tauris.

Driessnack, M. 2005. "Children's Drawings as Facilitators of Communication: A Meta-Analysis." *Journal of Pediatric Nursing* 20 (6): 415–23.

Dudgeon, Patricia and Abigail Bray. 2019. "Indigenous Relationality: Women, Kinship and the Law." *Genealogy* 3 (2): 23.

Duffy, Michelle. 2016. "Affect and Emotion in Children's Place-Making." *Space, Place, and Environment* 3: 379.

Eglash, Ron, Audrey Bennett, William Babbitt, Michael Lachney, Martin Reinhardt and Deborah Hammond-Sowah. 2020a. "Decolonizing Posthumanism: Indigenous Material Agency in Generative STEM." *British Journal of Educational Technology* 51 (4): 1334–53. https://doi.org/10.1111/bjet.12963.

Ekawati, Sri Aliah. 2015. "Children-Friendly Streets as Urban Playgrounds." *Procedia—Social and Behavioural Sciences* 179: 94–108. https://doi.org/10.1016/j.sbspro.2015.02.413.

Ellsworth, Elizabeth. 2005. *Places of Learning: Media, Architecture, Pedagogy.* Routledge.

Farrell, Betty, Maria Medvedeva Cultural Policy Center NORC and the Harris School of Public Policy at the University of Chicago. 2010. *Demographic Transformation and the Future of Museums.* AMA Press.

Fendrich, Roger. 1975. "The Problem of Anthropocentrism in Dewey's Metaphysics." *International Philosophical Quarterly* 15 (2): 149–59. https://doi.org/10.5840/ipq197515212.

Flanagan, Victoria. 2013. "'I Thought I Lived in a Country Where I Had Rights': Conceptualising Child Citizenship in the Posthuman Era." In *The Nation in Children's Literature*, Edited by Kit Kelen and Bjorn Sundmark, 261–76. Routledge.

Fornet-Betancourt, Raúl, Helmut Becker, Alfredo Gomez-Müller and J. D. Gauthier. 1987. "The Ethic of Care for the Self as a Practice of Freedom: An Interview with Michel Foucault on January 20, 1984." *Philosophy & Social Criticism* 12 (2–3): 112–31. https://doi.org/10.1177/019145378701200202.

Fors, Vaike, Åsa Bäckström and Sarah Pink. 2013a. "Multisensory Emplaced Learning: Resituating Situated Learning in a Moving World." *Mind, Culture, and Activity* 20 (2): 170–83.

Foucault, Micel. 1990. *The Care of the Self: The History of Sexuality V:3*. Penguin.

Fraser, Nancy. 1990. "Rethinking the Public Sphere: A Contribution to the Critique of Actually Existing Democracy." *Social Text* 25/26: 56–80.

———. 1999. *Another Pragmatism: Alain Locke, Critical "Race" Theory, and the Politics of Culture*. Duke University Press.

Fredericks, Rosalind. 2018. *Garbage Citizenship: Vital Infrastructures of Labor in Dakar, Senegal*. Durham: Duke University Press.

de Freitas, Elizabeth. 2017. "The Temporal Fabric of Research Methods: Posthuman Social Science and the Digital Data Deluge." *Research in Education* 98 (1): 27–43. https://doi.org/10.1177/0034523717723386.

Gere, Charlie. 2019. *I Hate the Lake District*. Goldsmiths Press.

Gerrard, Jessica, Sophie Rudolph and Arathi Sriprakash. 2017. "The Politics of Post-Qualitative Inquiry: History and Power." *Qualitative Inquiry* 23 (5): 384–94. https://doi.org/10.1177/1077800416672694.

Gleeson, Brendan and Neil Sipe. 2006. "Reinstating Kids in the City." In *Creating Child Friendly Cities: Reinstating Kids in the City*, Edited by Brendan Gleeson and Neil Sipe, 1–10. London: Routledge.

Glosbe. 2021. "Bar-Tailed Godwit in Korean—English-Korean Dictionary | Glosbe." https://en.glosbe.com/en/ko/Bar-tailed%20Godwit.

Goodley, Dan, Rebecca Lawthom and Katherine Runswick Cole. 2014. "Posthuman Disability Studies." *Subjectivity* 7 (4): 342–61.

Gordon, Lewis R. 1998. "African-American Philosophy: Theory, Politics, and Pedagogy." *Philosophy of Education Archive*, 39–46.

Gray, Chris Hables. 2000. *Cyborg Citizen: Politics in the Posthuman Age*. Routledge.

Guattari, Félix. 2014. *The Three Ecologies*. London; New York: Bloomsbury Academic.

Habermas, Jürgen. 1991. *The Structural Transformation of the Public Sphere: An Inquiry into a Category of Bourgeois Society*. MIT Press.

Hackett, Abigail and Margaret Somerville. 2017. "Posthuman Literacies: Young Children Moving in Time, Place and More-than-Human Worlds." *Journal of Early Childhood Literacy* 17 (3): 374–91. https://doi.org/10.1177/1468798417704031.

Hage, Ghassan. 2005. "A Not so Multi-Sited Ethnography of a Not so Imagined Community." *Anthropological Theory* 5 (4): 463–75.

Häkli, Jouni. 2018. "The Subject of Citizenship—Can There Be a Posthuman Civil Society?" *Political Geography* 67 (November): 166–75. https://doi.org/10.1016/j.polgeo.2017.08.006.

Halberstam, Jack. 2005. *In a Queer Time and Place: Transgender Bodies, Subcultural Lives*. Vol. 3. NYU Press.

———. 2020. *Wild Things: The Disorder of Desire*. Duke University Press.

Halilovich, Hariz. 2013. "Ethical Approaches in Research with Refugees and Asylum Seekers Using Participatory Action Research." *Values and Vulnerabilities: The Ethics of Research with Refugees and Asylum Seekers*, Edited by Karen Block, Elisha Riggs, and Nick Haslam, 127.

Haraway, Donna J. 2004. *The Haraway Reader*. Psychology Press.

———. 2008. *When Species Meet*. Minneapolis: University of Minnesota Press.

———. 2016. *Manifestly Haraway*. Vol. 37. Minneapolis: University of Minnesota Press.

Harris, Anne and Yvette Taylor 2016. "Sexualities, Creativities and Contemporary Publics." *Continuum: Journal of Media and Cultural Studies* 30 (5): 503–06.

Harwood, Valerie, Anna Hickey-Moody, Samantha McMahon and Sarah O'Shea. 2016. *The Politics of Widening Participation and University Access for Young People: Making Educational Futures*. Taylor & Francis Group.

Hast, Susanna. 2021. "In Touch with the Mindful Body: Moving with Women and Girls at the Za'atari Refugee Camp." In *Arts-Based Methods for Decolonising Participatory Research*, Edited by Tiina Seppälä, Melanie Sarantou, and Satu Miettinen, 43–58. Routledge Advances in Art and Visual Studies. New York, NY: Routledge.

Heitlinger, Sara, Marcus Foth, Rachel Clarke, Carl DiSalvo, Ann Light and Laura Forlano. 2018. "Avoiding Ecocidal Smart Cities: Participatory Design for More-than-Human Futures." In *Proceedings of the 15th Participatory Design Conference: Short Papers, Situated Actions, Workshops and Tutorial—Volume 2*, 1–3. PDC '18. New York, NY: Association for Computing Machinery. https://doi.org/10.1145/3210604.3210619.

Hickey-Moody, Anna. 2013. "Little Public Spheres." *Performance Paradigm* 9.

———. 2016. "Being Different in Public." *Continuum* 30 (5): 531–41.

———. 2018. "New Materialism, Space-Time Folds and the Agency of Matter." *Qualitative Inquiry* 26 (7): 724–32.

———. 2019a. "Faith." *Philosophy Today* 63 (4): 927–41.

———. 2019b. "Three Ways of Knowing Failure." *MAI: Feminism & Visual Culture* (blog). May 15, 2019. https://maifeminism.com/three-ways-of-knowing-failure/.

———. 2020. "New Materialism, Ethnography, and Socially Engaged Practice: Space-Time Folds and the Agency of Matter." *Qualitative Inquiry* 26 (7): 724–32. https://doi.org/10.1177/1077800418810728.

Hickey-Moody, Anna, Christine Horn, Marissa Willcox and Eloise Florence. 2021. *Arts-Based Methods for Research with Children*. Springer Nature.

Hickey-Moody, Anna and Marissa Willcox. 2019. "Entanglements of Difference as Community Togetherness: Faith, Art and Feminism." *Social Sciences* 8 (9): 264.

Hinton, Peta and Pat Treusch. 2015. *Teaching with Feminist Materialisms: Teaching with Gender. European Women's Studies in International and Interdisciplinary Classrooms*. Utrecht: ATGENDER.

Honkanen, Kati, Jaana Poikolainen and Liisa Karlsson. 2018a. "Children and Young People as Co-Researchers—Researching Subjective Well-Being in Residential Area with Visual and Verbal Methods." *Children's Geographies* 16 (2): 184–95.

Hossain, Sharif Tousif and Zarin Tasnim. 2020. "Study on the Importance of Open Space Due to Create Dhaka as a Child Friendly City." *Asian Journal of Social Sciences and Legal Studies* 2 (5): 96–103. https://doi.org/10.34104/ajssls.020.0960103.

Hovde, Sunniva, Asante Smzy Maulidi and Tone Pernille Ostern. 2021. "Towards Just Dance Research: An UMunthu Participatory and Performative Inquiry into Malawian-Norwegian Entanglements." In *Arts-Based Methods for Decolonising Participatory Research*, 59–80 Routledge Advances in Art and Visual Studies. New York, NY: Routledge.

Hultgren, John. 2017. "Representing Posthumans: Citizenship and the Political Production of Bodies and Technologies." In *Posthuman Dialogues in International Relations*, edited by Erika Cudworth, Stephen Hobden, and Emilian Kavalski, 181–98. Routledge. https://doi.org/10.4324/9781315613475-11.

Hunt, Peter. 2018. *Ancient Greek and Roman Slavery*. Hoboken, NJ: Wiley-Blackwell.

Huxley, Aldous. 2007. *Brave New World*. London: Chatto & Windus.

Iannelli, Laura and Carolina M Marelli. 2019. "Performing Civic Cultures: Participatory Public Art and Its Publics." *International Journal of Cultural Studies* 22 (5): 630–46. https://doi.org/10.1177/1367877919849964.

IPCC. 2018. "Summary for Policymakers." In: *Global Warming of 1.5°C. An IPCC Special Report on the Impacts of Global Warming of 1.5°C Above Pre-Industrial Levels and Related Global Greenhouse Gas Emission Pathways, in the Context of Strengthening the Global Response to the Threat of Climate Change, Sustainable Development, and Efforts to Eradicate Poverty* (Masson-Delmotte, V., P. Zhai, H.-O. Pörtner, D. Roberts, J. Skea, P.R. Shukla, A. Pirani, W. Moufouma-Okia, C. Péan, R. Pidcock, S. Connors, J.B.R. Matthews, Y. Chen, X. Zhou, M.I. Gomis, E. Lonnoy, T. Maycock, M. Tignor, and T. Waterfield (eds.). In Press.

Jacquez, Farrah, Lisa Vaughn, Alice Deters, Jody Wells and Kathie Maynard. 2020. "Creating a Culture of Youth as Co-Researchers: The Kickoff of a Year-Long Stem Pipeline Program." *Journal of STEM Outreach* 3 (1).

Jaskolski, Martina. 2016. "Youth Discources of Sustainability in Denpasar, Bali." In *Space, Place, and Environment*, Edited by Tracey Skelton, Karen Nairn, and Peter Kraftl, 3: 137–64. Geographies of Children and Young People. Singapore: Springer Singapore.

Knight, Linda. 2016. "Curious Hybrids: Creating 'not-Quite' Beings to Explore Possible Childhoods." *Discourse: Studies in the Cultural Politics of Education* 37 (5): 680–93. https://doi.org/10.1080/01596306.2015.1075706.

———. 2018. "Rearticulating Arts, Research and Education from the Disciplinary to the Affective in Public Arts Practices." In *Arts-Research-Education: New Connections and Directions*, Edited by Linda Knight, and Alexandra Lasczik Cutcher, 17–30. Studies in Arts Based Educational Research 1. Berlin: Springer.

———. 2019. "Childhood Art in Community Education: Postdevelopmental Learning through Feminist Leadership, Diversity and Pedagogic Invention." In *Postdevelopmental Approaches to Childhood Art*. Edited by Mona Sakr and Jayne Osgood, 29–46. London: Bloomsbury Academic.

———. 2020. "Inefficiently Mapping Boundaries: How Is an Urban Citizen?" *Mapping Meaning: The Journal* Summer 2020 (4): 66–75.

————. 2021. *Inefficient Mapping: A Protocol for Attuning to Phenomena*. Advanced Methods: New Research Ontologies 2. California: Punctum books. https://punctum books.com/titles/inefficient-mapping-a-protocol-for-attuning-to-phenomena/.

Knight, Linda, Felicity McArdle, Tamara Cumming, Jane Bone, Liang Li, Corinna Peterken and Avis Ridgway. 2015. "Intergenerational Collaborative Drawing: A Research Method for Researching with/about Young Children." *Australasian Journal of Early Childhood* 40 (4): 21–29. https://doi.org/10.1177/18369391150 4000404.

Knight, Linda and Hannah Rayner. 2015. "Hybrid Creatures as Complicating Visions of Early Childhood." *Complicity* 12 (1): 86. https://doi.org/10.29173/cmplct24242.

Koptie, Steve. 2009a. "Irihapeti Ramsden: The Public Narrative on Cultural Safety." *First Peoples Child & Family Review: An Interdisciplinary Journal Honouring the Voices, Perspectives, and Knowledges of First Peoples through Research, Critical Analyses, Stories, Standpoints and Media Reviews* 4 (2): 30–43. https://doi.org/10 .7202/1069328ar.

Lai, Ai-Ling. 2012. "Cyborg as Commodity: Exploring Conceptions of Self-Identity, Body and Citizenship within the Context of Emerging Transplant Technologies." *ACR North American Advances* 40: 386–394.

Lai, poh-Chin and Chien-Tat Low. 2019. "Provision of Convenient Play Space in a Densely Populated City." *International Journal of Environmental Research and Public Health* 16 (4): 651. https://doi.org/10.3390/ijerph16040651.

Latour, Bruno. 1992. 'Where are the missing masses? The sociology of a few mundane artifacts', In *Shaping Technology/Building Society: Studies in Sociotechnical Change Bijker*. Edited by W. E. and Law, J., Cambridge, MA, MIT Press, 225–58.

————. 1993. *We Have Never Been Modern*. Harvard University Press.

Lee, Pamela M. 1999. "Some Kinds of Duration: The Temporality of Drawing as Process Art." In *Afterimage: Drawing through Process*, 25–48. The MIT Press.

Lenette, Caroline. 2019. *Arts-Based Methods in Refugee Research*. Springer.

Luchtenberg, Malou L, Els LM Maeckelberghe and AA Eduard Verhagen. 2020. "'I Actually Felt like I Was a Researcher Myself.'On Involving Children in the Analysis of Qualitative Paediatric Research in the Netherlands." *BMJ Open* 10 (8): e034433.

Lundy, Laura, Lesley McEvoy and Bronagh Byrne. 2011. "Working With Young Children as Co-Researchers: An Approach Informed by the United Nations Convention on the Rights of the Child." *Early Education and Development* 22 (5): 714–36. https://doi.org/10.1080/10409289.2011.596463.

Lydon, Jane. 2021. *Anti-Slavery and Australia: No Slavery in a Free Land? Empire and the Making of the Modern World, 1650–2000*. Taylor & Francis Group.

MacRae, Christina, Abigail Hackett, Rachel Holmes and Liz Jones. 2018. "Vibrancy, Repetition and Movement: Posthuman Theories for Reconceptualising Young Children in Museums." *Children's Geographies* 16 (5): 503–15.

Malone, Karen. 2018. *Children in the Anthropocene: Rethinking Sustainability and Child Friendliness in Cities*. Palgrave MacMillan.

Malone, Karen, Marek Tesar and Sonja Arndt. 2020. "Re-Searching with Children in Posthuman Worlds." In *Theorising Posthuman Childhood Studies*, Edited by Karen Malone, Marek Tesar, and Sonja Arndt, 213–36. Springer.

Manning, Erin. 2013. *Always More than One: Individuation's Dance*. Durham: Duke University Press.

Marcus, George E. 2016. *Multi-Sited Ethnography*. Routledge.

Martin, Brian. 2013. "Immaterial Land." In *Carnal Knowledge: Towards a "New Materialism" through the Arts*, edited by Estelle Barrett and Barbara Bolt, 185–204. I.B. Tauris.

Monbiot, George. 2015. "The Child Inside." *The Guardian*, January 7, 2015. www.monbiot.com/2015/01/06/the-child-inside/.

Moreton-Robinson, Aileen. 2013. "Towards an Australian Indigenous Women's Standpoint Theory." *Australian Feminist Studies* 28 (78): 331–47. https://doi.org/10.1080/08164649.2013.876664.

———. 2017. "Relationality: A Key Presupposition of an Indigenous Social Research Paradigm." In *Sources and Methods in Indigenous Studies*, Edited by Chris Andersen and Jean M. O'Brien. 69–77.

Mould, Oli. 2016. "Parkour, Activism, and Young People." *Geographies of Children and Young People. Space, Place and Environment*. Edited by Tracey Skelton, Karen Nairn, and Peter Kraftl, Berlin: Springer.

Muecke, Stephen and Paddy Roe. 2020. *The Children's Country: Creation of a Goolarabooloo Future in North-West Australia*. Rowman & Littlefield Publishers.

Muñoz, José Esteban. 1999. *Disidentifications: Queers of Color and the Performance of Politics*. University of Minnesota Press.

Murphy, Laura. 2019. *The New Slave Narrative: The Battle over Representations of Contemporary Slavery*. Columbia University Press.

Murris, Karin. 2016. *The Posthuman Child: Educational Transformation through Philosophy with Picturebooks*. Contesting Early Childhood. Routledge.

Murris, Karin and Joanna Haynes. 2018. *Literacies, Literature and Learning: Reading Classrooms Differently*. Routledge.

Nagy, Kelsi and Phillip David Johnson II, eds. 2013. *Trash Animals: How We Live with Nature's Filthy, Feral, Invasive, and Unwanted Species*. Minneapolis: University of Minnesota Press.

Neimanis, Astrida. 2017. *Bodies of Water: Posthuman Feminist Phenomenology*. Bloomsbury Publishing.

Nelson, Sarah E. and Kathi Wilson. 2018. "Understanding Barriers to Health Care Access through Cultural Safety and Ethical Space: Indigenous People's Experiences in Prince George, Canada." *Social Science & Medicine* 218: 21–27.

Nolan, Justine and Martijn Boersma. 2019. *Addressing Modern Slavery*. NewSouth Publishing.

Noorani, Tehseen and Julian Brigstocke. 2018. *More-than-Human Participatory Research*. Connected Communities Foundation. Bristol.

Page, Tara. 2020. *Placemaking: A New Materialist Theory of Pedagogy*. Edinburgh University Press. https://www.jstor.org/stable/10.3366/j.ctv1453k6t.

Parker, Brenda. 2016. "Feminist Forays into the City: Imbalance and Intervention in Urban Research Methods." *Antipode* 48 (5): 1137–1358. https://doi.org/10.1111/anti.12241.

Pedwell, Carolyn. 2016. "De-Colonising Empathy: Thinking Affect Transnationally." *Samyukta: A Journal of Womens Studies* 16 (1): 27–49.

Petersen, Eva Bendix. 2018. "'Data Found Us': A Critique of Some New Materialist Tropes in Educational Research." *Research in Education* 101 (1): 5–16.

Pindar, Ian and Paul Sutton. 2014. "Translators' Introduction." In *The Three Ecologies*, translated by Felix Guattari, I. Pindar, and P. Sutton, 1–14, Editions Galilee.

Rankine, Claudia. 2014. *Citizen: An American Lyric*. Penguin.

Renold, Emma. 2018. "Privacies and Private: Making Ethical Dilemmas Public When Researching Sexuality in the Primary School." In *Ethical Dilemmas in Qualitative Research*, Edited by Trevor Welland and Lesley Pugsley, 121–34. Routledge.

———. 2019, "Reassembling the Rule(r)s: Becoming Crafty with How Gender and Sexuality Education Research Comes to Matter." In *Up-lifting Gender & Sexuality Study in Education & Research*, Edited by Jones, T., Coll, L., van Leent, and L., Taylor. Y London: Palgrave Macmillan.

Richards, Daniel P. 2019. "John Dewey, Nonhuman Agency, and the Possibility of a Posthuman Public." *Contemporary Pragmatism* 16 (4): 366–95.

Rogers Stanton, Christine. 2014. "Crossing Methodological Borders: Decolonizing Community-Based Participatory Research." *Qualitative Inquiry* 20 (5): 573–83. https://doi.org/10.1177/1077800413505541.

Savage, Mike and Roger Burrows. 2007. "The Coming Crisis of Empirical Sociology." *Sociology* 41 (5): 885–99.

Sencindiver, Susan Yi. 2017. "New Materialism." In *Oxford Bibliographies: Literary and Critical Theory*. Oxford: Oxford University Press. https://doi.org/10 :9780190221911–0016.

Seppala, Tiina, Melanie Sarantou and Satu Miettinen. 2021. "Introduction: Arts-Based Methods for Decolonising Participatory Research." In *Arts-Based Methods for Decolonising Participatory Research*, Edited by Tiina Seppälä, Melanie Sarantou, and Satu Miettinen, 1–18. Routledge Advances in Art and Visual Studies. New York, NY: Routledge.

Smit, Ben H. J. 2013. "Young People as Co-Researchers: Enabling Student Participation in Educational Practice." *Professional Development in Education* 39 (4): 550–73.

Snaza, Nathan. 2018. "Is John Dewey's Thought 'Humanist'?" *Journal of Curriculum Theorizing* 32 (2). https://journal.jctonline.org/index.php/jct/article/view/627.

Springgay, Stephanie and Zofia Zaliwska. 2016. "Learning to be Affected: Matters of Pedagogy in the Artists' Soup Kitchen", *Educational Philosophy and Theory* 49 (3): 273–283.

St Pierre, Joshua. 2015. "Cripping Communication: Speech, Disability, and Exclusion in Liberal Humanist and Posthumanist Discourse." *Communication Theory* 25 (3): 330–48. https://doi.org/10.1111/comt.12054.

Stengers, Isabelle. 2010. *Cosmopolitics*. University of Minnesota Press.

Taylor, Affrica. 2013. *Reconfiguring the Natures of Childhood*. New York: Routledge.

———. 2016. "Beyond Stewardship: Common World Pedagogies for the Anthropocene." *Environmental Education Research* 23 (10): 1448–61. https://doi.org/10.1080/13504622.2017.1325452

———. 2017. "Romancing or Re-Configuring Nature in the Anthropocene? Towards Common Worlding Pedagogies." In *Reimagining Sustainability in Precarious Times*, edited by Karen Malone, Son Truong, and Tonia Gray, 61–75. Singapore: Springer. https://doi.org/10.1007/978-981-10-2550-1_5.

Taylor, Carol A. and Jasmine B. Ulmer. 2020. "Posthuman Methodologies *for* Post-Industrial Cities: A Situated, Speculative, and Somatechnic Venture." *Somatechnics* 10 (1): 7–34. https://doi.org/10.3366/soma.2020.0298.

Till, Chris. 2015. "Žižek's Critique of New Materialism: Can We Theorise Natural Subjectivity?" *This Is Not a Sociology Blog* (blog). March 12, 2015. https://thisisn otasociology.blog/2015/03/12/zizeks-critique-of-new-materialism-can-we-theorise -natural-subjectivity/

Todd, Zoe. 2016. "An Indigenous Feminist's Take on the Ontological Turn: ' Ontology' Is Just Another Word for Colonialism." *Journal of Historical Sociology* 29 (1): 4–22.

Tsing, Anna Lowenhaupt and Sylvia Junko Yanagisako. 1983. "Feminism and Kinship Theory." *Current Anthropology* 24 (4): 511–16.

Tuck, Eve and Marcia McKenzie. 2015. "Relational Validity and the Where of Inquiry: Place and Land in Qualitative Research." *Qualitative Inquiry* 21 (7): 633–38. https://doi.org/10.1177/1077800414563809.

van der Tuin, Iris. 2008 "Deflationary Logic: Response to Sara Ahmed's 'Imaginary Prohibitions: Some Preliminary Remarks on the Founding Gestures of the 'New Materialism'" *The European Journal of Women's Studies* 15 (4): 411–16. https:// doi.org/10.1177/1350506808095297.

Ulmer, Jasmine B. 2017a. "Posthumanism as Research Methodology: Inquiry in the Anthropocene." *International Journal of Qualitative Studies in Education* 30 (9): 832–48. https://doi.org/10.1080/09518398.2017.1336806.

UNICEF. 2018. *Child Friendly Cities and Communities Handbook*. Geneva, Switzerland: UNICEF.

Vehmas, Simo and Nick Watson. 2016. "Exploring Normativity in Disability Studies." *Disability & Society* 31 (1): 1–16.

Vetlesen, Arne Johan. 2019. *Cosmologies of the Anthropocene: Panpsychism, Animism, and the Limits of Posthumanism*. Routledge.

Wake, Susan J. and Sally Birdsall. 2016a. "Can School Gardens Deepen Children's Connection to Nature." *Space, Place, and Environment. Geographies of Children and Young People* 3: 89–113.

Warner, Michael. 2002. "Publics and Counterpublics." *Public Culture* 14 (1): 49–90.

Warren, Wendy. 2016. *New England Bound: Slavery and Colonization in Early America*. New York, NY: Liveright Publishing Corporation.

Watson, Sophie. 2019. "City Water Matters: Cultures, Practices and Entanglements of Urban Water—An Introduction." In *City Water Matters*, 1–14. Springer.

Weir, Allison. 2017. "Decolonizing Feminist Freedom: Indigenous Relationalities." In *Decolonizing Feminism: Transnational Feminism and Globalization*, 257–87.

Welch, D. and N. Fitzgerald 2009. *"Return of the Godwit."* New Zealand Geographic. https://www.nzgeo.com/stories/return-of-the-godwit/.

Whitaker, Sally. 2018. *Hurdles to the Participation of Children, Families and Young People in Museums*. Kids in Museums, Arts Council England.

Williams, Robyn. 1999. "Cultural Safety—What Does It Mean for Our Work Practice?" *Australian and New Zealand Journal of Public Health* 23 (2): 213–14. https://doi.org/10.1111/j.1467-842X.1999.tb01240.x.

Wolfe, Cary. 2010. *What Is Posthumanism?* University of Minnesota Press.

Wolfe, Sylvia and Rosie Flewitt. 2010. "New Technologies, New Multimodal Literacy Practices and Young Children's Metacognitive Development." *Cambridge Journal of Education* 40 (4): 387–99.

Zembylas, Michalinos. 2018. "The Entanglement of Decolonial and Posthuman Perspectives: Tensions and Implications for Curriculum and Pedagogy in Higher Education." *Parallax* 24 (3): 254–67. https://doi.org/10.1080/13534645.2018.1496577.

Index

www.ingramcontent.com/pod-product-compliance
Lightning Source LLC
Chambersburg PA
CBHW021815270326
41932CB00007B/199